Families of Employed Mothers

Reference Books on Family Issues
(Vol. 24)
Garland Reference Library of Social Science
(Vol. 985)

Families of Employed Mothers
An International Perspective

Edited by
Judith Frankel

GARLAND PUBLISHING, INC.
New York & London
1997

Library of Congress Cataloging-in-Publication Data

Families of employed mothers : an international perspective / edited
    by Judith Frankel.
            p.   cm. — (Reference books on family issues ; v. 24)
    (Garland reference library of social science ; v. 985)
        Includes bibliographical references and index.
        ISBN 0-8153-1754-9 (alk. paper)
        1. Working mothers—Cross-cultural studies.   2. Children of
working mothers—Cross-cultural studies.   3. Work and family—
Cross-cultural studies.   4. Dual-career families—Cross-cultural
studies.   I. Frankel, Judith.   II. Series.   III. Series: Garland reference
library of social science ; v. 985.
HQ759.48.F35   1997
331.4'4—dc20   96-24090
                                                                    CIP

Printed on acid-free, 250-year-life paper
Manufactured in the United States of America

To Bob: Always

Contents

Acknowledgments

Many thanks and deep appreciation to Alethea Bennett and Dr. Rita Hoppert for their editing skills, their advice, and their assistance in the integration and preparation of this book. I could not have done it without them.

Introduction

The idea for this book arose in the late 1950s with my dissertation research. At that time the topic of maternal employment and its effects on the family, particularly the children, was under-researched in the United States; it was not discussed at all in other countries. My literature review for the dissertation was brief. Thirty-five years later, the situation had changed. The literature on the topic was extensive for the United States and showed that there had been some changes in both attitude and behavior regarding employed mothers and their families.

That led me to edit the book *The Employed Mother and the Family Context*. Written about the situation of families in the United States from a feminist perspective, it reviewed the present-day status of families of employed mothers. It included many topics and numerous articles and found that the status of the employed mother had changed. She now was in the numerical majority and the possessor of two jobs, one paid in the workplace, one unpaid at home. She was generally more satisfied being employed if she could manage the two jobs efficiently. If she could not, she felt stressed. The reasons for the "if not" were numerous, and foremost was the absence of adequate, affordable child care. The effects of her employment on her children were not noteworthy; in general they did as well as children of nonemployed mothers. Husbands of employed mothers had the benefit of more income and the disadvantage of fewer unstressed services from their wives.

In general, the major changes were in the increased number of employed mothers, the community's more accepting attitude toward them, and the terrible difficulties experienced by families in getting support for substitute child care. Domestic responsibilities for the most part remained the mother's task, and the family structure in two-parent households remained fairly patriarchal This picture is one that existed in the United States in the early 1990s.

In a global world, the next step seemed obvious. Did the same situation also exist around the world? What countries were affected by maternal employment, how were they affected, and what problems did this situation raise or redress?

This book examines the effects of maternal employment in selected countries other than the United States. Experts on this topic were invited to write about families of employed mothers in their countries. They were to use a framework that included the historical and cultural background of their country in discussing the effects of maternal employment on each member of the family and on public policy as it related to this topic.

While each author generally followed the outline, because of the unique history of each country, each chapter is distinct in the way that it approaches the topic, since there have been unique changes in the nature and effects of maternal employment on families in different countries. However, the conclusion reached in all the chapters is similar to the one reached by the authors of the first book: The more things change, the more they stay the same. This is best seen by analyzing the major themes that emerge from examining all the chapters and comparing how each nation relates to them.

The major theme to emerge is the idea of patriarchy. Each nation discussed is historically and presently patriarchal in some fashion. In some, like India, Taiwan, Puerto Rico, and Mexico, male dominance is very pronounced. In others, like the Philippines, Israel, Great Britain, and the United States, patriarchy prevails—but not to the extent it once did.

In India, for example, there may be some rhetoric and even legislative rulings about female equality, but the nature of the research process there, with mainly male researchers, challenges the practice of equality between the sexes. More research must be done that is not dominated by male researchers with their patriarchal perspective. Then we will be able to have more confidence in generalizations about equality reached by these studies. Chapter 3 questions the power differential of the sexes when it comes to property, position, status, and child custody in India. In Taiwan, male dominance is an entrenched position. On the other hand, in the United States, the glass ceiling remains in business and industry, and employed women suffer from dual roles that limit their access to promotion, even though they do have more equality and power in other realms, such as owning property and child custody decisions. The discussion on the Philippines reports a much closer equality of status between the sexes, with much more power in and out of the home for women than in other nations.

The changes brought about by maternal employment are seen in clashes between traditional and modern values. This is evident in all of the countries discussed, but in some it is much more of an issue. Developing countries seem to have the most difficulties reconciling old roles with new demands placed on those roles by changing social conditions, such as maternal employment outside the home. This is seen very clearly when comparing the discussions of this issue in chapter 10 on the United States and chapter 6 on Nigeria. Nigeria, a rapidly developing nation, still has a long way to go to ensure male/female equality.

The Mexican women in a study in chapter 5 reported that while they feel everything is fine and that their jobs do not affect their lives, many feel depressed. They related this depression to problems negotiating the complications of their double roles, since they considered that their status comes from their family position, and traditional domestic roles are valued as their first consideration. Chapter 4 discusses the clash of traditional and modern values in Israel as exemplified in the tension between family orientation versus self-fulfillment. On the other hand, even though women in the United States have difficulties navigating between two or more roles, they feel generally accepted as employed mothers by their social circle, and less tied to traditional role concepts than many of the other nationals.

The next theme to appear strongly is the theme of dual roles. Women in all the nations discussed in this book were often employed both inside and outside the home, domestically and for wages. In some countries, men share domestic work with their wives, but their share is usually minimal. In most instances domestic work remains women's work in all the countries mentioned. The extent of women's domestic work also depends upon the structure of their family, which varies in different countries. Women with extended families, for example, in the Philippines, have more support than those in many single-parent (read mother) families, such as in the United States.

In many countries, dual roles lead to role conflict and stress. In Mexico, for example, where the tradition of male financial support of family defines most of the men's status, wives' work outside the home causes dissatisfaction. The men, particularly those who were unemployed, were unhappy and shared their unhappiness with their wives. In turn, the employed wives were content to be employed but upset by their husbands' negative stance toward their employment in the face of their husband's unemployment.

This last theme leads to one of the major themes, or concerns, raised by all the authors—that of the problems of obtaining adequate substitute child care, either through personal family support or governmental assistance. The need for such assistance is clear in all countries, although some seem to have a head start on the issue, i.e., the Philippines. Germany has had a special problem since the reunification. In the former East Germany, women were educated and expected to be employed outside the home, and child care was provided. Now, in the unified German Republic, the situation is different. Many of the industries and assembly lines on which women worked have been closed, leaving the women unemployed and dissatisfied. Their self-esteem has dropped, and their confusion about their roles has increased.

Building on the previous theme, the life satisfaction of the employed mother is expressed in all the chapters. Most of the women in all of the countries were satisfied with their dual roles but felt that they needed more support in carrying them out. The support they needed was practical, like helpful substitute child care; value laden, like social acceptance by both sexes of the changing roles of women and the much-needed change in the roles of men; and active, like more governmental support for changing roles, practically, legislatively, and financially.

One of the countries that did not follow the above generalization was the unified German Republic. Prior to reunification, all women in East Germany expected to be employed outside the home and had governmental substitute child care available. They were comfortable with this position. However, after unification, and after the loss of industrial potential, many of the women lost their outside employment. The authors of the chapter describe the mothers as seeing many adverse effects of their unemployment and at-home status on their children. Studies, on the other hand, do not show any negative effects of mothers choosing to work exclusively at home as homemakers without wages. It will be interesting to note the development of this situation over time.

All of these themes combine to support my major thesis: Clearly there has been change in the nature and extent of maternal employment outside the home, resulting in significant changes in the workplace. However, domestic changes have not kept pace with workplace changes. Upon reading all the chapters, I conclude that a major and drastic reevaluation of male and female roles in family life needs to be undertaken, family structure needs reworking, and workplace and domestic roles need to be shared in a functional way, so that identity of each gender no longer remains the domain of that gender. I know I do not ask for an easy transition from the present structure of family form and function. But in terms of the material described in this book, I ask for a much-needed one if family life is to be satisfying and functional for all its members.

Contributors

Judith Frankel, Ph.D.
University of Cincinnati
Ohio

Nancy L. Galambos, Ph.D.
University of Victoria
Canada

Ruth Katz, Ph.D.
University of Haifa
Israel

Angela Lo, M.Ed.
Executive Secretary
Center for Research on Gender
Kaohsiung Medical College
Taiwan

Eileen M. Colberg Luciano, Ph.D.
University of Puerto Rico
Rio Piedras, Puerto Rico

Peter McCarthy, Ph.D.
University of Newcastle
England

Evelyn Ramos Marcano, Ph.D.
University of Puerto Rico
Rio Piedras, Puerto Rico

Justin A. Odulana, Ph.D.
University of Cincinnati
Ohio

Teresita Paed Pedrajas, Ed.D.
San Beda College
Manila, Philippines

G.N. Ramu, Ph.D.
University of Manitoba
Canada

Vincent Shieh, Ed.D.
Director
Center for Research on Gender
Kaohsiung Medical College
Taiwan

Dolores A. Stegelin, Ph.D.
University of Georgia

Emily Su, M.S.
Assistant Research Fellow
Center for Research on Gender
Kaohsiung Medical College
Taiwan

Elsa O. Valdez, Ph.D.
California State University
San Bernardino, California

Sabine Walper, Ph.D.
Institut fur Psychologie der
Universitat Munchen

Jane Wheelock, Ph.D.
University of Newcastle
England

Families of Employed Mothers

Chapter One
Employed Mothers and Their Families in Britain

Jane Wheelock and Peter McCarthy

We begin our survey of employed mothers and their families by setting out a framework for understanding the situation in Britain today. In doing so, we ask how the economic and social changes of the last half-century have influenced employment patterns of women and men in general and of mothers and fathers in particular. In considering the effects of these changes, it is important to take into account the role of the welfare state and of unpaid caring and domestic work, for it is not possible to understand the issues that concern families of employed women without giving attention to how the state and individuals outside the labor market contribute to the social reproduction of the family.

It is useful to view the past half-century in terms of two contrasting periods. The long boom, a period of relative prosperity, lasted until the mid-to-late 1960s. It was succeeded at the start of the 1970s by a period of long-run recession. These periods have come to be known as Kondratieff A and B cycles, respectively, after the Russian economist who first investigated long-run economic change.[1] What is surprising about Britain is that the number of women in the work force increased through both of these periods. On the other hand, employment patterns for men have been very different, with the Kondratieff B phase marked by substantial declines in rates of male participation in the labor market and escalating levels of male unemployment, thereby undermining men's role as economic providers.

The last half-century has also seen demographic and social change toward more diverse and unstable family forms, and, in particular, sharp differences between the labor-market behavior and economic fortunes of single-parent and two-parent families. As we shall demonstrate, there has been substantial change in the woman's relationship to the family—or household—economy over this period. At the start of the long boom, the British policy ideal of male breadwinners that had been developed by trade unionists and governments during the nineteenth century, and the corresponding notion of wives—if employed at all—as earning "pin money," might have corresponded to some sort of reality within the labor market. Today, the picture is radically different, and the British family economy relies on women and mothers not just to do unpaid domestic and caring work within the household but also to provide what can best be called a "component wage" (Humphries and Rubery, 1992). Given the low rate of pay commonly attached to "women's work," however, few families would be able to survive on mothers' earnings alone.

The impact of traditional, patriarchal ideology can never be far from the surface in considering how household work strategies play themselves out. Many of the socioeconomic changes that have taken place have put pressure on traditional views of gender divisions of labor. Yet state policy has often been slow to respond to the changes taking place, while the division of domestic labor has not changed at a pace corresponding to the changing structure of employment (Baldwin and Falkingham, 1994; Anderson, Bechhofer, and Gershuny, 1994). Consequently, women often carry the double burden of primary homemaker and important, or even essential, economic provider.

In the next section we take an overview of socioeconomic change in Britain in the postwar period, drawing attention to the effects of changes in the welfare state and in the traditional gender division of household labor on the families of employed mothers. The section that follows provides a descriptive overview of the labor-market participation of women in general and mothers in particular. We will then go on to look at the factors that affect the labor-market participation of mothers, asking why mothers want to work (supply) and why employers want to employ them (demand). We then ask what factors restrain mothers and make it difficult for them to go out to work, and what factors facilitate their taking up employment. Both policy and family contexts are significant here, where child care looms large as an issue for family members and policy-makers alike. In conclusion, we ask what the terms are on which mothers are employed, for themselves, for their husbands and children, and for the family as a whole. We suggest that a sane solution to the unacceptable aspects of these terms is to increase the chances for both mothers and fathers to combine the satisfactions of employment work with family work. In order to enhance the quality of family life, the dominion of paid employment—and its polar opposite, unemployment—over family lives needs to be diminished. This calls for a more egalitarian redistribution of the combined burdens—and rewards—of paid and unpaid work between men and women in Britain.

From Munitions Factory, to Home, to Office

Let us now go back to 1945, with its marriage and baby boom, full employment for men, and the return to the home of women who had contributed to the war effort in factories and fields. How has the picture changed so dramatically in a mere half-century? Mass production emerged in Britain in the years between the end of the war and the mid-1960s. The 1950s saw the simultaneous explosive growth of several new technologies (including electrical engineering, electrical consumer goods, chemicals, and petroleum products). This sustained an economic expansion that generated labor shortages and a demand for unskilled labor that drew married women in particular into employment. Mass production increased the number of standardized, simplified, and repetitive jobs, which were seen as "women's work." Labor-market segmentation was highly characteristic of women's employment, and by the 1960s the concentration of women in a few low-paid occupations had become ever more marked. Although Britain's older, nineteenth-century industries (such as coal, iron, and steel) remained static, the additional labor-market participation of women during this period was not at the expense of male employment. It should also be noted that in some parts of Britain—especially where textile production was located—there had always been a substantial female labor force.

Mass production required markets, and both women and the welfare state played a crucial role in the emergence of mass consumption. Mass production reduced costs, and led to real wage rises because wages were linked to rising productivity, but the substantial rise in postwar family incomes was also due to married women going out to work. Higher incomes sustained mass consumption, and private households became substantial centers of investment in consumer durable goods like refrigerators and televisions (Gershuny, 1983). Women were significant in this process, not only as wage earners, but also as the managers of household consumption—a crypto-servant class, as J.K. Galbraith (1975) put it.

Yet while women in general, and mothers in particular, continued to do the housework, bring up the children, and care for the elderly, so plugging substantial gaps in the provisions of the welfare state, this important set of economic and social activities was almost completely ignored (Waring, 1989). There was not even much interest in charting the growth of women's formal employment, as opposed to that of men (Massey, 1994). It is only recently that the importance of the multifaceted role of women in sustaining the postwar prosperity of the long boom has been recognized.

From the beginning of the 1960s, patterns of capital accumulation began to change. The colossal levels of investment required for mass production necessitated continuing expansion of markets, and this became more problematic as Britain faced growing competition, notably from West Germany and France. Economic growth led to labor shortages, and there was also a growing class struggle within the labor process (Armstrong, Glyn, and Harrison, 1991). As the relative costs of labor changed, capital became more concerned with cost-cutting, and employment of women, especially married women, became increasingly attractive to employers, though there was a growing tendency to employ them on a part-time rather than full-time basis. In addition, with economic growth the overall structure of demand in the economy was shifting away from manufacturing toward service industry, a sector that has long tended to employ more women than men.

The period from the mid-1960s to the beginning of the 1970s saw an international crisis of capital accumulation which, due to decline in national competitiveness, was experienced with particular severity in Britain. Internationally, it became difficult to extend Fordist mass production methods further: Reserves of labor had declined in the developed capitalist economies, so wage costs were rising. The limits to economies of scale were also becoming apparent. British capital, for example, was among that which sought new locations for production where labor costs were cheaper—either at the UK periphery (e.g., in Scotland, Wales, and Northern Ireland, where reserves of female labor in particular were often available) or outside Britain altogether. These trends were encouraged by the political priority given to internationally oriented financial capital over industrial capital. The shift of manufacturing employment to new locations—the new international division of labor—began to affect the availability of male manual jobs, and during the 1970s male unemployment began to rise (Rowthorn, 1986). Meanwhile, the proportion of women in the labor force continued to increase, though this was not due to absolute decline in the number of men employed but rather to women's jobs being concentrated in sectors of the economy, such as services, that were expanding and also happened to be labor intensive.

Married women returning to the labor market made up an inexperienced labor force that was unlikely to be unionized and consequently less likely to demand high wages. Women, and married women with children in particular, were a "flexible" source of labor, prepared to accept part-time jobs and willing to work unsociable hours: The "twilight shift," when husbands could look after the children when they came back from work, was particularly popular. The advantage of part-time employees was that they lacked statutory employment rights, and could therefore be easily laid off if demand fell.[2] Moreover, even women employed full time could be readily lost through "natural wastage" as they withdrew from the labor market to have children. Demand for female labor was further reinforced by the continuing deindustrialization of the British economy and the growing significance of the service sector. In addition, expansion in state social expenditure drew women into "caring" employment in the health, education and social services. On the supply side, because recession bit into men's income-earning potential, households were increasingly finding that they needed a second earner in order to maintain living standards.

The changing structure of employment during the 1970s, then, brought up issues of the *quantity* of employment available, particularly for male manual workers. It also raised the question of the *quality* of work available for women, despite some counteracting effects from the Equal Pay and the Equal Opportunities Acts, which came into effect in the middle of the decade. In sum, better paid male jobs (for fathers) were being lost, while lower paid part-time female jobs (for mothers) were being substituted.

During this same time period, William Beveridge emerged as an architect of the ideas behind the postwar democratic consensus in Britain. He had built the state benefit and insurance system around the concept of the male breadwinner in full-time, adequately paid employment. Married women were seen primarily as wives and mothers. Thus, women returning to the labor market were rarely insured against unemployment, and tended not to be officially defined as unemployed if unable to find work. Moreover, it was especially working-class, two-parent families who suffered from the collapse of the relatively well-paid manufacturing sector during the 1970s (Cutler, Williams, and Williams, 1986). As male unemployment grew, more and more men also began to fall out of the insurance net, leaving an increasing number of families without any social insurance coverage at all, and consequently wholly reliant on means-tested income support.

Since the start of the 1980s, the flexibility provided to employers by female labor has paved the way for a significant decline in employment conditions for men (see Wheelock, 1990). Features that were formerly chiefly in evidence in women's labor-market experiences have become part of male labor-market experience also. More frequent and longer periods of unemployment mean that men and fathers face problems similar to those experienced by mothers returning to the labor market. Successive modernizations—with lay-offs—as part of firms' responses to the squeeze on profitability have continued, but with the additional strategy of growing intensification of work. Internal labor markets—within large firms—have been reorganized, and core, skilled employees are expected to be "functionally flexible," able to turn their hands to a wider variety of tasks. Meanwhile, the peripheral, unskilled labor force becomes "numerically flexible" and readily expendable in times of lowered demand, thanks to temporary and short-term contracts of employment (see

Atkinson, 1984). This move to flexibility and work intensification has meant that male workers have become increasingly subject to the low pay and insecurity that already characterized female employment.

These are trends that have been vigorously encouraged by government policy since 1979. Legislation has curbed the role of trade unions and reduced employment protection. Flexible employment practices have been directly encouraged by government: the state sector, in particular, is characterized by deteriorating employment conditions. In addition, high rates of layoffs have led to increases in the number of small businesses and self-employed people, described by Foreman-Peck (1985) as "the chaff of economic recession."

Historically unprecedented rates of male unemployment requiring increased payment of state benefits combined with reductions in the tax base and a series of governments ideologically committed to "rolling back the frontiers of the state" have led to increasing pressure on the welfare state. The social insurance role of the benefit system is now all but abandoned, with means testing becoming an almost universal condition for the receipt of state benefits. With the low wages policy steadily pursued for the last fifteen years, benefits—such as family credit and housing benefits—have become a wage supplement that in effect subsidizes employers who pay wages that are so low that families are unable to survive on them. Indeed, some commentators have argued that the welfare state has become a tool of labor market policy, and that the Keynesian welfare state has been replaced by a "Schumpeterian workfare state" (Jessop, 1994). Cutbacks in the services provided by the state—education, health, social services—have pushed the burdens of caring back toward individual families, and particularly the women and mothers in them, and onto voluntary organizations whose volunteers also tend to be women.

Meanwhile, employment trends among women during the last fifteen years have reinforced previous trends in two respects. The integration of women into the labor market has continued, particularly markedly for mothers, and especially for mothers of preschool children, while the importance of women's component wages to incomes in most households is increasingly apparent. Also, the differentiation of women from men in terms of low pay has continued although the size of wage differences has narrowed (Humphries and Rubery, 1992). A new feature, however, or perhaps rather one that has become more noticeable as the absolute numbers of women involved have risen, is increased polarization between groups of women. Thatcherism and its legacy have seen women with higher educational qualifications in middle-class occupations, such as professional and managerial employment, gaining substantially in financial terms, particularly if they live in the south of England. On the other hand, women at the lower end of the income scale have seen their wages falling (Wilson, 1987; Humphries and Rubery, 1992).

Summing up the effects of changes over the last fifteen years, the combination of cuts in the welfare state and deterioration in the levels and conditions of men's employment has put mothers and children in a particularly vulnerable financial position. This vulnerability is further reinforced by continuing changes in family structures, with higher levels of divorce and more single-parent—both never-married and separated—households. Moreover, the contribution to financial independence that increasing employment of married women and mothers can make is limited by low levels of relative and absolute earnings.

There is of course a possibility that these new employment patterns will, in the long term, generate changes in the gender division of labor. So what then is the potential for changes in gender relations, both in the home and in paid work? If one takes the fairly widely accepted feminist model, which sees the status of women in the labor market as the result of the interaction between the two social systems of patriarchy and capitalism, the changes described threaten patriarchal structures, at the same time as being clearly of considerable importance to capitalism in its efforts to maintain profitability. During the 1980s, high rates of male unemployment and the increasing participation of women in the labor market, if only on a part-time basis, threatened patriarchal structures (Henwood and Wyatt, 1986). In the 1990s, as low-wage policies have continued, the potential for conflict between patriarchy and capitalism is even greater, for women's flexibility is being duplicated by lower wages and poorer conditions for men.

What is apparent is that economic changes have gone along with social changes, as well as changes in attitudes, though how far these are cause and effect is unclear. There is evidence from a large number of qualitative studies that women in general, and mothers in particular, are in the labor market and in the family on different terms from men (e.g., West, 1982; Wajcman, 1983). For low-paid mothers especially, part-time employment is a compromise that, in the absence of social child care, enables them to combine an income-earning role with their traditional caring role (Yeandle, 1984; Stubbs and Wheelock, 1990). Therefore, there has been some modification of the traditional division of household labor, for mothers now expect to combine their caring role with responsibility for income earning. Yet it has remained difficult for fathers, or indeed mothers, to accept that men, whether they are employed or unemployed, should abrogate their breadwinning responsibilities (Wheelock, 1990; Jordan et al., 1991).

It is consonant with such views that men are reluctant to take on the new types of jobs: After all, remuneration in part-time or low-paid jobs may be insufficient for a family breadwinner (Balls and Gregg, 1993). On the other hand, some men who are willing to take on the new jobs have found themselves unable to do so. This has been because of discrimination, or simply because of stereotyped notions of what occupations men could or should pursue. Indeed, it would seem that around half of the complaints about employment discrimination received by the Equal Opportunities Commission now come from men (Equal Opportunities Commission, 1993).

Despite evidence of widely held views that parental roles should be shared (see Martin, 1984), much of the policy discussion has been in terms of equal employment rights for mothers, rather than the equal rights of fathers to participate in care. This is replicated in policies concerned with postdivorce parenting, where the responsibilities of so called "absent" fathers are concerned with ensuring that they maintain financial responsibilities to their children, and ignoring issues of how they exercise the other responsibilities associated with being a father. During the long years of Conservative government, there has been the same lack of analysis as in previous decades concerning the impact of state policies on family life. Support for the principle of the traditional family has disguised the increasing participation of mothers in low-paid work. Thus, the British state has been able to maintain an apparently neutral stance on working mothers by defining the issue as a matter for private choice. Meanwhile, the impact of the employment of mothers on their partners, their children, themselves, and the rest of their families cries out for a policy lead.

Women and Mothers in the British Labor Market Today

Statistics about the British labor market reveal distinct increases in the rates of participation of women, and of women with children in particular. For instance, in 1951 the economic activity rate for women of working age (16 to 59 years) stood at 42%. By 1979, this rate had increased to 63%, and in 1992 it had increased to 71%. In contrast, the rate for men of working age fell from 91% to 86% from 1979 to 1992 (Sly, 1993). The Department of Employment has predicted that the size of the civilian labor force will increase by one million during the 1990s, and that 90% of those employed people will be women.

However, this growth in female economic activity owes much to the type of jobs that have been created. The majority of new jobs have been part time and low paid, and thus more suitable for secondary rather than primary earners. Given the structure of the family division of labor, which is historically based on the notion of male breadwinners, such jobs are regarded as more appropriate for women workers. In 1971, 15% of jobs in Britain were part time, but that had increased to 26% by 1991. The suggestion that women are more likely than men to take part-time jobs is supported by the fact that in 1992, 45% of women in work, compared with 6% of men, worked part time in their main job (Watson and Fothergill, 1993).

The largest increase in female employment has been among mothers of children under the age of five, the age at which children begin full-time education (see Figure 1). This increase has been particularly apparent among married or living-as-married women. Almost 50% of all married women with children younger than statutory school age are currently employed, compared with around 25% fifteen years ago (General Household Survey, 1992). This increase may be related to the increased availability of part-time work, but it has also been attributed to increasing numbers of women who return to work between births and to women returning to work earlier after childbearing. For instance, during the 1980s the proportion of women who returned to work within nine months of having a baby almost doubled (Harrop and Moss, 1994).

Single mothers are less likely to be employed: 42% of these mothers have jobs compared with 63% of mothers with partners. Nevertheless, those single mothers who do work are more likely than partnered mothers to have full-time jobs. Explanations for this differing pattern vary. The lower likelihood of employment among single mothers may result from the decline in availability of full-time jobs. An alternative explanation may be that the composition of families headed by single parents has changed in various ways: They have tended to get larger; an increasing proportion of single mothers have children of preschool age; and an increasing proportion of single mothers have never been married. As Harrop and Moss (1994) point out, these never-married mothers tend to have lower levels of education and training than other mothers. Consequently, they have less to offer prospective employers and are less likely than other mothers to be employed: 29% of never-married mothers, compared with 46% of divorced, single mothers are employed (General Household Survey, 1992). Jane Millar (1994) points to the complexities of build-

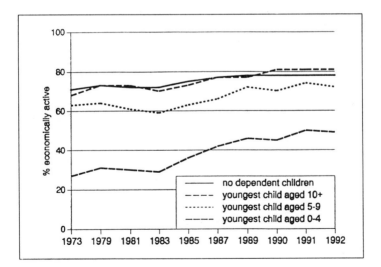

Figure 1. Economic activity rates of women (1973–1991). Source: General Household Survey 1992.

ing up an income package for single-parent families, and the impact
this may have on incentives to undertake employment. The income
derived from combining means-tested state benefits, uncertain
support payments, and low, insecure wages can prove extremely
unpredictable, particularly if there are also child-care costs to be
met.

    Although the economic activity rate of mothers has clearly in-
creased, they continue to be less likely to be in work than do women
who have no dependent children. Figure 2 shows the extent to which
the presence of children affects the economic status of women. Forty
percent of women of working age have dependent children, and the
economic activity rate of mothers is 63%, while it is 71% for all
women. The age of children is also a key determinant of economic
activity. Nearly half of all mothers had preschool children (aged 0 to
4 years), only half of these were economically active, and fewer than
one in five worked full time. Activity rates increased when the youngest child reached primary-school age (aged 5 to 10 years) and increased again when children became old enough for secondary school
(aged 11 to 15 years).

    Irrespective of the age of children, the majority of employed

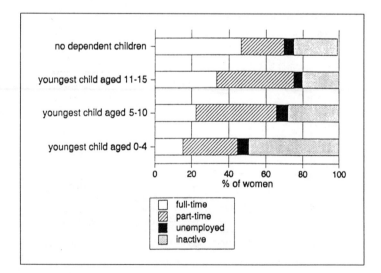

*Figure 2. Economic status of women by age of youngest child. Source: Sly
1993, Table 3.*

mothers work part time, whereas most other women in work have full-time jobs. This is further emphasized by Figure 3, which shows the hours worked per week by employed women. Unsurprisingly, women who have no children are most likely to work more than 35 hours per week. As far as the others are concerned, there is a clear relationship with the age of children, with those women who have younger children tending to have the shortest working week.

Clearly then, family structures have an important influence on whether women take up employment: Single mothers are less likely to have jobs than those who are partnered, and women with preschool children are the least likely to work either part time or full time. In addition, Harrop and Moss (1994) have reported a relationship between the mother's employment and education, ethnicity, and the father's employment status. The proportion of mothers of preschool children who were educated to A-level standard or higher and employed increased from 35% to 63% during the 1980s, while that of mothers with no qualifications increased significantly less: from 18% to 26%. Moreover, while nearly half of the qualified mothers worked full time, only a third of the unqualified mothers

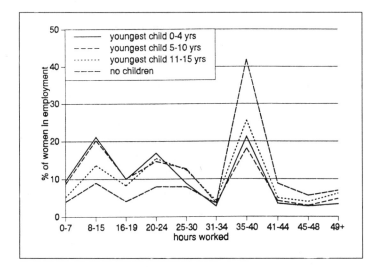

Figure 3. Hours worked per week by age of youngest child. Source: Sly 1993, Table 6.

did so (Harrop and Moss, 1994).

Employment rates grew more rapidly among white mothers than among either black mothers—for whom the rate actually fell—or mothers from South Asian backgrounds. At the end of the decade, 58% of white mothers, 54% of black mothers, and 36% of South Asian mothers were employed. However, black mothers were the most likely of these to have full-time jobs (Harrop and Moss, 1994), possibly because black mothers were more likely than others to be single parents and therefore not dependent on male breadwinners.

The number of two-earner families, in which both husband and wife were employed, increased from 43% to 60% between 1973 and 1992 (General Household Survey, 1992). Conversely, the number of families with no earners has also increased, creating discrepancies between "work-rich" and "work-poor" households. Clearly, having two earners increases the potential for economic well-being of families, but opportunities in this respect are by no means equally distributed. The rate of dual-earner households is significantly affected by the husband's social class, with wives of husbands who are in unskilled occupations being least likely to be employed.

Moreover, unemployment and nonemployment tend to be concentrated in particular families, just as employment is concentrated in others. Among families with children, only 13% of wives of unemployed men have jobs, whereas 69% of wives of employed men are employed themselves (General Household Survey, 1992). To a certain extent, economic inactivity among wives of unemployed men relates to disincentives connected with the state benefit system. The earnings of wives affect benefit levels so that working wives can, in some circumstances, have a negative impact on family income. However, a more important influence might be the tendency of those men who are more likely to experience unemployment—e.g., low-skilled and unqualified men—to marry women who have a low level of attachment to the labor market (Harrop and Moss, 1994). It is also possible that where nonemployed husbands fail to take on a share of the domestic work, their wives decide to give up employment rather than take on a double work burden (see Wheelock, 1990).

Women's Jobs and Earnings

The Equal Pay Act of 1970 stipulates that women cannot be paid less for doing the same work as men, or work of equal value. Since the introduction of the act, gender differences in earnings have narrowed, albeit slowly: In 1992, women's earnings from full-time employment were 71% of those of men, compared with 63% in 1979. However, as men tend to work longer hours the hourly rate is probably a more reliable indicator of equality. Even these suggest there is still some considerable difference: The hourly rates of pay for women working full time are currently just 79% of those of men (New Earnings Survey 1992, Table 1). Consequently, even when women work full time they are considerably less well off than male workers. So, for instance, the New Earnings Survey (1992) revealed that only one in four women in full-time work were earning more than the average weekly wage of their male counterparts.

Women who work part time are noticeably worse off than full-time workers, with those doing part-time jobs receiving on average just 74% as much per hour as women who work full time, and 83% as much as male part-time workers (New Earnings Survey, 1992). In addition, women workers compare unfavorably with male workers in other respects. For instance, 89% of men working full time belonged to either an occupational or personal pension scheme, while only 75% of women in full-time jobs did so. Just 32% of women working part time had some form of pension provision (General Household Survey, 1992).

The continuing gap between the earnings of men and women stems primarily from the difficulty that women have in getting access to certain types of job. As indicated by Figure 3, women tend to congregate in particular categories of occupation. In some areas of employment, such as clerical/secretarial, sales, personal, and protective services, women make up the majority of employees. However, they are very much in the minority when it comes to higher-status occupations such as management and administration and the professions. Indeed, the only professions in which women outnumber men are those of teaching and associated health professions such as nursing—professions related to women's traditional caring roles (from Sly, 1993, Table 7). Figure 4 also shows that women without children are more likely than other women to be in the management and administration category, indicating that the pursuit of a career may for women preclude taking time out from their jobs to have children.

Of all women employed, 26% are in clerical or secretarial occupations: 14% are in personal service occupations; and 11% are in sales occupations other than those of buyers, brokers, and sales representatives. Women are noticeable by their absence from science, engineering, and craft and related occupations. In the science and engineering professions, men outnumber women by almost ten to one; in skilled construction trades by almost seventy to one; in skilled engineering trades by more than forty to one; and among drivers and mobile machine operators by thirty to one (Sly, 1993). According to Haskey (1993), the occupational status of employed single mothers is not significantly different from that of working mothers who have partners. However, as suggested above, single mothers are significantly less likely to be employed.

The fact that part-time jobs are disproportionately allocated to women emphasizes gender differences in earnings. Part-time work tends to receive lower levels of pay, and part-time workers are often deprived of rights available to full-time workers. Nevertheless, it

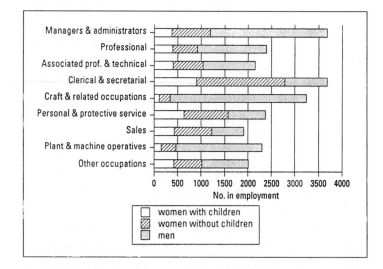

Figure 4. Occupation type by gender and presence of children. Source: Sly 1993, Table 7.

appears that most mothers who take part-time jobs do so out of preference for that type of work. Figures tend to suggest that they are content to be part-time workers and that they have no desire for full-time employment. In fact, 93% of women in part-time work say that they are not looking for full-time jobs, while only 6% suggest that they are doing part-time work because they are unable to get full-time employment (Watson and Fothergill, 1993). However, women's aspirations for employment are likely to be restricted by their other responsibilities, and the shortage of alternative sources of child care. Thus, part-time female workers who do not have dependent children are more likely to be dissatisfied with part-time work. In addition, attitudes are likely to change as children get older. Initial reasons for choosing part-time work can quickly become invalid, so that even those women who are currently satisfied with part-time jobs may not continue to be so. It remains the case that many women see nonstandard work as essential to their domestic and income requirements (Horell, Rubery, and Burchell, 1994).

Why Do Mothers Want to Work?

We have seen that large numbers of mothers work outside the home, and they are doing so in steadily increasing numbers. Why do they do it? Studies of women in the labor market have identified six major reasons why wives, living-as-married women, or mothers undertake paid work, including: economic need; a desire to contribute to family income; a desire for independent income; concerns about maintaining an established career; and to keep touch with the labor market. It is recognized that employment—of men—fulfills a number of psychological and social needs as well as earning income (see Jahoda, 1982). Correspondingly, studies have shown that women may go out to work for social reasons, as well as for self-fulfillment.

Views of women's employment as marginal, along with ideas that British women are uncommitted to the labor market, have had to be reassessed in recent years. Indeed, much evidence suggests that women's wages have become an essential part of household income. Even at the start of the 1980s, male earnings accounted for less than half of household income in Britain (the rest deriving from women's and children's earnings and from state benefits), while it was estimated that if women didn't work, the number of households in poverty would quadruple (Phillips, 1983). Chaney (1980), in a study in northeast England, found that 85% of the women interviewed reported that money was the reason for returning to work. Economic motivation for seeking employment is more apparent among single parents than it is for married women (Morris, 1990). Eighty-five percent of employed single parents suggest that they work out of financial necessity, compared with 37% of married women (Martin, 1984). The most striking rise regarding the contribution of female earnings to household income has been in households where there are children present: During the 1980s, the proportion of family income provided by mothers' earnings rose by over 50%. If earning less than half the national average income is taken as a poverty line, in 1990 one in twelve couples fell below it. Without women's earnings, the proportion would have been 50% higher (Harkness, Machin, and Waldfogel, 1994).

Despite the increasing evidence that men are rarely able to support their family without help, women themselves may tend to underplay the importance of their wages to family incomes. For example, a study of women's employment potential in north-east England found that women defined their financial contribution as an "extra," even though their wages might be used for such basic necessities as the mortgage, debt repayment, or buying children's clothes. It was also shown that women, as paid workers, had a strong commitment both to the idea of paid employment in general, and a strong pride in their own status as workers. Thus few of those who were currently out of the labor market, whatever their domestic situation, were happy with the prospect of remaining out of a job for long. The paradox was that although paid employment was seen by the vast majority as necessary for their own self-confidence and esteem, as well as to support their families, it was also perceived as involving tensions, additional work, and often the guilt of not living up to the ideal of the "good" wife, mother, or daughter (Stubbs and Wheelock, 1990).

Other members of the family and society have also shown some animosity toward working mothers. Brannen and Moss (1991) studied women who returned to work after childbirth and found that many experienced hostility from relatives, friends, and work colleagues. In a study of dual-earner families carried out by Watson and

Fothergill (1993), some female respondents suggested that the fact that they worked did not meet with the approval of partners who tended to feel that "a woman's place should be in the home," while other women reported that they had actually given up employment because of the hostility demonstrated by their partners.

Why Should British Employers Want to Employ Mothers?

We have already seen that sectors of the economy that have traditionally employed women have expanded during the decades of British deindustrialization. As a result, women are more likely to find themselves in expanding sectors of the economy, while men are more at risk of being in contracting sectors and risking unemployment. However, female service workers are under a threat from a number of sources. The fiscal crisis of the state initially, then the rise of the New Right and cuts in public-service provision, have already limited prospects in the public sector. Technological change now threatens employment in both public and private-sector services. The effects of new technology are already apparent in the retail sector, and also affect clerical occupations. Of course, there are areas in which female employment tends to be concentrated. It is interesting to note that professional occupations are also now under threat from restructuring—with growing unemployment among middle management for example—and from intensification. The extent to which this will feed through in terms of loss of employment potential among predominantly male professionals has yet to be seen.

It is when we come to the characteristics of the labor force, rather than its structure, that the advantages of employing women, especially mothers, becomes apparent. Specifically, it is the flexibility and value for money of mothers that makes them attractive to employers. As we have already seen, the fact that mothers in particular enter and leave the labor market because of family responsibilities, and are also prepared to work part time, fits in with cost-cutting. Natural attrition and restricted contracts for part-timers means that employers do not have to retain mothers in their jobs if they are no longer needed.

In addition to their flexibility in employment, women (mothers in particular) tend to be cheap to employ. Part-time working mothers do not need to be paid as many benefits. However, a recent (1994) European Union ruling gave part-time workers retrospective rights to pensions, and there has been much comment in Britain that this may discourage employers from using part-time workers in the future. However, there are other factors that make mothers an attractive labor force. When women reenter the labor market after a break, they usually experience downward mobility in the sense that the jobs they do tend to be lower paid, are labeled as less skilled, and are more likely to involve less desirable hours than their previously held jobs (Martin, 1984). Indeed, it has been argued that for many British women, maternity is not so much a career break as a career rupture (Glasner, 1992).

Yet many women return to work in jobs which, though traditionally labeled as unskilled, in reality carry considerable responsibility and require a substantial range of skills. Serving in a busy bar, for example, requires a good memory and skills in dealing with people and handling money (Stubbs and Wheelock, 1990). Mothers of young families would not cope with their unpaid domestic duties if they did not develop precisely the type of interpersonal, management, and financial skills that employers find so useful.

Mothers, constrained by child-care requirements, are often prepared to work early morning or evening hours, when husbands or other family members are available for child care. There is increasing recognition among employers that it is important to retain highly skilled and trained women after they become mothers. Demographic changes, and the drop in the numbers of young people entering the labor market, have led employers of more educated women, including many of the big banks and financial institutions, to introduce programs designed to encourage mothers to return to work after maternity leave.

Facilitating and Restraining Mothers' Employment and the Impact on Families

In this section, we examine the factors that may encourage or discourage individual mothers from undertaking paid work. For example, major institutional changes introduced in the British economy during the 1980s had a significant impact on family expenditure. Rising household expenses have put increased pressure on mothers to undertake paid employment. The promotion of home owner-ship, as well as liberalization of financial markets, encouraged house-hold debt. The Policy Studies Institute conducted a study in 1989 on the debt held by British households. This study found more than 2.5 million households in debt, mostly because of low incomes. Those who had the most debt were living on benefits or low pay (Policy Studies Institute, 1992). Rising house prices during the 1980s seemed to be a boon for the fortunate owner/occupiers. With little thought for the possibility that the boom might collapse, households were committing a higher and higher proportion of their income to mort-gage repayments. Many found that the financial institutions were happy to remortgage at current higher valuations. In 1988 mort-gage holders were, on average, spending nearly twice as much on discretionary spending—on holidays, consumer durables, and so forth—as nonmortgage holders. But the boom in house prices came to an abrupt end at the start of the 1990s, and by 1993 it was esti-mated that some 1.7 million households faced a situation of nega-tive equity, owing more to the financial institutions than the value of their houses. Interest rates had also risen, as had unemployment. Indebtedness became a severe financial burden for better-off house-holds, too (for further details, see Wheelock, 1995).

The extension of the period of financial dependency of young people on their families has also put pressure on family incomes and on mothers as component wage earners. Unemployment among the young, and particularly young men, has been consistently well above that for other age groups. At the same time, the availability of state benefits for this group has been severely curtailed. Government-spon-sored training schemes for the young pay such meager wages that families are inevitably subsidizing their sons and daughters (Hollands, 1990). Full-time students are increasingly expected to be financed by their parents, or to go in to debt; they have no right to claim a whole variety of state benefits. Mothers, for example, may find them-selves working to pay the rent for their student son's or daughter's lodgings.

There are, then, a set of growing pressures on mothers to con-tribute to the family income package. Will they actually do so? Dis-incentives may arise from inside the family household as well as from outside it. Behavior in the labor market can be understood only with respect to access to, uses of, and benefits from earned income. Jan Pahl (1989) has researched the way in which British married couples manage their money, and found that both men and women seem to see the family as a unit within which money is shared, with this being particularly so for men when thinking of the money they earn. But while in theory the man is seen as the breadwinner, in practice, women are more family-centered in their spending. Wives are more likely to make economies when there is financial stringency, such as missing a meal, turning down the heat, or borrowing money, and they are also likely to have less spending money than their partners. The greatest inequalities are associated with low household income, and in households where the husband has the greatest control over finance. As Pahl points out, the implication for child welfare is that a pound that enters the house through a woman's pay packet is more likely to be spent on the children than a pound coming in through the husband's pay packet.

The system of money management also has significant implications for the living standards of individuals within the household, and it is interesting to note that female-managed systems are associated with the lowest family income levels. Morris (1990) draws a distinction between household income and domestic income, where the latter is spent on joint household needs. She points out that there are three levels of financial responsibility: control over how money is allocated; money management, which puts control into operation; and budgeting, or spending within particular expenditure requirements. In the lowest income families, it is women who have the responsibility for managing and budgeting a tight household income, though men may still control the finances since, in most female-managed systems, the husband's personal spending money is a protected category. The policy implication is that when households are dependent on income maintenance schemes, money is likely to be used more efficiently if it is paid directly to women, as has always been the case with the universally available child benefit.

The disparity of income between men and women, especially in the child-rearing years, means that there has to be some sharing of resources if women and children are not to have a lower standard of living than men. Pahl's research (1989) into British families shows that such sharing may not be complete. Thus a further implication of her research is that unequal patterns of income distribution and money management and control inside the household may reinforce the incentives for mothers to enter the labor market simply to ensure that their children's and their own individual spending needs are met.

Despite the increase in economic activity among women, wives continue to bear the main responsibilities for work in the home. According to Jowell, Brook, Taylor, and Prior (1991), in three-quarters of the families surveyed for the 1991 study of social attitudes, women did most of the housework. In two-thirds of the households in which both partners worked full time, women were primarily responsible for domestic duties. There tend to be two views of the household's response to changes in its relation to the formal labor market. The first highlights the undoubted fact that employed married women bear a disproportionate double burden, and sees women's labor as secondary to men's, arguing that women's proportion of domestic labor is insensitive to changes in outside commitments. An alternative view is that of "adaptive partnership," in which the division of domestic labor reflects changes in labor market participation. Thus Gershuny, Godwin, and Jones (1994) show husbands' proportion of housework rising over the decade 1975–1985, whether their partners were working full time, part time, or as housewives, but with the greatest shift for those with working wives. They argue that comparisons between cross-sectional studies of couples in varying employment positions have been illegitimately used to draw longitudinal conclusions about lack of change over time in the division of domestic labor. They suggest a model of "lagged adaptation," in which the adjustment in roles does not take place through short-term redistribution, but through extensive processes of household negotiation, or even reconstitution, over many years and indeed over generations.

One study that confirms the idea of lagged adaptation, albeit over a relatively short time scale, is Wheelock's investigation (1990) of northeast England households with children, in which husbands had become unemployed or left the labor market while mothers continued to undertake paid work. In-depth interviews with a representative sample of thirty such households showed shifts toward husbands' undertaking more domestic and child-care work in nearly 70% of the group, though none with complete role reversal. While few of the couples found it easy to adapt to the changes in traditional roles that they had made, there was a general feeling that the shift was only fair. Most husbands were devastated by the loss of their breadwinner role, but commented on the compensations given by the greater opportunities to bring up their children and be with their families. There was some evidence that where there was no shift in the division of domestic labor, wives might abandon paid work.

Other studies of households with unemployed men have not shown the same shift in who does what in the house, but overall household circumstances were different, with wives usually full time at home too. Role insecurity has been posited as at least part of the explanation for the lack of change in such cases (Morris, 1985; McKee and Bell, 1985). A further study, of women returning to work after childbirth, found that "fathers did not equally share child-care or other domestic tasks nor did they accept equal responsibility for these areas" (Brannen and Moss, 1991, p. 251). Nevertheless, the women concerned tended to praise partners for the help they did give and valued the emotional support partners provided. Moreover, almost a half of the parents who participated in the Cooper and Lewis study (1993) said they shared child care equally, indicating growing awareness of the importance of fathering. Nevertheless, the majority of couples did feel that child care is predominantly the mother's job and consequently, when asked who would be more likely to take time off work in a domestic crisis, the majority of respondents, men and women, indicated that it would be the mother (Cooper and Lewis, 1993, p. 85). Gregson and Lowe (1993) show paid (female) nannies and cleaners substituting for wives' domestic roles in two-earner professional households, in addition to some extra contributions from fathers.

Clearly, it remains the case that irrespective of whether they have jobs outside the home, women continue to carry the main responsibility for housework, homemaking, and child care. Nevertheless, the degree to which men get involved in these activities is undoubtedly changing. It is important to realize that men's capacity to be more involved may well be restricted by the extra hours they work outside the home. For instance, whereas only one in 166 women usually works more than 48 hours per week, as many as a third of their partners do so. Employed men work longer hours in Britain than anywhere else in the European Union. Hence, although men may recognize that responsibilities in the home ought to be shared, if they are employed the increasing pressures of work mean it is difficult for them to spend as much time as partners doing unpaid domestic work. For unemployed men, the story, of course, is different.

Opportunities for mothers to take up employment in two-earner households are dependent on the availability of alternative forms of child care. However, in Britain, very little child care is provided by the state. For instance, state facilities are available for only one in a hundred under-fives, and those places have come to be regarded as "essentially a social work resource for the use of families with major problems rather than a service for the general run of employed parents" (Brannen and Moss, 1991, p. 29). A report produced by the International Year of the Family (1994) has suggested that "failure by organizations to support the family life of their employees is, arguably, one of the biggest barriers to commercial performance and effectiveness." Yet, despite increases in female employment, only 1% of working mothers have access to nursery provision connected with their workplaces (Condy and Roberts, 1995). Nevertheless, more enlightened employers are beginning to recognize that provision of child care facilities for employees makes economic sense. For instance, the Midland Bank has calculated that it costs £18,000 to replace an assistant manager with 11 to 15 years of experience, but a subsidy toward a nursery place is a mere £2,500 per year. Over four years, the bank saves £8,000 by retaining a manager (Commission on Social Justice, 1994). The use of workplace nurseries by mothers is now no longer taxable.

When children reach school age, their attendance at school takes them out of the home, at least for parts of the day. Consequently, mothers are then more likely to work, though the hours after school continue to present child-care problems, and some mothers are unable to continue employment during school holidays. Where help is required with after-school or vacation child care, the most common sources are partners, followed by the children's grandmother. It is the absence of a partner with whom to share responsibilities that is a major reason why single mothers are less likely to work. Moreover, a consequence of the high level of labor-market participation among women without children is that grandmothers have become less available for looking after grandchildren while mothers work. For instance, 73% of women aged between 45 and 54 years and 55% of those aged 55 to 59 are economically active (Social Trends, 1992, Table 4.5). On the other hand, increasing rates of male unemployment and enforced early retirement of male workers may mean that grandfathers are more available to carry out traditional grandparenting roles, which have in the past been the province of grandmothers. The range of options available for care of children depends to a large extent on the age of the children. Mothers are more likely to work after children start school because help is more readily available. For instance, of women with children aged five to eleven, 16% ask a friend or neighbor to help out, compared with 1% of mothers with children under five (Harman, 1993, p. 95).

Despite the support that working mothers receive from partners, families, friends, and neighbors, many women can work only because they pay someone to look after children. Outside the family unit and schools, most child care is provided by the private sector. However, the cost of this means that it is not an option available to women in low-paid jobs, especially when added to the costs of getting to work. A survey carried out by the Scottish Low Pay Unit found that although most working mothers relied on informal child-care arrangements, a third used formal child-care services such as day care and nurseries. Where costs were involved, they were invariably met by mothers rather than fathers, and payments made represented between 10% and 50% of earnings; in some cases more than 50% (cited in Harman, 1993). A recently introduced tax concession that allows single parents to offset child care costs against their tax provides some assistance for single mothers. This is an example of differing government attitudes toward single mothers and partnered mothers working outside the home.

The right to maternity leave is an important factor in enabling mothers to retain jobs, yet such leave is generally not provided. As Brannen and Moss (1991) have argued,

In a proper maternity leave scheme, women maintain their status as employees while absent from their work due to pregnancy and childbirth. Instead, under British legislation women have their contract terminated with a guarantee of reinstatement in similar work, though not necessarily their previous job, and are not entitled to non-statutory benefits such as bonuses during their absence (p. 29).

In order to qualify for maternity leave women need to have been with the same employer for at least two years, a stipulation that excludes many women, especially those having a second or subsequent child and thus who are more likely to have had broken periods of employment. Moreover, benefit payments are paid for only eighteen of the legally allowed forty weeks of absence. The attitude of the British government toward the notion of parental leave after childbirth is further emphasized by its decision to reject a European Union directive that fathers should have statutory entitlement to unpaid paternity leave. This provides further evidence of the failure of the British state to recognize that mothers and fathers have equal responsibilities toward children.

Given the constraints that mothers face in entering or remaining in the labor market, it is scarcely surprising to find mothers adopting a whole variety of compromise solutions so that they can successfully juggle their domestic and paid work responsibilities. As we have seen, part-time employment is the route chosen by many mothers. Others include home employment—notoriously exploitative, whether it involves machining clothes, stuffing envelopes, assembling Christmas novelties or electronic equipment, or more high-tech telecottage work. Job sharing remains a rare phenomenon, with employers often wary of its costs rather than enthusiastic about its benefits. Some mothers take up the option of setting up in business, where they feel more at liberty to determine their own hours of work, and it is certainly true that the rate of increase of self-employment among women is higher than it is among men (for case study material on this, see Wheelock, 1993). Given employed mothers' continuing double burden, it is scarcely surprising that such evidence as there is points to married women being more responsive to tax- and benefit-induced incentives and disincentives than their husbands (Dilnot and Kell, 1989).

Sharing Work

The years since the Second World War, and the last two decades in particular, have been marked by dramatic changes in the structure of family life in Britain: The marriage rate has fallen; the divorce rate has increased; more families are headed by a single parent; increasing numbers of children are born outside marriage; and more women are choosing to start families later in life, or opting not to have children at all. These changes have been accompanied by transformations in the structure of employment to the extent that, if present trends continue, more women than men will be participating in the labor market by the end of the century. The consequence of this labor market change as far as families are concerned has been two distinct forms of polarization: between the employment potential of men and women, and between "work-rich" and "work-poor" families. These trends are part and parcel of a further polarizatio:., that between relatively well-paid managerial/professional women, and poorly paid working-class women.

In addition, growing flexibility of work is likely to have a significant impact on working time patterns. If unpaid domestic and child-care work is also be done, the move to two-earner families and more continuous female participation requires greater predictability of working hours so that domestic and employment timetables can be intermeshed (Horrell, et al., 1994). Women's double burden has in part been cushioned by state-provided welfare services, but these are also under threat from the very same forces of economic change.

The challenge for policy is how to address the implications of these changes for the social reproduction of the family. The situation calls for strategies that not only facilitate opportunities for women to take advantage of the growing availability of work, but also that address ways to allow men to share in the benefits of economic growth while at the same time increasing their commitment to other aspects of family life that involve them in roles going beyond that of economic provider. It is also important to ensure that children do not lose out. The report from the Commission on Social Justice (1994) pointed to the need to establish a balance between two objectives: to empower women to share financial as well as emotional responsibility for children, and to encourage and enable men to share the emotional and practical, as well as the financial, responsibilities for parenting.

This requires the means by which men and women can participate fully in both paid employment work and unpaid domestic work. It requires new attitudes toward work, family, and gender. Women may be helped into employment by increased provision of low-cost child care and reforms in the taxation and social security systems, and each of these are urgently required. But one of the priorities surrounds encouraging men to take more time to participate in domestic and child-care work. Rubery (1994) has suggested that the best way to achieve this would be by raising the pay of women workers, an action that would enable families to attain reasonable standards of living without fathers working excessive overtime. Policies to shorten the working week would be an important complement.

It is clear that current employment patterns are set to continue into the next millennium. These have not necessarily been the intention of state policy. Yet they have consequences that place them clearly in the policy arena, calling for imaginative approaches to family life and gender relationships. Britain needs a policy framework that allows a fit between work and family for fathers as well as mothers, otherwise the current generation of parents and their children will lose out.

Notes

1. See Smith and Wallerstein (1994) on how Kondratieff cycles relate to the household.
2. A variety of European Union rulings in the 1990s are increasingly challenging this situation.

References

Anderson, M., Bechhofer, F., and Gershuny, J. (Eds.) (1994). *The social and political economy of the household*. Oxford: Oxford University Press.

Armstrong, P., Glyn, A., and Harrison, J. (1991). *Capitalism since 1945*. Oxford: Blackwell.

Atkinson, J.S. (1984). *Flexibility: Uncertainty and manpower management* (Institute of Manpower Studies Report 89). Falmer, UK: University of Sussex.

Baldwin, S., and Falkingham, J. (Eds.) (1994). *Social security and social change*. Hemel Hempstead: Harvester/Wheatsheaf.

Balls, E., and Gregg, P. (1993). *Work and welfare: Tackling the jobs deficit*. London: Institute of Public Policy Research.

Brannen, J., and Moss, P. (1991). *Managing mothers: Dual earner households after maternity leave*. London: Unwin Hyman.

Burrows, R., and Loader, B. (Eds.) (1994). *Towards a post-Fordist welfare state?* London: Routledge.

Chaney, J. (1980). *Social networks and job information*. Report to Joint SSRC/EOC Research Committee.

Commission on Social Justice (1994). *Social justice: Strategies for national renewal*. London: Vintage Press.

Condy, A., and Roberts, C. (1995). Families and work. In R. Bayley, A. Condy, and C. Roberts (Eds.) *Policies for families: Work, poverty and resources*. London: Family Policy Centre.

Cooper, C.L., and Lewis, S. (1993). *The workplace revolution: Managing today's dual career families*. London: Kogan Page.

Cutler, T., Williams, K., and Williams, J. (1986). *Keynes, Beveridge and beyond*. London: Routledge and Kegan Paul.

Dilnot, A., and Kell, M. (1989). Male unemployment and women's work. In A. Dilnot and I. Walker (Eds.) *The economics of social security*. Oxford: Oxford University Press.

Equal Opportunities Commission (1993). *Annual report*. Manchester: EOC.

Folbre, N. (1994). *Who pays for the kids? Gender and the structures of constraint*. London: Routledge.

Foreman-Peck, J. (1985). Seed corn or chaff? New firm formation and the performance of interwar economy. *Economic History Review, 8* (3), 402–422.

Galbraith, J.K. (1975). *Economics and the public purpose*. London: Andre Deutsch.

General Household Survey. (1992). Office of Population Censuses and Surveys. London: HMSO.

Gershuny, J. (1983). *Social innovation and the division of labour*. Oxford: Oxford University Press.

Gershuny, J., Godwin, M., and Jones, S. (1994). The domestic labour revolution: A process of lagged adaptation. In M. Anderson, F. Bechhofer, and J. Gershuny (Eds.) *The social and political economy of the household*. Oxford: Oxford University Press.

Glasner, A. (1992). Gender and Europe: Cultural and structural impediments to change. In J. Bailey (Ed.) *Social Europe*. Harlow: Longmans.

Gregson, N., and Lowe, M. (1993). Renegotiating the domestic division of labour? A study of dual career households in northeast and southeast England. *Sociological Review, 41*, 475–505.

Harkness, S., Machin, S., and Waldfogel, J. (1994). *The decline of the male breadwinner*. London: STICERD, London School of Economics.

Harman, H. (1993). *The century gap*. London: Vermilion.

Harrop, A., and Moss, P. (1994). Working parents: Trends in the 1980s. *Employment Gazette 102*, 18, 343–351.

Haskey, J. (1993). Lone parents and married parents with dependent children in Great Britain: A comparison of their occupation and class profile. *Population Trends, 72*, 33–44.

Henwood, F., and Wyatt, S. (1986). Women's work, technological change and shifts in the employment structure. In R. Martin and B. Rowthorn (Eds.) *The geography of deindustrialisation*. London: Macmillan.

Hollands, R.G. (1990). *The long transition: Culture, class and youth training*. London: Macmillan.

Horrell, S., Rubery, J., and Burchell, B. (1994). Working-time patterns, constraints and preferences. In M. Anderson, F. Bechhofer, and J. Gershuny (Eds.) *The social and political economy of the household*. Oxford: Oxford University Press.

Humphries, J., and Rubery, J. (1992). The legacy for women's employment: Integration, differentiation and polarisation. In J. Mitchie (Ed.) *The economic legacy: 1979–1992*. London: Academic Press.

International Year of the Family. (1994). *Making the connection: Competition, effective working and the family*. Ottawa, Canada: The Committee.

Jahoda, M. (1982). *Employment and unemployment: A social psychological analysis*. Cambridge: Cambridge University Press.

Jessop, B. (1994). The transition to post-Fordism and the Schumpeterian workfare state. In R. Burrows and B. Loader (Eds.) *Towards a post-Fordist welfare state?* London: Routledge.

Jordan, B., James, S., Kay, H., and Redley, M. (1991). *Trapped in poverty? Labour market decisions and low-income households.* London: Routledge.

Jowell, R., Brook, L., Taylor, B., and Prior, G. (1991). *British social attitudes: The 18th report.* Dartmouth: Aldershot.

McKee, L., and Bell, C. (1985). Marital and family relations in times of male unemployment. In B. Roberts, R. Finnegan, and D. Gallie (Eds.) *New approaches to economic life.* Manchester: Manchester University Press.

Martin, J. (1984). *Women and employment: A lifetime perspective.* London: HMSO.

Martin, R., and Rowthorn, B. (Eds.) (1986). *The geography of deindustrialisation.* London: Macmillan.

Massey, D. (1994). *Space, place and gender.* Cambridge: Polity.

Millar, J. (1994). *Poor mothers and absent fathers: Support for lone parents in comparative perspective.* Social Policy Association Conference, University of Liverpool.

Mitchie, J. (Ed.) (1992). *The economic legacy: 1979–1992.* London: Academic Press.

Morris, L. (1985). Renegotiation of the domestic division of labour in the context of redundancy. In B. Roberts, R. Finnegan, and D. Gallie (Eds.) *New approaches to economic life.* Manchester: Manchester University Press.

Morris, L. (1990). *The workings of the household.* Cambridge: Polity.

New Earnings Survey. (1992). Department of Employment. London: HMSO.

Pahl, J. (1989). *Money and marriage.* Basingstoke: Macmillan.

Paul, R.E. (1984). *Divisions of labour.* Oxford: Blackwell.

Phillips, A. (1983). *Hidden hands: Women and economic policies.* London: Pluto Press.

Policy Studies Institute. (1992). *Credit and debt: The PSI Report.* London: PSI.

Roberts, B., Finnegan, R., and Gallie, D. (Eds.) (1985). *New approaches to economic life.* Manchester: Manchester University Press.

Rowthorn, B. (1986). De-industrialisation in Britain. In R. Martin and B. Rowthorn (Eds.) *The geography of deindustrialisation.* London: Macmillan.

Rowthorn, B. (1992). Government spending and taxation in the Thatcher era. In J. Mitchie (Ed.) *The economic legacy: 1979–1992.* London: Academic Press.

Rubery, J. (1994, June). *What do women want from full employment?* Paper presented at TUC Conference: Looking Forward to Full-Employment. London: Congress House.

Sly, F. (1993). Women in the labour market. *Employment Gazette* (November): 483–495.

Smith, J., and Wallerstein, E. (1992). *Creating and transforming households.* Paris: Cambridge University Press.

Social Trends. (1992). Office of Population Censuses and Surveys. London: HMSO.

Stubbs, C., and Wheelock, J. (1990). *A woman's work in the changing local economy.* Aldershot: Avebury.

Wajcman, J. (1983). *Women in control: The dilemmas of a workers' co-operative.* Milton Keynes: Open University Press.

Waring, M. (1989). *If women counted: A new feminist economics.* London: Macmillan.

Watson, G., and Fothergill, B. (1993). Part-time employment and attitudes to part-time work. *Employment Gazette,* (May), 213–220.

West, J. (Ed.) (1982). *Women, work and the labour market.* London: Routledge and Kegan Paul.

Wheelock, J. (1990). *Husbands at home: The domestic economy in a post-industrial society.* London: Routledge.

Wheelock, J. (1993). The flexibility of small business family work strategies. In K. Caley, E. Chell, F. Chittenden, and C. Mason (Eds.), *Small enterprise development: Policy and practice in action.* London: Paul Chapman Publishing.

Wheelock, J. (1995). People and households as economic agents. In M. Macintosh, et al., *Economics and changing economies*, (pp. 79–112). Milton Keynes, UK: The Open University.

Wheelock, J., and Oughton, E. (1996). The household as a focus for research. *Journal of Economic Issues, XXX* (1) (March), 1–17.

Wilson, E. (1987). Thatcherism and women: After seven years. In R. Meleband, L. Panetch, and J. Saville (Eds.) *Socialist Register* (pp. 199–235). London: Merlin Press.

Yeandle, S. (1984). *Working women's lives: Pattern and strategies.* New York: Tavistock.

Chapter Two
Employed Mothers in Germany

Sabine Walper and Nancy L. Galambos

A consideration of the employment situations of German women and the impact of employment on their lives and on family members affords a rare and unique opportunity to observe how the experiences of women in the labor force are intimately connected with sociohistorical change, political and economic ideologies, and cultural beliefs about gender roles. The historical changes in Germany in the second half of this century, especially the development of two separate states with dramatically different political and economic systems and the reunification of those states in 1989–1990, are fascinating in the differential impact that they have had on women's labor-force participation rates, their career trajectories, the availability of support for women with families (e.g., day care), the male-female earnings differential, and gender segregation in occupations. As we will see, in the space of five decades, ideological differences between the two states were associated with distinct changes and characteristics in the structure of society—a structure that was translated into differences in the very fabric of women's lives and work.

This chapter explores the differences and similarities in women's employment in the former Federal Republic of [West] Germany (FRG) and the [East] German Democratic Republic (GDR), and in the process offers an understanding of how these two republics shaped the experiences and expectations of women. We will also examine the current situation of employed women in Germany. Although the results are not yet in, owing to the relative recency of reunification, there are indications of the significance of this startling social change on former East German women in particular. After considering the broad sociohistorical context of employed women in Germany, we move to an examination of the empirical literature on

these women and their families. What does the research tell us about
the stresses and strains, the challenges, and the rewards that employed mothers experience? What is the impact of mothers' employment on children, on the division of labor in the household, and on
husbands? Finally, the chapter will conclude with the implications
of the current situation in Germany for social policy and the implementation of initiatives that follow from it.

Historical and Economic Background: Women in the German Democratic Republic

The labor-force participation of women in the former GDR
was firmly rooted in a political and economic climate that valued
the contributions of every worker. Indeed, the East German constitution declared not only that women and men had the right to
work but that they were obligated to do so (Rudolph, Appelbaum,
and Maier, 1990). In order to procure the labor of every individual,
equality of the sexes and the emancipation of women were explicitly
stated political goals that resulted in women's high level of
participation in the labor force, relatively easy access to vocational training and education, and entrance into traditionally male-
dominated occupations. Provisions were made for placement of children in day care, and generous maternity leaves were available (Maier,
1993).

The net result for women living in this centrally planned
economy was that by 1989, 49% of the labor force in East Germany
was composed of women, a figure that is substantially higher than
in industrialized countries, where on average the female share of the
labor force is about 41% (Maier, 1993; Nuss, 1989). Moreover, an
astonishingly high 85% of women between the ages of 15 and 65
were employed. Unlike the situation in the FRG, women with children were no less likely to be employed than women without children (Maier, 1993), except during the first year following the birth
of a child, when the majority of East German mothers took advantage of extended, paid parental leave from their guaranteed jobs.

The high labor-force participation rate of women with children
was made possible by the wide availability of state-subsidized day
care centers, nursery schools, and kindergartens that were open all
day and that provided hot meals to children. In the 1980s, places

were available for over 80% of all children not yet in school, including infants and toddlers. Women's involvement in the labor force was also made easier by the fact that companies served hot meals to workers, and laundry services were located on site such that the family's clothing could be dropped off and picked up the same day (Rudolph, et al., 1990). To facilitate the continued involvement of mothers in the work force after the birth of a child, mothers received one year of fully paid parental leave; and for those with more than one child, work hours were shortened without any subsequent reduction in pay (Maier, 1993).

Not only did these measures relieve women of some of their household burden, but we suspect that mothers experienced little of the guilt that is typical among many West German and North American mothers who are employed when their children are young (Krüger, Born, Einemann, Heitze, and Saifi, 1987; Scarr, 1984; Sommerkorn, 1988). After all, women in the GDR saw work as a moral obligation and access to child care as a right of the worker. This is much unlike the situation for women in the FRG, where it was, and continues to be, widely believed that day care is harmful to children (Beer and Mueller, 1993).

Women in East Germany were relatively highly educated and well trained for their occupations. As of 1989, about 90% of women who were employed had completed skilled vocational training or college/university (which is equivalent to a master's degree in the United States). They also accessed typically male-dominated degree programs in medicine, mathematics, and natural sciences. For example, 20% of engineering students were women, compared with 10% in the former West Germany (Maier, 1993; Rudolph, et al., 1990). Significantly more women in the GDR than in the FRG were employed in occupations such as manufacturing, agriculture, and the trades (Maier, 1993).

Lest we begin to see the GDR as a utopia in which the sexual division of labor was completely absent, it is important to recognize that women were still expected to carry out most of the domestic work in addition to their paid labor (Beer and Mueller, 1993). Equality of the sexes was not only a goal for its own sake but was also promoted in the service of economic survival of the state. And since the state could well survive with women having a larger share of the domestic burden, there was little questioning of "traditional" roles in the household.

While East German women were ahead of their sisters in the West on many indices such as availability of day care, status of occupation, and levels of education and training, there was still a gap between what men and women were paid. On average, the monthly income of a full-time employed woman was 76% of the full-time employed man's earnings, a figure that compared favorably with the 66% in the former West Germany (Rudolph, et al., 1990). And although women in the GDR had gained entrance into nontraditional occupations, there were still fewer women than men in those occupations. About 30% of managers were female (a high percentage relative to industrialized nations in general), but even these were positioned at lower or intermediate levels. Given the high level of East German women's integration into the occupational and educational network, the inferior earnings of East German women compared with East German men was attributable in part to wage discrimination based on gender rather than on educational or vocational experience (Gerlach, 1987; Hannan, Schoemann, and Blossfeld, 1990; Maier, 1993).

Women in the Federal Republic of Germany

In contrast to the overriding political focus on enabling women's employment in East Germany, the West German state has been characterized by a conservative ideology on gender roles that underscores women's primary duties as mothers and homemakers (Schneewind, 1995). The old German maxim *Kinder, Kirche, Kueche* ("children, church, kitchen") aptly captures the predominant view of women's appropriate roles in the past, a view that was officially dismissed in the 1970s but still shapes family policies, at least as far as child care is concerned. It was only in 1977 that the Marriage and Family Law was reformed, a law that lauded full-time motherhood and had granted men some control over their wives' right to work (Lane, 1993). And even now, women's main responsibility for child care and household duties is hardly questioned, thus limiting their options on the labor market.

With this conservative gender ideology in place, the labor-force participation of women in the former West Germany stands in stark contrast to that in the former East Germany. In the FRG, about 40% of the total labor force in the late 1980s was composed of women (Rudolph, et al., 1990). Of those women of working age, 55% were in the labor force, a figure that until recently had not changed much over the course of this century. For example, in 1925, 48% of women in the FRG were employed; by 1982, that figure had grown only to 51% (Maier, 1993; Sass, 1986).

These overall statistics, however, mask some significant changes in demographic features of the female labor force. First, due to the general increase of educational level and years spent in school and job training, the timing of first entry into the labor market has been postponed markedly. Hence, the mean age of women in the labor force has increased. And second, the percentage of women who were never employed or who remained out of the labor market until age 45 dropped from 53.5% for the birth cohorts 1900–1919 to only 28% for women born in 1940–1949. At the same time, the percentage of women who were employed continuously up to age 45 increased dramatically from 2.8% (for the 1900–1919 cohort) to 18.7% (for the 1940–1949 cohort) (Kirner and Schulz, 1992, p. 40). Especially significant increases in labor-force participation occurred among married women and mothers with children under age 18, mostly in the 1980s (Gensior and Schoeler, 1989).

The typical pattern in the FRG is for women to leave the labor force after the birth of a child, and remain out of it for six to eight years (Maier, 1993). In 1987, the percentages of mothers employed was 37% for those whose children were less than 2 years, 42% for those with 3- to 5-year-old children, and 52% of those with children aged 6 to 13 years (Lane, 1993). Inadequate provisions for day care make it difficult for women in the FRG to combine work with parenting, and the fact that school children return home at noon makes even part-time work a difficult act to juggle (Lane, 1993). In the late 1980s there was day care space for only 4 percent of children under three, 30 percent of children between ages three and four, and 70 percent of children between four and five (Rudolph, et al., 1990).

Compared with women in the GDR, women in the FRG attained lower levels of education and training. As of 1990 about 65% of employed women in West Germany had completed skilled vocational training or some postsecondary education (compared with

87% in East Germany). Women in the FRG also had limited access
to typically male-dominated degree programs. Given these training
differences, occupational segregation was more prominent in the
FRG, with women positioned most frequently in the service sector
(Maier, 1993; Rudolph, et al., 1990). Indeed, the number of West
German women employed in service occupations increased and the
number of women employed in manufacturing occupations decreased
during the 1980s (Gensior and Schoeler, 1989). Of course, occupational segregation contributes to male-female wage differentials, a
factor that helps to explain the higher wage differential in West than
in East Germany. There are signs, however, that this wage differential in the FRG may be decreasing (Hannan, et al., 1990).

It is against this backdrop of differences between East and West
that reunification occurred. Naturally, such a merging of formerly
diverse ideologies, situations, and expectations will not occur without presenting adjustment difficulties to some, if not a large portion, of the population. As we will see, it is perhaps women from the
former GDR who have experienced the most dramatic changes in
their lives, not only because they have had to adjust to a market
economy, but also because imposed on them is an ideology that
challenges their very right to work and the high value that they place
on work outside of the home.

Present Demographics: Women in a Unified Germany

Immediately upon reunification, predictions were that former East
German women would shoulder the costs of reunification. These
predictions were based on several lines of reasoning. First, those sectors in which women played prominent roles would be most likely
to lose in a restructured economy (e.g., light industry, textiles, and
clothing; administrative positions). Second, child care facilities would
be closed because of economic exigencies. Third, where East German men would be looking for work, discriminatory hiring practices would occur, keeping East German women out of the labor
force (Rudolph, et al., 1990).

In large part, these predictions have been realized, as many
former East German women now find themselves at home unemployed. While 4 million East German women were employed
in November 1989, that figure had dropped to only 2.9 million in

May 1992. The average unemployment rate during 1992 was twice as high among women (19.6%) as among men (10.5%) (Bundesministerium für Familie und Senioren, 1994, p. 154). In evaluating these unemployment rates, it is important to know that special labor market policies such as "short labor" (i.e., reduced working hours with reduced pay for former full-time jobs), early retirement, occupational training, and publicly subsidized temporary jobs have kept the unemployment statistics for East Germany lower than they actually are. If these measures did not ease the squeeze on the labor market, the unemployment rate would amount to about 40% (Bundesministerium für Familie und Senioren, 1994, p. 153).

Where cutbacks have been made, more women than men have been dismissed, and where there has been expansion, recruitment policies have favored the hiring of men. Reemployment has also been slower among women than among men. Among women from the former East Germany who are employed, many are in lower-paying and lower-prestige positions than they held previously, many are underemployed, and still others are employed in female-dominated occupations rather than in the nontraditional type of work to which they had been accustomed (Maier, 1993).

In this situation of dramatic economic changes—not only in the labor market, but in public child care as well—children (and potential child-bearing) emerge as major handicaps for East German women who seek employment. Compared with women without children, unemployment rates are higher among married mothers with children below age 16 and highest for single mothers, who are hit most frequently by long-term unemployment (Beckmann and Bender, 1993).

It is a new experience for former East German women to struggle to find adequate day care for their children (Beer and Mueller, 1993; Maier, 1993). Indeed, a stark and dramatic rise in the numbers of abortions and sterilizations has occurred among women from the former GDR, as they have chosen work over motherhood in a system that, from their perspective, forces them to make such a choice. "No woman can be certain that this renunciation of motherhood will actually achieve what she desires, namely economic independence, but many women do seem convinced that with a child their chances of attaining that goal are zero" (Beer and Mueller, 1993, p.

292). Surveys have shown that women from the former East Germany are extremely unwilling to give up their roles as workers. About 70% would prefer to work, even if their husbands could financially support the family (Beer and Mueller, 1993; Maier, 1993). There are almost no differences in preferences for working between women with children below age 16 and women with older or no children (Bundesministerium für Familie und Senioren, 1994, p. 169).

In the West, more so than in the East, children and marital status determine women's labor-force participation. Women's employment rates in the West vary between 55% for those without children to 24% for mothers with five children, while the respective difference in the East is only 69% to 50% (data for 1991; Bundesministerium für Familie und Senioren, 1994, p.152). Separated, divorced, and never-married women in the West are more likely to be employed than married women and widows, a finding that clearly reflects differences in the economic "pull" into the labor market.

This brings us to the more general question of women's motives for being employed. However, before addressing this issue, we will turn to the effects of maternal employment on children, the most controversial issue in the public debate in West Germany.

Effects on Children

Concern about the consequences of maternal employment for children's development and well-being has guided scientific inquiry into women's employment in West Germany from the very beginning of studies in this area after World War II. In early studies, however, the focus was primarily on expected negative effects of employment on mothers' role performance in the family—that is, their caretaking competencies and attitudes and their ability to devote energy, patience, and tender caring to their children. Several assumptions that guided early research on maternal employment and its consequences for children were summarized by Pfeil (1961, p. 325): (a) When mothers are employed, they are not available to supervise their children. (b) Time available for education and caretaking by mothers is, thus, reduced to a few hours per day. (c) In addition, the physical and psychological strains experienced by mothers in dual roles make it difficult to nurture their children with the necessary concentration and care. (d) No form of day care, no matter how good, can replace the mother (see Schütze, 1988).

Considering these assumptions, it came as a surprise that empirical findings did not support what seemed to be the logical consequences of these assumptions. For example, in a comparison of teachers' judgments of 113 children with employed mothers to 145 children with nonemployed mothers (Speck, 1956), only minor—largely insignificant—differences emerged. Differences were particularly small with regard to objective data (days absent from school: 2.5% more among children with employed mothers) and largest for subjective evaluations (personality problems: 17.5% more among children with employed mothers), suggesting some bias on the teachers' side (Schütze, 1988). Significant costs of maternal employment regarding children's cleanliness, their active participation during lessons, and their social contacts were not observed. A closer look, however, revealed that girls, in fact, seemed to benefit: They had better grades in mathematics, and were more differentiated and self-controlled than were daughters whose mothers were not employed (Schreiner, 1963).

During the late 1960s and 1970s, John Bowlby's concept of maternal deprivation provided the scientific framework for the continued search for disadvantages accruing to children with employed mothers in West Germany (Schütze, 1988). Although a critical review of the literature showed that maternal employment had only very limited effects on mothers' parenting and no direct effect on children (Lehr, 1974), the debate still continues today. Opponents of maternal employment, mostly pediatricians, stress the risks of mothers' working to children's health, well-being, and attachment to their mothers, particularly in the early years. Others such as Koch (1975) point to advantages for: (a) mothers' personality development; (b) the nature of mothers' interactions with their children, which may foster independence, assertiveness, and an achievement orientation; and (c) an increased variety of social experiences for children because of their involvement with multiple caretakers. Surprisingly, this controversy has not stimulated many empirical studies in Germany. Instead, researchers have relied on findings from the U.S.A.

One of the few studies in Germany, still in progress (Roos, 1993), compared the daily activities of the primary-school children of mothers in nuclear families with full-time, part-time, or no employment. So far, the findings have revealed only a few differences. Children whose mothers are not employed report more visits of friends to their homes than children with employed mothers, but there are no differences concerning their own visits to friends' homes. There were also no differences in the amount of TV watching or in children's fixed activities during the week (e.g., music lessons or sports). Children with employed mothers had more contact with their grandparents, who were often relied on as caretakers in the mother's absence (see also Lang, 1985). Hardly any children, however, have mentioned a desire for more contact with their mother. Peers have been much more favored in this regard irrespective of maternal employment status. Hence, this study finds little indication that the daily activities and experiences of school-aged children differ strongly depending on their mothers' employment status.

In line with these findings, a representative survey of school children aged 8 to 12 years in former West Germany revealed no effects of maternal employment on children's psychological well-being (Lang, 1985). And a careful study of children aged 10 to 15 years in Austria showed an advantage to children with employed mothers as indicated by their higher independence, security, and higher readiness for social engagement (Rollett and Reisel, 1988). When mothers felt strained by a high work load, however, children tended to develop less favorably. This effect was stronger when the mother's reports, rather than objective measures (e.g., personality tests on anxiety and irritability) of her children's well-being, were used. This study suggests that difficulties on the job have more impact on children's development, particularly mothers' perceptions of their children's development, than does employment status per se.

Although conclusive data are lacking, it seems plausible that maternal employment affects children's involvement in household tasks. In this respect, gender roles are still quite pronounced. In both parts of Germany, daughters are much more likely than sons to be involved in household tasks. In addition, East German girls more often play an instrumental role in the family than do West German girls, most likely because of the higher rate and longer daily duration of maternal employment in the East (Jugendwerk der Deutschen Shell, 1992; see Walper, in press).

A major issue in the debate over maternal employment is public child care. In line with West German family policies favoring family-based child care (see below), the supply of public child care is especially scarce for children up to 3 years of age. Little has changed in West Germany during the past 200 years concerning the attitude toward public child care for infants and toddlers (Beller, 1993). Parents' skepticism is still high, with many viewing child care outside the family in the early years as a rather unfavorable alternative for those who cannot afford to have the mother stay at home or to find a better "private" child care solution. The respective East-West difference in attitudes about day care is startling: Full-time day care up to age 3 is considered detrimental to children's development by almost two-thirds of West German adults, while two-thirds in East Germany believe it is not. Even later, during the preschool years, beneficial effects of full-time kindergarten are acknowledged by only about 20% of West German women and men, but over 60% of East German women and men (Institut für praxisorientierte Sozialforschung [IPOS], 1992, p. 63ff.).

Empirical findings, although scarce, do not support this prejudice against public day care (Beller, 1993). After all, a variety of features of the institution, such as its size and the training and interaction styles of the caretakers, play a major role in determining how effective and supportive of the child's development the child care situation is—and these features can be found in many public day care settings. Furthermore, findings from the Austrian study indicate that the timing of a mother's return to the workplace—and, hence, children's entry into day care—may be important. For instance, a one-year leave from work was related to higher levels of emotional problems in children than was continuous employment (after the legally prescribed maternal leave) or an extended interruption (or termination) of employment (Rollett and Reisel, 1988).

Finally, mothers of "difficult" children may place them more readily in a day care than mothers of "easy" children, thereby leading to selection instead of socialization effects (Beller, 1993). Hence, although the Austrian study suggests that child care outside the family during the first three years is negatively related to mothers' later evaluation of their children's development, such findings need to be qualified in future research. Furthermore, future evaluation is warranted, since this finding is restricted to mothers' subjective views of their children, which may well be shaded by feelings of guilt.

Effects on the Mothers

In West Germany, the question of how mothers are affected by employment has a long-standing history in social science. Not surprisingly, the issues addressed reflect prevailing ideological views on maternal employment as they have changed over time. Two distinct phases are characterized by different "scientific" concerns. The first phase dates back to the 1950s and the early 1960s and was dominated by the theory of polar sex-based character attributes defining natural personality differences between women and men (Schütze, 1988). Women were thought to complement men's activity, aggressiveness, and intellectuality with their passivity, patience, and emotionality, providing the basis for healthy family functioning. Women's main role was considered to be in the home, buffering children from the increasing influence of the evils of capitalism. Hence, women's entry into the labor market with its capitalistic and achievement-oriented demands seemed not only to contradict women's natural talents, but also to threaten the emotional richness and caring skills that were a necessary resource for intimate relationships.

Confronted with women's high employment rate in the postwar era, the first study on maternal employment found that economic pressure was a woman's main motivation to work outside the home (Schelsky, 1960). If other motives such as "liking the job" and "striving for independence" were also raised, they were almost always evaluated negatively (e.g., Speck, 1956; Pfeil, 1961). Although some investigations noted positive outcomes of maternal employment such as a strengthening of women's self-esteem and their growing self-reliance and security (e.g., Pfeil, 1961), the main focus was on possible negative effects on parenting competencies, a concern that was neither directly tested nor supported by the findings on children's well-being (see above).

The second phase of research on the effects of employment for mothers began in the 1980s and has been driven by entirely different questions (Schütze, 1988). Given the demand for equal opportunities and women's increasing level of education and occupational training, the focus shifted from children (and mothers' parenting competencies) to women's options for individualized life planning (Beck-Gernsheim, 1980, 1992), the instituional and work-related barriers against combining employment and child-rearing (Krüger, et al., 1987), the living conditions of employed mothers and full-time homemakers (Becker-Schmidt, Knapp, and Schmidt, 1984; Nauck, 1993) and—most recently—effects of employment on women's personality development and health (Brüderl and Paetzold, 1992).

Women's Work Orientation

It has become evident that women's main motivation in seeking employment is not economic pressure, at least as far as married women are concerned. As shown by a West German survey in 1986, only 16% of employed married women indicated that they needed the income for family living expenses (Bundesministerium für Familie und Senioren, 1994, p. 168ff.). Of course, other economic motives may be important, as well, such as wanting to improve one's standard of living (16%) and securing one's retirement pension (12%). However, in most cases intrinsic motives such as enjoying the work and the social contact with colleagues are also important. In the economically tight situation of East Germany, however, about 35% of employed married women work primarily to support their families, 12% to improve the family budget, and about 5% to improve their retirement situations.

Even in a reanalysis of older (1975) survey data of about 1,600 employed mothers—a sample that included a disproportionately large share (40% to 50%) of single mothers—economic motives emerged as less important than previously thought (Bertram and Bayer, 1984). Thirty-three percent of the mothers did not indicate any financial reason to work, and an additional 23% indicated economic as well as intrinsic motives. The findings of this as well as other studies were well suited to challenge widespread beliefs about a typical "female" work orientation. Most important, mothers' employment motivation and work orientation depend largely on the same factors that are important for men's work orientation: occupational prestige and work conditions such as self-directedness, lack of supervision, and decision-making power. Comparable to Kohn's findings (1969) for men in his classic study on occupational orientation, employed mothers endorsed intrinsic motives more strongly and considered their employment more often as necessary for their personal life satisfaction when they experienced greater self-directedness in their work and had more decision-making power. Thus, any comparison of men's and women's work orientation has to take into account differences in the specific demands of men's and women's jobs instead of referring to gender roles only. Interestingly, family-related factors such as number and ages of children and even problems in combining work and children did not matter for women's work orientation. Only husbands' positive attitudes to their wives' employment were related to a somewhat stronger intrinsic motivation among mothers.

These findings on women's employment motives caution against common causal explanations concerning maternal employment: What may be considered a "determinant" (e.g., work orientation) may actually turn out to be an "effect," and vice versa. Such interdependencies seem to occur in many respects for factors that we discuss as "effects" for mothers, but since we have to rely mostly on cross-sectional data, mutual influences across time cannot be disentangled.

Workload in Household, Child-Care, and Decision-Making Power

One of the extensively discussed and investigated effects of mothers' employment on mothers relates to their overall workload resulting from combining occupational and family duties. A recent survey conducted in East and West Germany shows high similarities for the distribution of time women spend in the household (Dannenbeck, 1992). Of all women between age 18 and 55, 63% in the West and 56% in the East say that they work over 20 hours a week in the household, despite the strong differences in employment rates. Household chores are still largely a female domain and thus contribute to the substantively larger combined workload of employment and household work among women than men. While 52% of East German women indicated working over 60 hours per week in both domains altogether, only about 30% of the men do so. In West Germany, the overall pattern is very similar, despite a somewhat lower overall workload: 41% of the women but only 25% of the men work over 60 hours per week in employment and household chores combined. Women's time spent on household chores decreases with increased employment hours, but 18% of those with 40 hours' employment per week still run a full "second shift" of over 40 hours in the household.

A closer look at the distribution of specific family tasks among couples shows that traditional patterns still prevail (Dannenbeck, 1992; Keddi and Seidenspinner, 1991; Oberndorfer, 1993). Women are mostly in charge of shopping, cleaning, cooking, child care, keeping contact with the child's teacher, and taking care of older, handicapped, or ill relatives. Men take care of repairs and renovations, while some tasks (e.g., playing with children, keeping contact with friends and relatives) are more equally distributed between both partners. As might be expected, maternal employment reduces the likelihood of a traditional role distribution in these domains, but the effects are moderate. While 73% of the couples with a full-time homemaking mother run their household according to the prevailing traditional pattern, the same holds true for 61% of the couples with employed mothers (Keddi and Seidenspinner, 1991, Table 12).

It seems that it is not so much "rational choice" that determines patterns of labor distribution between men and women but rather deep-rooted gender ideologies and idealizations of mother-child interdependencies—which function as a psychological barrier against more symmetrical role patterns and, hence, cause stress for employed mothers (Brüderl, 1992; Schröder, 1992). Women's subjective responsibility for family tasks and their high standards of housework and child care often leave employed mothers with feelings of personal failure, dissatisfaction, and guilt (Krüger, et al., 1987), especially concerning the time they devote to the children and family (Lang, 1985). As indicated by a representative survey on the compatibility of employment and child care in West Germany, women feel particularly responsible for managing the household efficiently on their own, when their employment is not due to financial reasons but to a need for social contact, activity, and personal competence (Born and Vollmer, 1983). And even though the majority of young mothers think that an "ideal" mother should be interested in things other than the child (Erler, Jaeckel, Pettinger, and Sass, 1988), they tend to have a guilty conscience when becoming reemployed again after the birth of a child (Bundesministerium für Arbeit und Sozialordnung, 1986). As Mueller (1991) pointed out: "Being anxious that the child could feel neglected turns out to be the heaviest burden of gainfully employed mothers, if they refer to problems caused by their way of life" (p. 164).

Thus, it is not surprising that in a study of European countries, West German women showed the lowest feelings of self-assurance and self-esteem, with a strong ambivalence in the evaluation of their full-time homemaking and employment (Erler, Jaeckel, and Sass, 1983). Family-oriented women who were not employed evaluated the situation of a full-time homemaker most negatively and held a rather positive image of employed women; the reverse pattern of evaluation was observed for employed women.

In general, there is a strong push into gender-typed family roles exerted by the birth of the first child, which holds true even for couples with previously nontraditional role patterns (Reichle and Montada, 1994; Schneewind and Vaskovics, 1992; Sieverding, 1992). Not surprisingly, the transition to parenthood is a crucial point for women's occupational planning as well as for the distribution of responsibilities among both partners. In West Germany it mostly requires women's renunciation of employment and, hence, often involves subjectively distressing losses in this respect. That mothers' withdrawal from the labor market is not fully voluntary is suggested by their evaluation of the multiple changes (Reichle and Montada, 1994): Those mothers who remained employed after child-bearing had the most positive balance in gains and losses resulting from the birth of their first child.

As mothers' workload increases with their participation in the labor market, so should their influence in the family. This expectation, derived from resource theory, finds mixed support. While some studies show that employed mothers indeed have more decision-making power than nonemployed mothers (Bertram and Bayer, 1984), others suggest that full-time homemakers more often consider themselves to be fully responsible and autonomous in decision-making compared with employed mothers, who more strongly endorse shared decision-making (Keddi and Seidenspinner, 1991). It seems as if maternal employment at least partly supports more cooperative patterns of decision-making, thus preventing the segregation of male and female domains of responsibility. However, as we will see when discussing the effects of maternal employment on fathers, the transition to parenthood turns out to be a crucial period for establishing role patterns in the partnership.

Women's Health

Given the high workload of employed mothers, one might expect negative effects on maternal health, deriving from the stress they experience. On the other hand, mothers with health problems may be more likely to leave the labor market, contributing to a positive selection bias for employed mothers. Finally, employed mothers may profit from the diversity of experiences in different role domains, which might compensate for any potential negative effects. Because homemakers often face a lack of intellectual stimulation combined with high emotional demands placed on them by family members (Ochel, 1992), working as a full-time homemaker may actually be more stressful than gainful employment.

As suggested by the diversity of hypotheses, findings are not consistent. In a large survey on women in Bavaria (the largest state in southern West Germany), employment was not related to mothers' subjective health status nor their report of psychosomatic symptoms (Gavranidou, 1993). However, employed mothers who worked more than 24 hours per week indicated higher feelings of strain than full-time homemakers and part-time employed mothers. This was irrespective of the age of the youngest child; that is, it could be observed in all phases of the family cycle.

In contrast to these findings, Borchert and Collatz (1992) reported findings from three studies that indicated higher well-being and health among work-oriented women and mothers in particular. In a large sample of pregnant women, those who were employed had markedly better health than those who were not employed. Contrary to household demands, which were mostly considered as stressful and had negative effects on the course of pregnancy and delivery, employment had positive effects on health behavior, pregnancy, and delivery. Most important, although employment and the respective expansion of women's domains of activity contributed to a larger number of life events experienced by employed women, they seemed to be better able to cope with these events than nonemployed women.

In their analyses of work and family orientation as determinants of women's well-being, Borchert and Collatz (1992) found that women's occupational qualifications and a higher number of children emerged as very important factors. The highest subjective stress was reported by nonskilled mothers with more than two children who worked full-time. Employment in nonskilled jobs also related to women's low life satisfaction, while, in general, well-trained employed women had the best health status. This was found to be true not only among women in general, but also among women with children. Compared with family-oriented mothers with many children, job-oriented mothers (who have higher occupational qualifications and are employed) seem to experience lower stress, are better able to cope with multiple demands, can rely on more social support, and enjoy better health. One of the rare longitudinal studies that allows us to look at mutual influences between women's health and employment across time assessed the status of women four months after the birth of a child and six years later. No relationship was found between maternal employment history and their self-reported and interviewer-rated health (Gavranidou and Heinig, 1992). Earlier health problems and maternal depressiveness four months after delivery did not have any prognostic influence on their later employment status. Much more important was mothers' satisfaction with their employment status and with their partner: Twelve of the 14 women who were dissatisfied with not being employed four months after the birth of their child had entered the labor market six years later, and all women who had been dissatisfied with their partners had later sought employment, most likely to achieve financial independence. However, because this study is restricted to a small sample of 39 mothers, it certainly warrants replication.

Overall, there does not seem to be a simple relationship between maternal employment and health. Women's job qualifications and job situations play a major role in moderating the effects of employment, and working as a full-time homemaker is not always considered the worst option—at least in West Germany.

Effects of Unemployment

While any comparison between employed mothers and homemakers has to deal with many factors related to the number of children, the availability of child care, and appropriate jobs in the area, a look at the effects of unemployment on mothers provides further insight into the meaning of employed work for mothers. As evident from unemployment surveys in West Germany, women experience less stress during unemployment than men (e.g., Brinkmann, 1986), which has mostly been explained by the higher availability to women of alternative roles in the family and household, their lower employment orientation, and lower financial strain in the face of income loss (see also Mohr, 1993). In this respect, East Germany is a special case, since women were socialized for full-time employment and they placed high importance on their work role. Accordingly, even among the long-term unemployed in East Germany, almost no woman indicates that she does not want to become reemployed (Hahn, 1993). If we look at those aspects of their previous work that the unemployed miss most, the multiple losses become evident. Aside from the regular income, which is considered most important, the large majority of women strongly miss "the feelings of being needed" and "the chance to use my skills"—with little signs of change across time (Ehrhardt, 1993; Hahn, 1993). The lack of approval gained through work was felt even more strongly as unemployment continued. Although these women are well aware of their poor chances for reemployment given the high unemployment rate among East German women, they are very reluctant to withdraw into the "silent reserve" of women who do not actively seek employment.

According to longitudinal data, there have been almost no changes in individual value orientations among unemployed women in East Germany (Hahn, 1993). As to the availability of alternative roles in the family, it is interesting to note that the value women place on the family does not increase during the course of unemployment (Ehrhardt, 1993). Although 41% of the women enjoyed having more time for the family after half a year of unemployment (as compared with 26% of the unemployed men), this percentage was significantly reduced to 27% about one year later, when it matched the figures for men. Almost 70% of these women missed the regular contact with colleagues, over 50% were anxious about not finding new employment, over 40% indicated that being at home gets on their nerves, and more than a third of the women sometimes felt really uncared for. Although some of the negative social consequences were lower among women who lived with a partner, children did not affect women's reactions to unemployment. Most important, there were no differences between East German women and men—supporting the notion that occupational socialization rendered the employment role for women in East Germany so focal to their self-concept and social network that it cannot permanently be compensated for by activities in the family domain.

Effects on Fathers

When discussing "effects" of maternal employment on fathers, we need to keep in mind that the available cross-sectional data on differences between men's attitudes and behavior depending on their wives' employment status are open to speculation concerning the causal direction of effects. Nonetheless, the findings concerning men's participation in household tasks are quite telling with respect to indicating prevailing role constellations in the domestic domain.

Effects of maternal employment on men's gender attitudes are a case in point. As suggested by a representative study of men, their wife's or female partner's employment seems to affect men's sensitivity toward questions of equality, discrimination, and the problem of coordinating family and work demands (Metz-Göckel and Müller, 1986). Somewhat surprisingly, this increased sensitivity is even reflected in men's perceptions of their own workplace. Those men with an employed female partner stated more often than men with a nonemployed partner that they work in companies with an equal proportion of male and female employees, and they even acknowledged more often having female supervisors and female colleagues at the same occupational level. Most important, this finding holds true even when the husbands do not approve of their wives' employment. Hence, it seems as if men are less likely to stick to a gender-segregated world view if their wife is gainfully employed, irrespective of how they evaluate their own wives' employment situation (Mueller, 1991).

As to the division of labor in the household, maternal employment has only very limited effects on fathers. According to findings from the West German family survey, the overall time men spent in household chores increases just slightly with their wives' involvement in the work role (Krombholz, 1991). While 25.6% of the fathers with a full-time employed wife work between 11 and 20 hours in the household, only 18.7% of those with a nonemployed wife do so. Higher involvement in household tasks remains women's duty. Only 15% of the fathers invest more than 20 hours per week in household tasks, no matter if the mother is full-time employed or a homemaker. In contrast, 90% of the mothers who are not employed and 60% of the full-time employed mothers do so. Nonetheless, if we look at the distribution of gender-typed tasks, families with employed mothers have slightly less traditional patterns (61%) than families with nonemployed mothers (75.3%) because of a higher preference for task sharing (Keddi and Seidenspinner, 1991).

Findings for East Germany show a very similar asymmetry in fathers' and mothers' household work (Dannenbeck, 1992). If both partners are employed, 49% of the men but only 9% of the women report spending not more than 10 hours a week on household chores. As might be expected, men's higher education contributes to less traditional division of labor patterns (i.e., men's higher participation in family tasks).

Although a number of findings suggest that contemporary men participate more in child care than men did some decades ago (Erler, et al., 1983), this increased involvement obviously does not generalize to other "feminine" family tasks. Men who are willing to assume the homemaker role either part time or full time, along with a corresponding reduction in their employment, are rare. Findings on their activities and life satisfaction indicate that full-time homemaking men fare less well than those who are homemakers only part time (Strümpel, Prenzel, Scholz, and Hoff, 1988). For most men, the primary importance of the work role remains unchanged (Sieverding, 1992). For example, if the child is ill and one of the parents has to take a leave to care for the child, only 4% of the fathers with an employed wife would do so (Ochel, 1992). The vast majority leave this duty to the mother.

Surprisingly, this gender inequality was not publicly addressed as problematic in East Germany, and in both parts of Germany women seem to have accepted the given role distribution. According to the IPOS-survey (1992), 89% and 88% of the women in the East and West, respectively, are satisfied with the division of labor in the household, and even among the employed, only 10% (East) to 13% (West) wish that their husbands would do more household chores. It seems as if women accept the given arrangement—perhaps because they know that men's higher participation would be "costly." Detailed analyses from a West German survey suggest that in the early phase of the family cycle, husbands' higher participation in routine household duties even relates to slightly increased tensions between family and work experienced by employed mothers (Nauck, 1987). However, since these cross-sectional data leave the causal direction open, it is similarly possible that mothers' felt strain in family life calls for husbands' higher involvement in household work.

From a developmental viewpoint, one may suspect that men's participation in household and child-rearing tasks is not only dependent on mothers' current employment status but also on the division of labor established in earlier phases of the family cycle. Indeed, the transition to parenthood may be a "sensitive period" in this respect, given that maternal employment after the birth of the first child seems to affect the later division of family tasks among both partners (Walper, 1993a). In families with preschool or school-age children, fathers assumed a larger share of family tasks on their own if the mother had returned to her job after the birth of the first child. Task sharing was not higher in families with continuously employed mothers, but both partners seem to have established a pattern of assigned responsibilities, as indicated by a similarly enhanced rate of tasks being performed by the mother only. This holds true irrespective of the mothers' current employment status and of their attitudes toward maternal employment.

Aside from these immediate effects, there are less obvious influences of maternal employment on fathers. As shown by a study on effects of economic deprivation on parents' well-being and family life, maternal employment may buffer against the negative consequences of income loss on fathers (Walper, 1988). However, this finding does not hold true across various socioeconomic groups. Better educated families profit the most from maternal employment, in terms of fathers' psychological well-being and their communication with children following income loss. The lower traditionalism in these families may be important here, allowing for a positive interpretation of maternal employment as a resource in coping with the main breadwinner's economic loss, as opposed to viewing this "role change" as a threat.

Finally, the father's role in child-rearing and his relationship to the children seem to be affected by the mother's employment. This not only holds true for the often-cited increase in fathers' participation in child-care as a function of mothers' entrance into the work force, but also for their resulting influence on children. Data from adolescents indicate that in families with full-time homemaking mothers, the father's (and mother's) subjective importance to the child (i.e., how important children consider the praise or negative evaluations provided by their father) is largely dependent on the marital relationship, with higher marital cohesion leading to the higher importance of parental feedback. Negative effects of parents' role strain on their importance to children are entirely mediated through the marital relationship. In families with full-time employed mothers, however, the quality of the marital relation does not matter, but with mothers' increasing role strain fathers gain in subjective importance to children (Walper, 1993b).

Effects on Family Structure

Although there is a correspondence between the increasing rate of maternal employment and a decrease in birth rates in Germany, the desire for children has not decreased substantially, and the percentage of childless couples has changed only slightly (Nave-Herz, 1994). Although young couples—not necessarily married—enjoy many economic advantages because of the earnings of both partners, only a small minority consider this lifestyle as a lifetime preference (Schneewind and Vaskovics, 1992).

However, child-bearing has become a step in family development that is increasingly postponed by well-educated women of the younger cohorts (Huinink, 1989). This strategy has clear advantages, as it allows time to establish one's occupational career before committing one's time and energy to child-rearing or confronting the stress of combining both tasks. However, it has its risks, too, particularly the result of the increasing chances of involuntary childlessness (Nave-Herz, 1994). Less educated women, in contrast, opt for an increasingly earlier family formation, most likely because of the earlier independence from parents achieved by younger cohorts (Huinink, 1989). Furthermore, women with highly qualified jobs more often decide against a second child, trying to return to the labor market after the birth of the first child. In contrast, men's occupational status relates positively to the number of children born to the family, indicating quite different effects of men's and women's achievements in the labor market on family development.

It is important to note that it is not maternal employment per se but rather women's options for higher-qualified jobs that seem to determine their decisions concerning child-bearing, a finding that can well be explained by the likely loss of costly resources resulting from mothers' absence from the labor market. Most likely, these decisions would look quite different if the barriers to combining employment and child-rearing were lower.

As to the relation between maternal employment and divorce, relevant studies are lacking. Even if the divorce rate is higher among dual-earner couples, we would not know whether employment contributed to problems in the marital relationship and thus "caused" its instability, or whether it allowed women to get divorced, as suggested by data showing that mothers in an unsatisfying marital relationship are more likely to seek employment (Gavranidou, 1993), most likely to gain financial independence from a nonrewarding, possibly unstable relationship.

Effects on Policy

As previously noted, family policy in West Germany strongly emphasized families' responsibility for child care, while the former GDR needed mothers in the labor market and, hence, mobilized substantially more public resources to that end. If all demands of caring for the generation of young are translated into monetary values, less than 30% of the total in West Germany and over 80% in the former GDR had been provided by public sources (Liegle, 1991).

Particularly in the supply of public child care, West German policy has not been sensitive to the changing demands of families with employed mothers. As noted above, public child care is especially scarce for children up to 3 years of age, and even during the preschool years, when about 75% of all children in West Germany visit the kindergarten (Fried, 1993), the supply is mostly restricted to part-time day care without lunch for children. Full-time day care is available for only 7% of the 3- to 6-year-olds (Liegle, 1991).

Furthermore, school-age children generally leave school between noon and 1 P.M., and often spend irregular and few hours in school during the elementary years. Hence, this period in children's lives puts strong demands on parents (in practice, on mothers) in terms of child care. Public after-school day care is available for only 3.5% of West German elementary-school children (grades 1 to 4), while 82% of their agemates in the former GDR were in such institutions (Liegle, 1991). As a consequence, employed mothers in West Germany had to find private solutions for the child care problem, mostly relying on grandparents or baby sitters.

As one may guess from these figures, West German family policy favors a three-phase model of women's participation in the labor market. The first phase is when women are employed before the child-bearing years; the second phase is when mothers stay home until their children are sufficiently independent (i.e., up to their late school years); and the third phase is after the child-raising years, when women return to the labor market. To support family-based child care, especially during the early years, a parental leave act was introduced in 1986. This allows mothers or fathers who had been employed before the birth of the child to stay at home taking care of the child with a pay of up to DM 600 per month and guaranteed return to their former jobs. Currently, parental leave may be taken for up to three years, with payment being dependent on the spouse's earnings. This payment is limited to two years. Although fathers have the same right to parental leave, it is almost always mothers (85%) who use this option. Because access to preschool day care favors older children, places are scarce for the youngest group eligible for kindergarten, the 3-year-olds. Hence, the current model of a three-year parental leave after the child's birth often leaves a gap between parental leave and the child's entry into kindergarten, making it difficult for mothers to enter the labor market at that point.

Because of the many limitations of available child care, several companies have developed their own policies to allow for a better combination of work and child care. It is particularly large companies that either grant extended parental leave up to 7 or sometimes 10 years, provide their own child care, offer part-time jobs with a more flexible work schedule, or allow for home-based work (Schwartz, Schwarz, and Vogel, 1993). However, the effects of extended parental leave are very limited. Of 1,000 women who took advantage of the 7-year maternal leave granted by Siemens AG, only 100 returned to work after that period (*Sueddeutsche Zeitung,* May 20/21, 1995, p. V1/13). The rapid change in technology meant an equally rapid loss in job qualifications for those who do not remain in their jobs. Since only a very small minority of the companies (about 6%) provide training for mothers with extended leave, reemployment turns out to be quite difficult, for the employers as well as for the employees.

Company-provided child care has been quite controversial. Although it clearly helps parents to combine employment and family duties, it has its disadvantages. First, children have to be transported to the facilities, which are often far away from their homes. Thus, they have few chances to develop a social network of friends and playmates in the neighborhood. Second, as changing one's employer means losing the child care facility, parents become more dependent on the company. There are recent efforts to find improved solutions, such as providing open child care, which includes a certain percentage of noncompany children from the neighborhood and guarantees child care even if the parents are no longer employed by the company (Busch, Doerfler, and Seehausen, 1991; Schwartz, et al., 1993). These measures are motivated mostly by the companies' need to keep highly qualified mothers in their workplace. Whether unskilled workers would also profit from the same measures is quite questionable.

Summary

The comparison of families with employed mothers in East and West Germany shows evidence of strong differences before unification in the need for and public support of maternal employment in both societies. While maternal employment was normative in the former GDR with equal labor-force participation for women and men and little gender segregation in job training as well as access to occupational sectors and qualified positions, mothers in West Germany still struggle to combine family tasks and employment. Part-time employment, although a preferred means to reduce the overall workload and leave more time for the family, restricts women's chances for qualified positions and promotion, thus contributing to stronger gender segregation in the West German labor market. Furthermore, the preference for family-based child care along with traditional views of motherhood puts West German mothers in charge of full-time child care for a considerable phase in the family cycle. West German mothers who delegate this task and seek employment experience feelings of guilt and personal inadequacy with respect to meeting the demands of their family roles—unlike their East German counterparts.

Nonetheless, the comparison of East and West points to striking similarities with respect to the division of labor in the domestic domain. While mothers increasingly entered the labor market, little changed in fathers' involvement in household chores, and even though their participation in child care increased somewhat, this increase pertained mostly to engagement in "fun" activities. This imbalance cannot be sufficiently reduced by employed mothers reducing the amount of time they spend on household chores. Domestic responsibilities clearly limit women's options for occupational involvement. Mueller (1991) quotes various findings and sources "free from any suspicion of being feminist (that) pointed out that with the division of domestic work as it is today, the family will tend to remain the last refuge for women's suppression" (p. 159). Men, women, employers, and work councils all agree: "It is neither lack of qualification, nor resistance to stress, nor adversity toward responsibility—but women's responsibilities for domestic work that prevents them from having an equal chance" (p. 161).

Despite the multiple demands, a substantial share of employed mothers enjoy the psychological and social—not only financial—advantages of their employment, gains from which the whole family may profit. Particularly East German women seem to consider their work role as a crucial part of their identity and indicate little desire for returning to a full-time homemaker role. Empirical studies have not found support for the idea that there are costs to the development and well-being of children if mothers are employed, unless the mothers feel strained by an overly high workload. Yet the perceived costs are still a major concern. Interestingly, East German youths' attachment to their mothers and fathers does not seem to have suffered from the high degree of maternal employment and extrafamilial child care, and in fact exceeds that of West German youth (see Walper, 1995).

It remains to be seen how reunification will be played out in women's and their families' lives in the long term. Undoubtedly, there will be further changes, as social forces from both East and West combine to shape women's lives. At the same time that the ideology of the West will hold some women back, the ideology brought from the East may act to further a less conservative view of the sexes.

References

Becker-Schmidt, R., Knapp, G.A., and Schmidt, B. (1984). *Eines ist zu wenig—beides ist zuviel. Erfahrungen von Arbeiterfrauen zwischen Familie und Fabrik.* Bonn: Verlag neue Gessellschaft.

Beck-Gernsheim, E. (1980). *Das halbierte Leben. Männerwelt Beruf, Frauenwelt Familie.* Frankfurt/M: Fischer.

Beck-Gernsheim, E. (1984). *Vom Geburtenrückgang zur Neuen Mütterlichkeit? Über private und politische Interessen am Kind.* Frankfurt/M.: Fischer.

Beck-Gernsheim, E. (1992). Anspruch und Wirklichkeit—Zum Wandel der Geschlechtsrollen in der Familie. In K.A. Schneewind, and L. v.Rosenstiel (Eds.), *Wandel der Familie* (pp. 37–47). Göttingen: Hogrefe.

Beckmann, P., and Bender, S. (1993). Arbeitslosigkeit in ostdeutschen Familien. Der Einfluß des Familienkontextes auf das individuelle Arbeitslosigkeitsrisiko. *Mitteilungen aus der Arbeitsmarkt- und Berufsforschung, 26,* 222–235. Stuttgart: Kohlhammer.

Beer, U., and Mueller, U. (1993). Coping with a new reality: Barriers and possibilities. *Cambridge Journal of Education, 17,* 281–294.

Beller, J. (1993). Kidnerkrippe. In M. Markefka and B. Nauck (Eds.), *Handbuch der Kindheitsforschung* (pp. 535–545). Neuwied: Luchterhand.

Bertram, H., and Bayer, H. (1984). *Berufsorientierung erwerbstätiger Mütter.* München: Deutsches Jugendinstitut.

Borchert, H., and Collatz, J. (1992). Empirische Analysen zu weiblichen Lebenssituationen und Gesundheit. In L. Brüderl, and B. Paetzold (Eds.), *Frauenleben zwischen Beruf und Familie: psychosoziale Konsequenzen für Persönlichkeit und Gesundheit* (pp. 189–209). Weinheim: Juventa.

Born, C., and Vollmer, C. (1983). *Familienfreundliche Gestaltung des Arbeitslebens. (Schriftenreihe des Bundesministeriums für Jugend, Familie, Frauen und Gesundheit, Bd. 135).* Stuttgart: Kohlhammer.

Brinkmann, C. (1986). Finanzielle und psychosoziale Folgen der Arbeitslosigkeit. *Materialien aus der Arbeitsmarkt-und Berufsforschung, 8.*

Brüderl, L. (1992). Beruf und Familie: Frauen im Spagat zwischen zwei Lebenswelten. In L. Brüderl and B. Paetzold (Eds.), *Frauenleben zwischen Beruf und Familie: psychosoziale Konsequenzen für Persönlichkeit und Beruf* (pp. 11–34). Weinheim: Juventa.

Brüderl, L., and Paetzold, B. (Eds.). (1992). *Frauenleben zwischen Beruf und Familie: Psychosoziale Konsequenzen für Persönlichkeit und Beruf.* Weinheim: Juventa.

Bundesministerium für Arbeit und Sozialordnung (Ed.) (1986). Erwerbstaetigkeit und Mutterschaft. Bonn: Bundesministerium für Familie und Senioren.

Bundesministerium für Familie und Senioren. (1994). Familien und Familienpolitik im geeinten Deutschland—Zukunft des Humanvermögens. Fünfter Familienbericht. Bonn: Bundesministerium für Familie und Senioren.

Busch, C., Doerfler, M., and Seehausen, H. (1991). Frankfurter Studie. Perspektiven und Möglichkeiten betrieblicher Förderung von Kinderbetreuungsangeboten. Frankfurt/M.: Bildungswerk der Hessischen Wirtschaft und Deutsches Jugendinstitut.

Dannenbeck, C. (1992). Zeitökonomische Aspekte der organisation des Familienalltags. In H. Bertram (Ed.), Die Familie in den neuen Bundesländern (pp. 187–212). Opladen: Leske + Budrich.

Ehrhardt, G. (1993). Ost-Berliner erwerbslose Frauen und Veränderungen im Rollenverhalten. In G. Mohr (Ed.), Ausgezählt. Theoretische und empirische Beiträge zur Psychologie der Frauenerwerbslosigkeit (pp. 126–152). Weinheim: Deutscher Studien Verlag.

Erler, G., Jaeckel, M., Pettinger, R., and Sass, J. (1988). Kind? Beruf? Oder Beides? Eine repräsentative Studie über die Lebenssituation und Lebensplanung junger Paare zwischen 18 und 33 Jahren in der Bundesrepublik Deutschland im auftrag der Zeitschrift Brigitte. München: DJI Verlag.

Erler, G., Jaeckel, M., and Sass, J. (1983). Mütter zwischen Beruf und Familie. München: Juventa.

Fried, L. (1993). Kindergarten. In M. Markefka and B. Nauck (Eds.), Handbuch der Kindheitsforschung (pp. 557–565). Neuwied: Luchterhand.

Gavranidou, M. (1993). Wohlbefinden und Erwerbstätigkeit im Familienverlauf. In B. Nauck (Ed.), Lebensgestaltung von Frauen: Eine Regionalanalyse zur Integration von Familien- und Erwerbstätigkeit im Lebensverlauf (pp. 235–260). Weinheim: Juventa.

Gavranidou, M., and Heinig, L. (1992). Weibliche Berufsverläufe und Wohlbefinden: Ergebnisse einer Längsschnittstudie. In L. Brüderl, and B. Paetzold (Eds.), Frauenleben zwischen Beruf und Familie: psychosoziale Konsequenzen für Persönlichkeit und Gesundheit (pp. 105–121). Weinheim: Juventa.

Gensior, S., and Schoeler, B. (1989). Women's employment and multinationals in the Federal Republic of Germany: The job-export question. In D. Elson and R. Pearson (Eds.), Women's employment and multinationals in Europe (pp. 60–79). New York: Macmillan.

Gerlach, K. (1987). A note on male-female wage differences in West Germany. Journal of Human Resources, 22, 584–592.

Hahn, T. (1993). Erwerbslosigkeitserfahrungen von Frauen in den neuen Bundesländern. In G. Mohr (Ed.), Ausgezählt. Theoretische und empirische Beiträge zur Psychologie der Frauenerwerbslosigkeit (pp. 87–125). Weinheim: Deutscher Studien Verlag.

Hannan, T.M., Schoemann, K., and Blossfeld, H.P. (1990). Sex and sector differences in the dynamics of wage growth in the Federal Republic of Germany. American Sociological Review, 55, 694–713.

Huinink, J. (1989). Ausbildung, Erwerbsbeteiligung von Frauen und Familienbildung im Kohortenvergleich. In G. Wagner, N. Ott. and H.J. Hoffmanbn-Nowotny (Eds.), Familienbildung und Erwerbstätigkeit im demographischen Wandel. Proceedings der 23. Arbeitstagung der Deutschen Gesellschaft für Bevölkerungswissenschaft am 28. Februar–3. März 1989 in Bad Homburg v.d.H. (pp. 136–158). Berlin, Heidelberg: Springer.

Institut für praxisorientierte Sozialforschung (IPOS). (1992). Gleichberechtigung von Frauen und Männern—Wirklichkeit und Einstellungen in der Bevölkerung. Stuttgart: Kohlhammer.

Jugendwerk der Deutschen Shell. (1992). Jugend '92. Im Spiegel der Wissenschaften (Band 2). Opladen: Leske + Budrich.

Keddi, B., and Seidenspinner, G. (1991). Arbeitsteilung und Partnerschaft. In H. Bertram (Ed.), *Die Familie in Westdeutschland* (pp. 159–192). Opladen: Leske + Budrich.

Kirner, E., and Schulz, E. (1992). Das Drei-Phasen-Modell der Erwerbsbeteiligung von Frauen—Begründung, Normen und empirische Evidenz. In N. Ott and G. Wagner (Eds.), *Familie und Erwerbstätigkeit im Umbruch* (pp. 17–55). Berlin: Duncker and Humblot.

Koch, R. (1975). *Berufstätigkeit der Mutter und Persönlichkeitsentwicklung des Kindes.* Köln: Pahl-Rugenstein.

Kohn, M.L. (1969). *Class and conformity: A study in values.* Chicago: University of Chicago Press.

Krombholz, H. (1991). Arbeit und Familie: Geschlechtsspezifische Unterschiede in der Erwerbstätigkeit und die Aufteilung der Erwerbstätigkeit in der Partnerschaft. In H. Bertram (Ed.), *Die Familie in Westdeutschland* (pp. 193–231). Opladen: Leske + Budrich.

Krüger, H., Born, C., Einemann, B., Heintze, S. and Saifi, H. (1987). *Privatsache Kind— Privatsache Beruf.* Opladen: Leske + Budrich.

Lane, C. (1993). Gender and the labour market in Europe: Britain, Germany and France compared. *Sociological Review, 41,* 274–301.

Lang, S. (1985). *Lebensbedingungen und Lebensqualitaet von Kindern.* Frankfurt/M.: Campus.

Lehr, U. (1974). *Die Rolle der Mutter in der Sozialisation des Kindes.* Darmstadt: Steinkopff.

Liegle, L. (1991). Vorschulerziehung und Familienpolitik vor und nach der Vereinigung. In P. Büchner and H.H. Krüger (Eds.), *Aufwachsen hüben und drüben* (pp. 137–145). Opladen: Leske + Budrich.

Maier, F. (1993). The labour market for women and employment perspectives in the aftermath of German unification. *Cambridge Journal of Economics, 17,* 267–280.

Metz-Göckel, S., and Müller, U. (1986). *Der Mann. Die Brigitte-Studie.* Weinheim: Beltz.

Mohr, G. (1993). Frauenerwerbslosigkeit: Spekulationen und Befunde. In G. Mohr (Ed.), *Ausgezählt. Theoretische und empirische Beiträge zur Psychologie der Frauenerwerbslosigkeit* (pp. 17–48). Weinheim: Deutscher Studien Verlag.

Mueller, U. (1991). The Family: Space for self-development or privatization of social problems? In W.R. Heinz (Ed.), *The life course and social change: Comparative perspectives* (pp. 159–168). Weinheim: Deutscher Studienverlag.

Nauck, B. (1987). *Erwerbstätigkeit und Familienstruktur.* München: DJI Verlag.

Nauck, B. (Ed.). (1993). *Lebensgestaltung von Frauen.* Weinheim: Juventa.

Nave-Herz, R. (1994). *Familie heute. Wandel der Familienstrukturen und Folgen für die Erziehung.* Darmstadt: Wissenschaftliche Buchgesellschaft.

Nuss, S. (1989). Women in the world of work: Statistical analysis and projections to the year 2000. Geneva: International Labour Office.

Oberndorfer, R. (1993). Aufgabenteilung in Partnerschaften. In B. Nauck (Ed.), *Lebensgestaltung von Frauen: Eine Regionalanalyse zur Integration von Familien- und Erwerbstätigkeit im Lebensverlauf* (pp. 145–175). Weinheim: Juventa.

Ochel, A. (1992). *Kinderbetreuung in Deutschland.* Brigitte-Untersuchung '92. Hamburg: Gruner und Jahr.

Pfeil, E. (1961). *Die Berufstätigkeit von Müttern.* Tübingen: J.C.B. Mohr.

Reichle, B., and Montada, L. (1994). Problems with the transition to parenthood. Perceived responsibility for restriction of losses and the experience of injustice. In M.J. Lerner and G. Mikula (Eds.), *Entitlement and the affectional bond: Justice in close relationships* (pp. 205–228). New York: Plenum Press.

Rollett, B., and Reisel, B. (1988). Entwicklungspsychologische Reanalyse der IFES-Untersuchung. In Österreichischer Arbeiterkammertag (Ed.), *Elternerwerbstätigkeit und Kindesentwicklung. Entwicklungspsychologische Determinanten und Konsequenzen des Frauenerwerbsverhaltens im Arbeitnehmer-Milieu.* Wien: Österreichischer Arbeiterkammertag.

Roos, J. (1993). Der Kinderalltag von Grundschuelern mit berufstaetigen und nicht berufstaetigen Muettern. Paper presented at the 11th Meeting of Developmental Psychology, Osnabrueck.

Rudolph, H., Appelbaum, E., and Maier, F. (1990). After German unity: A cloudier outlook for women. *Challenge, 33,* 33–40.

Sass, J. (1986). The German debate. In T.S. Epstein, K. Crehan, A. Gerzer, and J. Sass (Eds.), *Women, work and family in Britain and Germany* (pp. 109–117). London: Croom Helm.

Scarr, S. (1984). *Mother care—other care.* New York: Basic.

Schelsky, H. (1960). *Wandlungen der Deutschen Familie in der Gegenwart.* Stuttgart: F. Enke.

Schneewind, K.A. (1995). German Family: Changed patterns of marriage and family life. *Family Perspective, 29* (4), 337.

Schneewind, K.A., and Vaskovics, L.A. (1992). *Optionen der Lebensgestaltung junger Ehen und Kinderwunsch (Verbundstudie) (Schriftenreihe des Bundesministeriums für Familie und Senioren, Bd. 9).* Stuttgart: Kohlhammer.

Schreiner, M. (1963). Auswirkungen mütterlicher Erwerbstätigkeit auf die Entwicklung von Grundschulkindern. *Archiv für die gesamte Psychologie, 115,* 334–361.

Schröder, A. (1992). Berufstätige Mütter—zur Vereinbarkeit von Ideal und Wirklichkeit. In L. Brüderl and B. Paetzold (Eds.), *Frauenleben zwischen Beruf und Familie: psychosoziale Konsequenzen für Persönlichkeit und Gesundheit* (pp. 89–103). Weinheim: Juventa.

Schütze, Y. (1988). Mütterliche Erwerbstätigkeit und wissenschaftliche Forschung. In U. Gerhardt and Y. Schütze (Eds.), *Frauensituation. Veränderungen in den letzten zwanzig Jahren* (pp. 114–138). Frankfurt/M.: Suhrkamp.

Schwartz, W., Schwarz, T., and Vogel, C. (1993). *Mütter und Väter zwischen Erwerbsarbeit und Familie: Probleme—Praxisbeispiele—Orientierungshilfen.* Stuttgart: Ministerium für Arbeit, Gesundheit, Familie und Frauen Baden-Württemberg.

Sieverding, M. (1992). Wenn das Kind einmal da ist . . . Die Entwicklung traditionellen Rollenverhaltens bei Paaren mit ursprünglich egalitären Rollevorstellungen. In L. Brüderl, and B. Paetzold (Eds.), *Frauenleben zwischen Beruf und Familie: Psychosoziale Konsequenzen für Persönlichkeit und Gesundheit* (pp. 155–170). Weinheim: Juventa.

Sommerkorn, I.N. (1988). Die erwerbstätige Mutter in der Bundesrepublik: Einstellungs- und Problemveränderungen. In R. Nave-Herz (Ed.), *Wandel und Kontinuität der Familie in der Bundesrepublik Deutschland* (pp. 95–144). Stuttgart: Enke.

Speck, O. (1956). *Kinder erwerbstätiger Mütter.* Stuttgart: Enke.

Strümpel, B., Prenzel, W., Scholz, J., and Hoff, A. (1988). *Teilzeitarbeitende Männer und Hausmänner. Motive und Konsequenzen einer eingeschränkten Erwerbstätigkeit von Männern.* Berlin: Edition Sigma Bohn.

Walper, S. (1988). *Familiäre Konsequenzen ökonomischer Deprivation.* München: Psychologie Verlags Union.

Walper, S. (1993a). Berufsbiographie und Partnerschaft: Auswirkungen von Erwerbsunterbrechungen beim Übergang zur Elternschaft auf die Gestaltung der Partnerbeziehung. In B. Nauck (Ed.), *Lebensgestaltung von Frauen: Eine Regionalanalyse zur Integration von Familien- und Erwerbstätigkeit im Lebensverlauf* (pp. 177–208). Weinheim: Juventa.

Walper, S. (1993b). *Auswirkungen elterlicher Belastungen auf das Erziehungsverhalten: Erwerbstätige und nicht erwerbstätige Mütter im Vergleich.* Paper presented at the 11th Biennial Meeting of Developmental Psychology, Osnabrueck, September 28–30, 1993.

Walper, S. (1995). Youth in a changing context: The role of the family in East and West Germany. In J. Youniss (Ed.), *After the wall: Family adaptation in East and West Germany. New Directions for Child Development.* San Francisco: Jossey-Bass.

Chapter Three
Paid Work, Married Women, and the Family in India

G.N. Ramu[1]

This chapter briefly examines the nature of dual-earner families in India, with a special emphasis on women. India is one of the oldest civilizations in the world, with the majority of its population still living in villages, but it is also one of the fifteen major industrial countries. Its social system is hierarchic in terms of caste and wealth, while its political system is governed by democratic norms and practices. It is a society in which tradition and modernity not only coexist but also reinforce each other. Given such complexities and contradictions, it is rather difficult to provide a general model of dual-earner families that is applicable to all groups in India. The task has also been made very difficult by the absence of systematic studies of rural families, and this is striking given that most Indians live in rural areas. Consequently, the profile of dual-earner families depicted is incomplete.

This chapter is divided into five sections. The first section provides some background information on India, especially on its demographic, economic, political, and cultural dimensions. In the second section, issues concerning the status of women in general and their role in the labor force in particular are considered. The third section examines the positive and negative effects of women's paid work on their domestic roles, their well-being, their children, their husbands, and the structure of the family system. The fourth section considers social policies that would help or hinder working women's role in India. This is followed by a fifth, concluding section.

Indian Society: A Background
An objective understanding of the position of women in India is contingent upon understanding its demographic patterns, religious

traditions, political processes, family values, and legal framework. Historically, all these have coalesced to entrench inequalities between men and women both within and outside the home, regardless of economic contribution.

Demographic Patterns

Although geographically India is the seventh largest country in the world, it is the second most populous, with nearly 844 million people in 1991. Since 1951 the population of India has grown by about half a billion. With an annual average growth rate of over 2%, India's population is expected to exceed one billion by the year 2000, when it would constitute 28% of Asia's population and nearly 17% of the world's population (Premi, 1991). The birth rate for the period 1986–1991 was 27.5 per 1,000 population, although this was considerably lower than what it was in 1901 (49.2 per 1,000 population). The high proportion of those in their prime fertility period in the 1980s has kept the birth rate correspondingly high (Registrar General of India, 1991). The magnitude of the population growth in India has undoubtedly offset the economic gains the country has made since its independence. Despite its centralized planning for development in both the agricultural and industrial sectors, India has not succeeded in generating enough resources to provide even the most basic necessities for its ever-increasing population. One consequence of this failure is that some groups have remained on the fringe with no hope of relief in sight. Women are one such group.

A number of factors have contributed to India's unmitigated population growth. First, given the predominantly agrarian nature of the society, where manual labor is critical for the survival of the family, couples tend to bear many children, as they consider them an economic security blanket. Second, because of the preference on the part of most Indian couples for at least two male children, they continue to procreate until their goal is reached, and this naturally increases the fertility rate (Ramu, 1988). Male children are preferred because sons provide security to their parents in their old age, as well as play a critical role in funeral rites. Therefore, the primary responsibility of most Indian women is to bear male children and to rear them properly with the hope that they will become good providers. Third, improved health care, among other factors, has contributed to the decline in mortality rates in recent decades. For example, the death rate for the decade 1901–1910 was 42.6 per 1,000 population, but it declined rather dramatically to 10.3 for the period 1986–1991. Fourth, the infant mortality rate has also been declining— from 106 in 1984–1985 to 90 in 1989–1990 (Agrawal, Varma, and Gupta, 1992). Fifth, longevity is increasing. The average life expectancy at birth for Indians between 1901 and 1910 was 23 years (for men, 22.6 years and for women, 23.3 years), but it rose to 61.1 years (60.6 years for men and 61.2 years for women) for the period 1986–1990. Finally, a major hurdle in controlling India's population growth has been the level of illiteracy, particularly among women. For example, in 1991 about 64% of men and 40% of women were defined as literate. As demographers have pointed out, there is a close relationship between literacy and the level of education among women on the one hand and the fertility rate on the other. That is, the lower the educational status of women, the higher the fertility rate. A consequence of these trends is the dramatic rise in the number of persons per square kilometer from 77 in 1901 to 257 in 1991.

Society: Rural/Urban Dichotomy, the Economy, and the Polity

Despite all its efforts to modernize and industrialize, India still remains largely an agrarian society. In the past ninety years India's urban population has increased slowly, from about 11% of the total population in 1901 to 26% in 1991. Even though only one in four Indians lives in a town of over 5,000, the urban population exceeded 217 million in 1991 (Agrawal, et al., 1992). Nonetheless, what should not be ignored, especially when we are considering gender issues, is the immensity of the rural population, with its adherence to traditions and customs that have a bearing on the roles men and women play both within and outside the households. For example, about 73% of India's 844 million people live in roughly 500,000 villages. As a result, agriculture and related activities remain the primary source of livelihood for most Indians. About 70% of employment and 35% of the gross domestic product (about $350 billion in 1993) comes from agriculture. The average farmer in India does not own more than three acres of land, and there are severe social cleavages. According to one source, roughly 59% of Indians are in the lowest income category or can be considered poor, 37% are lower and middle income, and only 4% are high income (Stern, 1993).

India has been a parliamentary democracy since 1952, and according to Stern (1993), "By any comparative measurement parliamentary democracy in India is genuine, stable, and adapted to its social environment" (p. 13). All levels of political units, ranging from village councils to national parliament, are based upon adult franchise. And yet, when we consider the composition of the state legislatures and parliament by gender, clearly the electoral politics in India are still in the hands of men.

Religion, Caste, and Language

In India, religious and caste values play a critical role in determining the economic, social, and familial roles of men and women. For example, some Muslim women are segregated by *purdah* (veil), which prevents them from seeking jobs that bring them face-to-face with men other than their parents, husbands, and siblings. According to purdah customs, women should confine their activities to segregated quarters, wear a *burkha* (typically a black robe that covers the entire body and veils the face), and travel in closed vehicles. Likewise, upper-caste Hindu women have been precluded from working in the fields or elsewhere to maintain status and ritual distance from inferior castes.

While it is true that in terms of numbers India is a country of Hindus (82.6% of the population in 1981[2]), there is an enormous religious diversity. For example, in 1981 there were over 75 million Indian Muslims (11.4% of the total population), one of the highest concentrations of the followers of Islam in the world. Other religious groups included Christians (2.4%), Sikhs (2.0 %), and Parsis, Buddhists, Jains, and others (1.6%). Religion continues to play an important part in the personal sphere, if the frequency of visits to places of worship is any indication. For example, a *Sunday* poll asked its respondents how often they visited places of worship. About 20% visited one regularly, another 35% went at least once a week, and 28% on special occasions (*Sunday*, January 22, 1994, p. 64). In recent years, religion has become a critical factor in elections because the ideology and the platform of many political parties are formulated to attract specific segments of the electorate. As a result there have been few major changes in recent years in religion-based laws and practices that work against equality between men and women (Parashar, 1992).

It is impossible to discuss Indian society without reference to its caste system. The caste system can be interpreted in at least two ways. Most introductory sociology textbooks describe it as a four-fold hierarchical division of society according to occupations. Thus, in descending order, there are Brahmins (priests and scholars), Kshatriyas (rulers, soldiers), Vaishyas (traders), and Shudras (peasants, and artisans). Since the hierarchy was based originally on ritual considerations, there was considerable social distance between groups and this was reinforced by food habits, endogamy, and, of course, a hereditary occupational system. However, this approach, often known as the *varna* classification or scheme, excludes a significant proportion of the population—the so-called Untouchables and tribal groups. The second way of interpreting the caste system, which takes into account *jati,* or subcastes, provides a more realistic picture. For instance, even though Brahmin is one category, there are several regionally based endogamous Brahmin subcastes. Likewise, among Shudras, there are numerous peasant and artisan endogamous *jatis* who maintain distinct ways of life. (For more on caste, see Srinivas, 1962, 1966.) Since the census does not ask people their *varna* or *jati* status, a distribution of the Hindu population by *varna* is not available. However, as the constitution requires that those traditionally deemed "Untouchables" and the tribals be given special consideration to ensure that their historically oppressed status does not continue in modern India, they are enumerated in the decennial censuses. All those who were known as "Untouchables" are now enumerated as *Scheduled Castes.* Similarly, the people who live in forests and on hills are defined as *Scheduled Tribes.* To be considered a member of the scheduled caste, one's caste must be recognized in the list or the schedule of the government. Thus, of the 840 million Indians in 1991, over 138 million, or 16%, belonged to scheduled castes (the so-called Untouchables), and nearly 68 million, or 8%, belonged to scheduled tribes.[3] It is women from the scheduled castes and tribes who provide the labor critical to the agricultural and informal sectors of the Indian economy.

Although there are 14 "principal" languages listed in the 1991 census, there are hundreds of local dialects and languages that are not officially recognized but are used in daily transactions by various ethnic and tribal groups.

Status of Women in the Labor Force
Social and Legal Dimensions

What women can or cannot do within and outside their households depends on not just religion but also their position in law, the family, their personal life cycle, their caste, and the economic status of the husband or father. Thus poor women from the Untouchable caste have had fewer restrictions on their movements and role in the labor force than, for instance, upper-class or upper-caste women. Likewise, older women have greater autonomy than unmarried young women. Nonetheless, religious traditions have always provided the normative framework for women's conduct within and outside their households regardless of their economic status.

Although the constitution defines India as a secular state to be governed by rule of law, all citizens are ensured of equality as a fundamental right regardless of their race, religion, and sex. However, in matters of inheritance, marriage, and divorce, there are separate and unequal laws, inspired and shaped by particular religions, that generally apply only to their followers (see Parashar, 1992). Consequently, at least four sets of marriage and family laws govern Indians, some working against the interests of women more than others (Mulla, 1970; Mehta, 1987; Chatterji, 1988; Monteiro, 1990; Parashar, 1992; Agnes, 1992). These laws do not treat women equally with regard to age at marriage, inheritance, divorce, and maintenance. For instance, the legal reforms of 1955 and 1956, which cover Hindus, Sikhs, and Parsis, removed disadvantages that women suffered in terms of inheritance, age at marriage, divorce, abortion, widow remarriage, dowry, maternity leave, job opportunities, education, and so on. Yet laws governing Muslim women in marriage and divorce remain archaic. Also, mere legislation is not effective in an agrarian society in which the majority of people, especially women, are ignorant about such issues and continue to be governed by patriarchal values and norms. Consequently, traditional attitudes shaped by religious tenets still largely determine the status of women in urban and rural India.

The religious texts that stipulate codes of conduct for women were written by men and put women in a disadvantaged position in matters of property and personal, as well as marital, rights. To illustrate, the depiction of women in Hindu scriptures, mythology, and folklore has been uneven and ambivalent. The *Rig Veda*, one of the earliest Hindu religious texts, not only considered women equal to men but extolled their virtues. Hindu women enjoyed this unquestioned equality for only a brief period. Restrictive social codes and sanctions laid down in religious texts between 200 B.C. and A.D. 200 still carry weight even today. Of these, the *Laws of Manu* are critical in that they portray woman as the most divine creation but also the scum of the earth. For instance, one verse implores that "women must be honored and admired by their fathers, brothers, and husbands" because "where women are honored, the gods are pleased." By contrast, another verse denigrates them: *Day and night, women must be kept in dependence by the males (of) their families and if they attach themselves to sensual enjoyments, they must be kept under one's control. Her father protects (her) in childhood, her husband protects (her) in youth, and the sons protect (her) in old age; a woman shall never be fit for independence* (Buhler, 1982, p. 328). Manu said that a woman should never be allowed autonomy because her "nature" as a woman "is innately as impure as falsehood. The Lord created woman as one who is full of sensuality, wrath, dishonesty, malice, and bad conduct" (Sharma, 1988, p. iv). While such harsh assessments are now seen as crude and conservative, the belief that women ought to be overseen by men is widely acknowledged, certainly by men.

Since Muslim personal law has been resistant to change, Muslim women in India are more oppressed than Hindu and Christian women. Muslim personal law, based on the *Quran*, accords women a subordinate position in marriage, divorce and, more important, property rights (see Parashar, 1992). In essence, customary law permits Muslim men to marry as many as four wives (although few ever do) while prescribing monogamy for women. It also gives men the informal right to divorce, whereas women have to seek divorce in law courts where the grounds are restricted to cruelty, desertion, failure to provide the necessities of life, incurable diseases, and the like. When the divorce becomes effective, the wife gets whatever her ex-husband chooses to give, which is often barely enough to survive. The practice of *purdah* precludes women from competing for jobs with other women or men. Consequently, many end up as piece-rate workers at home while taking care of household chores and children. In other ways, Christian women fare better than their Muslim and Hindu counterparts in terms of their access to education and employment. In areas of marriage and divorce, however, the laws are antiquated. The Indian Christian Marriage Acts, enacted by the British Parliament in 1869 and 1872, have never been amended. In 1990, some Christian women's groups proposed reforms that are consistent with the thinking and practice of the majority of Indian Christians, but the Indian Catholics Bishops Conference opposed them. The government of the day deferred to the wishes of the bishops rather than the demands of the reformers, saying that official religious leaders represented their followers, not the so-called reformers (Monteiro, 1990).

Until recently, Indian fiction and secular writing reflected the religion-inspired consensus on the domestic role of women. An ancient Sanskrit proverb characterizes the ideal Hindu wife as follows: "In work a slave, in business a diplomat, in sex a courtesan, in virtue as firm as the earth, and in looking after the husband, as good as the mother" (Sharma, 1988). A contemporary study of life in a village in Andhra Pradesh (Dube, 1955) observes that "according to the traditional norms of the society, a husband is expected to be an authoritarian figure whose will should always dominate the domestic scene. The wife should regard him as her master and should serve him faithfully. The husband is superior, the wife is subordinate" (p. 14). In rural India, with a few exceptions, the foundation of the patriarchal and patrilineal joint family depends on the sacrifices women make. Even when they are the major breadwinners, they play a passive role so that the honor of their dependent husband is not sacrificed.

There are clear signs that old views concerning the place and role of women are slowly changing, thanks to legal reforms and a growing awareness on the part of both sexes of the need to improve the status of women. But only when the traditional patriarchal premises of family and kinship have been successfully challenged will there be equality both within and outside the household. Secularism and individualism have yet to be universally understood and acknowledged as essential to people's well-being. Men and women differ in how they respond to these modern values and in the degree of flexibility they demonstrate in accommodating them to their normative framework. In this regard, one of the earliest studies on dual-earner households found that cultural norms, the superiority of the patriarch in particular, were upheld by husbands whereas most of the wives upheld the equalitarian norms of modern times (Kapur, 1970).

A Demographic Profile

A review of selected demographic indicators reveals some of the conditions that marginalize Indian women in the labor force. As the World Bank's report *Gender and Poverty in India* noted, "India has invested, and continues to invest, far less in its women workers than in its working men. Women are less endowed with productive resources in terms of education, health, and productive assets—all of which could bring them higher returns for their labor" (p. 1).

The constitution of India and various government policies have acknowledged that the eradication of female illiteracy is a first step toward equality. Progress has been slow, however. After four decades of the so-called concerted efforts to improve the educational status of women, about two-thirds of all Indian women remain illiterate. The literacy rate for women climbed from 8% in 1951 to 39% in 1991. By comparison, the rates for men were about 27 and 64% for 1951 and 1991, respectively (Census of India 1991, Series 1, Paper 3 of 1991). Even though there has been some improvement in the school enrollment rates, there are still twice as many boys enrolled as girls.

All of the social, cultural, and familial reasons for limiting women's educational opportunities are rooted in patriarchy. Most rural parents do not consider their daughters as part of their household, since they move out after marriage. Therefore, an investment in them is not profitable. From the point of view of poor parents, their labor (taking care of siblings, tending cattle, doing domestic chores) is valuable only in the short run, and there is no financial return on the time, effort, and scarce resources spent sending them to school. In urban areas, however, the situation is improving, not because there has been an attitudinal change about the value of women, but because women's education, especially if it is job-oriented, enhances their prospects in the marriage market.

The female-male ratio in India has always been low. What is striking is that the ratio is decreasing as the economic gains the country has made are increasing. For example, there were 972 females per 1,000 males in 1901, but the number declined to 927 per 1,000 males in 1991 (Census of India, 1991, Series-1, Paper 2). Such an adverse sex ratio is a result of systematic discrimination against female children leading to malnutrition and sickness, which in turn raises the proportion of maternity-related deaths. The lack of adequate prenatal care has also contributed to the high mortality rate among Indian women. The World Bank (1991) study reports that the "mortality rates among women are higher than those among men up to the age of 35, but the most dangerous periods for female survival in India are between the age of one month and four years and the span between ages 15 and 34 when women are in their peak child-bearing years" (p. 2). Another factor in India's lopsided sex ratio is the increasing demands by grooms for large dowries, which has led to many tragic consequences (e.g., bride-burning, bankruptcy of bride's parents). To forestall such tragic family events, many parents now use amniocentesis and abort female fetuses.

The infant mortality rate in India is reported in aggregate, and thus it is not possible to establish statistically that female infants have a higher rate than males. Even though the total infant mortality rate has dramatically declined in the last four decades (from 134 per 1,000 live births in 1950 to 80 in 1990), there are signs that more female infants die of neglect (Census of 1991, Paper 3).

The mean age of rural women at marriage in 1981 was 16.7 years, compared with 17.6 years for urban women. The age at which Indian women marry corresponds to their level of education. For instance, illiterate women marry when they are around 16, while women with a college degree tend to marry when they are about 21. According to 1981 data, an Indian woman will bear an average of four children during her lifetime. Unlike their counterparts in the developed world, Indian women now have a lower life expectancy at birth than men according to estimates for 1991–1996: 61.2 years as opposed to 61.7 for men (Agrawal, et al., 1992, pp. 83–89).

Labor-Force Participation

In spite of the forces promoting change, the lives of Indian women center on the home. Their activities—whether domestic, economic, or a combination of both—are an integral part of the patriarchal family. Even well-educated women seeking "modern" jobs are guided by family concerns in their choice of work and their dedication to it (Rath, 1987; Ramu, 1989). Consequently, work for pay for the majority of Indian women becomes an extension of domestic obligations and responsibilities. Furthermore, "What is considered appropriate—whether it is the form of marriage, female demeanor, or the nature of women's work—is closely linked with the family's position (ascribed or aspired) in the social-status hierarchy. The family's caste ranking and the community's ethnic ranking constrain women far more than men by the status-hierarchy of work, confining them to certain areas or kinds of work and excluding them from certain others" (Bardhan, 1985, p. 2207).

When examining the data on the labor-force participation in India we should keep the following points in mind. First, even though the census collects fairly systematic information on the work-participation rates of men and women (e.g., Census of India, 1991, Paper 3), the data are incomplete and do not reflect the total picture of the labor force because of changing definitions of the *worker* in the decennial censuses prior to 1981 (Mitra, Ashok, Pathak, and Mukherji, 1980; Karlekar, 1982; Nayyar, 1987). Thus it is virtually impossible to draw any firm conclusions about long-term changes in the status of women in the labor force. Second, it appears that a significant proportion of girls and women aged seven and over are not recorded as workers. This is because often it is the male head of the household who gives the information to the census enumerator. Men usually are reluctant to admit that their daughters and wives are co-providers, since it might reflect on their own shortcomings as men. Third, there is no way of determining the work-participation rate of women by marital status, since the census does not collect such information. Fourth, the actual number of women who combine housework (which is supposedly of no economic value) with farm work (without which a good many rural families could not survive) is not accurately enumerated, and thus we are left with guesses. Finally, there are no reliable data on the unemployment rate by gender, making it difficult to determine whether there is discrimination in hiring practices, particularly in the formal and industrial sectors.

Although women constitute about 48% of the total population, they constitute only a small proportion of the labor force in India, a proportion that is one of the lowest among developing nations as well as in the history of modern India. Of the 840 million or so Indians in 1991, 315 million, or 37%, were in the labor force.[4] The distribution of worker by gender was 223.5 million men (51.2% of all men) and 91 million women (22% of all women). In effect, every second man and just about every fourth woman were in the labor force. The total work participation rate increased between 1981 and 1991, an increase that can be credited to the increase in the female work participation rate from 19.7% in 1981 to 22.3% in 1991. By contrast, the rate for men actually declined by 1% from 52.6% in 1981 to 51.6% in 1991. The decline was experienced (as registered in percentages) only in rural areas. As far as women workers are concerned, their numbers declined slightly in rural areas, while those in urban areas registered a marginal increase.

Another datum that sheds light on the marginality of women in the labor force is the proportion of women in the categories of "main" and "marginal" workers. For enumeration purposes, main workers were those who worked for wages for six months or more, while those who worked for less than six months were called marginal workers. For instance, in the 1991 census, 285 million, or about 34%, were main workers and about 48 million, or 3.5%, were marginal workers. But when these numbers are considered by gender the picture that emerges is rather stark. Over 50% of men were main workers while only 16% of women were in this category. Thus, according to inferences drawn by the Indian census, over 85% of marginal workers in India were women, and nine out of ten of these were in rural areas. The data from the 1991 census reveal that out of 285.42 million main workers some 110 million, or nearly 39%, were cultivators (those who cultivated land they owned or leased from others), 74 million, or 26%, were agricultural laborers (who worked for others for wages), 10 million, or about 4%, were household industry workers, and nearly 90 million, or 31%, were in other occupations. Most urban women workers were concentrated in the categories of "household" and "other" workers (Census of India, 1991, Series 1, Paper 3).

In essence, the main source of employment for women in India is agriculture. The majority of them are from the scheduled castes and tribes (Ambewadikar, 1986; Dunn, 1993). Women's share in white-collar, managerial, and professional employment is rather restricted (various estimates suggest that no more than 3% of working women are in these categories), even though some marginal gains have been made in recent decades, the extent of which is yet to be systematically documented.

Paid Work, Women, and Family

Most Indian women, whether in rural or urban areas, whether married or not, have worked and continue to work (with or without wages) outside the home. Their work is critical given the agrarian and poverty-stricken nature of the society. The largest and the most conspicuous section of India's working women (mostly married) are agricultural laborers, toiling under the most oppressive conditions for wages that are arbitrarily determined by landowners. Little research has been conducted on the impact of these women's nondomestic work on their children, families, and marriages.

By contrast, middle-class working women in urban India, who are a minority, have received greater attention from researchers, and their problems seem to be the focus of many policies. The reasons for such special attention is the concern about how a wife's employment will affect family values and roles. In this regard, Desai and Anantram (1985) note, "Middle-class women's outside work participation is not merely an economic activity, but it affects norms regarding the proper sphere of women, her status vis-à-vis her husband, values underlying patriarchal family structure, redefinition of the roles of family members, care of children, mixing with other men and remaining outside the house for long periods. These are questions which are of concern for sociologists" (p. 308).

Because of the apprehension that urban women's work may bring structural changes in family life, a great deal of attention has been focused on them in recent years (for an annotated bibliography, see Rao, Ramani, Ghosh, Joshi, and Archarya [Eds.], 1994). With the expansion of the industrial and service sectors and the rising cost of living in urban areas, there is an expectation that more and more urban women will enter the formal labor sector, thus bringing about dramatic changes in marital and family dynamics. This expectation is further reason for there being more studies of working women in urban than in rural economies. Another reason is that researchers are city dwellers who find it easier to conduct research where they live.

Most of the studies of dual-earner households in urban settings have focused on the impact of work on the family—more specifically, on how the mother's out-of-home employment affects child care (especially of preschool children), the husband's status both in and outside the home, and services normally provided by full-time housewives. Some studies have also examined whether married women's employment affects their physical and psychological well-being as well as the domestic balance of power (for a review, see Ramu, 1989, Chapter 1). While these concerns are quite legitimate, they are pertinent only to a minority of dual-earner households in India. In what follows, a profile of dual-earner households based on the author's research, as well as from other sources, will be presented.

Women's Paid Work and Socialization of Children

The belief that men and women have "natural" propensities that make them competent in segregated spheres of activity is firmly entrenched in the minds of most Indians. To be feminine is to be a good mother and a good wife, in that order. In the words of Caplan (1985), "The position of a wife is one of subordination, that of a mother is much more powerful. It is through her status as a mother that a woman is able to ameliorate her position as a wife" (p. 59). Among Indians, particularly among Hindus, motherhood is venerated (see Ramu, 1994), and as a result women's identity, self-respect, and honor are dependent on their success as mothers. In this regard Kakar (1981) observes:

Whether her family is poor or wealthy, whatever her caste, class or region, whether she is a fresh young bride or exhausted by many pregnancies and infancies already, an Indian woman knows that motherhood confers upon her a purpose and identity that nothing else in her culture can. Each infant borne and nurtured by her safely into childhood, especially if the child is a son, is both a certification and a redemption (p. 56).

Because of this cultural edict, child care has remained the primary responsibility of women whether they are employed or not.

The question that has been repeatedly examined is to what extent the mother's employment influences the child's psychological and physical development. For the majority of working mothers—i.e., the unskilled and marginal workers—this is an irrelevant issue because they have little choice in the matter. They simply cannot afford to stay home and look after their children: If they did, they all would starve. Women in rural areas consider themselves fortunate if elderly relatives can mind their children when they are away at work. Those who do not have such kin support depend on older children to mind the younger children. If these arrangements are not practical, then young children simply accompany their mothers to the place of work. Even though such an arrangement puts additional burdens on women, they prefer to have their children within view rather than leaving them alone or leaving them with others—to whom they would be indebted forever. In such circumstances, husbands seldom offer to share child care chores even when they are unemployed or have the time to do so.

In urban areas it is not uncommon to see unskilled women workers periodically attend to their children, who are left in the shade to play by themselves. Such an arrangement suits both employees and employers for their own reasons. As the World Bank's report (1991) points out,

Although children are allowed informally (i.e., without any special facilities) at the mother's workplace, neither this nor the flexibility in hours of work are socially motivated by concern for the working mother. It is rather a strategy that permits the small entrepreneurs who employ these women to retain their own flexibility. . . . To them it is an advantage to have workers they can call on to work longer hours when needed or fewer hours when demand is low (p. 97).

When children reach the age of six or seven, they are often forced to seek work themselves either as farm-hands or as helpers in urban tea stalls or shops. With no education or skills, they, like their parents, end up as marginal workers.

Among the urban middle class, most tasks that center around children (feeding, bathing, dressing, disciplining, and preparing them for school) fall to females. Whether a woman is employed or not is of little consequence because of the belief that their primary task is not just to bear children but also to rear them properly. The concerns that were expressed in the 1960s by U.S. researchers about the negative impact of the mother's employment on children (e.g., Nye and Hoffman, 1963) were repeated in the 1980s by urban, middle-class Indians (e.g., Rani, 1976; Wadhera, 1976; Devi, 1987; Ramu, 1989). The belief that children of working mothers are deprived of maternal care and attention, and as a result experience a variety of problems, is widely shared by both men and women. This belief weighs heavily in a woman's decision to seek employment. If she does, there is always guilt about compromising her domestic responsibilities. In a study of married professional women in Banares, Saxena (1995) notes, "The mental stress to which a working woman is subject is compounded by a guilt factor that she is being a bad mother, an inadequate parent, a woman who does not feed her child or spend enough time with the children, one who neglected her child because of an overwhelming ambition and lust for a career" (p. 79). However, there can be some relief if there are elder relatives at home who are willing to babysit or if the couple can afford to hire full-time servants.

In a study of dual- and single-earner households in a large city in South India, it was found that the wife's employment had little impact on the husband's role in child care (Ramu, 1989). The vast majority of women wanted their husbands to share the tasks but the latter were unwilling because of conservative conceptions and professed incompetence. Some women themselves contribute to the gender-segregation of child care tasks. From their point of view, allowing a man to do what is clearly perceived as a womanly task violates their self-concept as a competent mother and wife. In effect, working mothers in India, whether they are unskilled part-time workers or professionals, consider child care an integral part of their becoming and being a normal woman. They are the first ones to admit that their employment does result in the neglect of children, and most stretch their physical resources to reduce such a neglect to the minimum (Ramu, 1989).

Among the urban, middle-class, dual-earner households, the perceptions of husbands on the issue of child neglect are important because they add to the domestic burdens and psychological stress among working mothers. This is because they have to be extra alert in matters of child care in order to avoid being blamed by their husbands for neglecting their maternal obligations. Most working wives are extremely sensitive to their husbands' evaluation of their domestic performance. In this regard, Rani's respondents (1976) reported that their daily routine upon returning home from work was to listen to complaints by husbands or in-laws about the neglect of children or their misbehavior, the inefficiency of the servants, or chores left undone. These problems are attributed to the wife's giving greater attention to work than to domestic responsibilities. In view of this, many women seek only those jobs that allow them the flexibility to attend to their domestic obligations first (Rath, 1987).

Although the vast majority of poor women in both urban and rural India as well as an increasing number of middle-class women with preschool children are in the labor force, there has not been any public discussion about the need for universal day care. Instead, at the insistence of feminist groups, the Department of Labor now requires employers to provide day care if their firm has more than fifty employees. To circumvent this rule, most small firms restrict the size of their staff to forty-nine and simply do not hire women with children. Some large industries and corporations do provide day care to their female employees on a cost-sharing basis, but such privileges are enjoyed by very few working women. There are also a few privately run day care centers in large cities; however, these are not within the reach of lower- and middle-class families. Only in a minority of instances do kin or servants care for children while their mother is at work, with the result that children in most dual-earner households have to fend for themselves.

The Positive and Negative Impact of Double Duty on Women

Most married women workers in India are in the labor force because of economic necessity. Professional women who enter the labor force to fulfill themselves—or to compete to put their specialized skills to use—are the exceptions. In general, however, whether they work in the agricultural or urban-industrial sectors, women end up doing the housework, which includes caring for children, in-laws, and husband. While their economic contribution to the family gives them an advantage in some areas, it also takes a toll on their own psychological and physical resources. Let us first consider the benefits to women of gainful employment.

For many women employment means no longer being confined to their homes. They are freer to go places independently and to make acquaintances at their places of work. They may also have more discretionary money than full-time homemakers. But the most important consequence of work for married women is their ability to increase their domestic power. The extent to which their employment gives them the power to bargain and renegotiate the balance of power in domestic decision-making depends on the magnitude of their financial contribution and the level of their husband's reliance on such a contribution. Unskilled women workers in particular seem to have gained considerable ground in domestic decision-making. This is because men's source of domestic and nondomestic power in a patriarchal and patrilineal society lies in landed property. Among the marginal groups such as the lower castes, few ever own land; if they do, the land may not be very fertile. As a result, women's wages are extremely critical, and by bringing more money into family coffers, women gain concessions from their husbands (Bardhan, 1985; Parthasarathy, 1988; World Bank, 1991).

By all indications (see, for example, World Bank, 1991), rural women's earnings are not only recognizable but are substantial relative to what their husbands earn, and tend to improve their domestic status. To illustrate, a study by Bidinger, Nag, and Prabhu (1986) of 40 households of agricultural workers in Andhra Pradesh found that working women had a greater role in household decision-making, particularly regarding food. This pattern was confirmed by Mencher's findings (1988) from twenty villages in Kerala and Tamil Nadu, where women retained discretionary authority over a substantial portion of their income.

Studies of unskilled women workers in urban areas offer contradictory results on the relationship between their earnings and their ability to influence various family decisions. For instance, studies of poor working women in Calcutta (Bannerjee, 1985) and in Allahabad (Bhatty, 1981) found that their decision-making power increased with their economic contribution to the household. Kalpagam (1988) found that among the poor families in Madras men and women shared not only their earning responsibilities but the domestic chores as well. By contrast, studies by Standing (1985) of lower-class women in Calcutta, and by Karlekar (1982) of women sweepers in Delhi, found that employment had little effect on their domestic status. A number of studies (Sharma 1980; Mies,1986; Karlekar, 1982; Mencher, 1988) suggest that in poor families women tend to have greater domestic responsibilities. Apart from earning an income, these women are compelled to ensure that the income is not spent unwisely by their husbands. They want to make sure that the fruits of their labor are expended on the basic family needs (e.g., food and clothing). In the process of negotiating a budget plan, some women may encounter abuse by their husbands, who disapprove of their wives' money-making decisions, while others may earn the respect of their husbands. These issues need further exploration before firm conclusions can be drawn.

Studies that have dealt with issues of marital power have concluded that employment enables women to demand and get equality on most issues pertaining to savings, miscellaneous expenditures, or children's education. To illustrate, a comparison of dual-earner and single-earner couples who are professionals and white-collar workers in Hyderabad found that education and employment gave women more power in all areas of domestic decision-making except in the purchase of high-priced items such as a car or a motor scooter. Even so, the husbands in this study had a major say in whether their wives should seek employment, and what kind of employment (Devi, 1987). These findings were confirmed by another study of dual- and single-earner households in Bangalore (Ramu, 1989). The wife's income gave her greater explicit authority in domestic matters.

Having noted the positive effects of gainful employment on women's domestic authority, we will now briefly focus on the major disadvantages that employment brings. The research in India on these issues has focused more on urban middle-class women than on the unskilled marginal workers in cities and villages. Clearly, women who are on the fringe keep long hours in the field, in quarries, construction sites, and so on, and they return home to cook, clean, and perform other domestic services while their husbands are chatting with their friends in tea or *arrack* (country liquor) shops (Mencher, 1988). Karlekar (1982) argues that poor women are more concerned about their jobs than psychological complexities, because the wages that their jobs generate are critical for the survival of their families. Her respondents, women sweepers in Delhi, seldom reported role conflict or ambivalence. While lower-class women may not report any role conflict, the impact of extended hours of strenuous work on their physical and psychological capacities is severe. It is interesting to note that this impact has yet to be documented in research.

Now turning to the urban scene, there is a consensus among researchers that work has many negative effects on married women. Given the primacy of the traditional roles of wife and mother, women find it difficult to cope with the competing demands of work and family. The burdens of doing double duty could be partly relieved if husbands shared domestic work, but this has not happened. It is an article of faith among men, and among some women too, that women are naturally endowed for housework. Any woman who neglects her domestic responsibilities and concentrates on her job or occupation not only betrays her lack of feminine virtues but also violates the rights of other family members to receive her services. Accordingly she has to earn her legitimacy as a wage earner by simultaneously performing her domestic role well. Alternatively, she could find help from relatives or servants; however, most middle-class women cannot afford full-time servants.

Most of the role conflict and the fatigue experienced by employed wives indicate that husbands do not generally assist their wives (Rani, 1976; Chakrabortty, 1978; Khanna and Verghese, 1978; Mies, 1980; Caplan, 1985; U. Sharma, 1986; Savara, 1986; Devi, 1987; Ramu, 1989; Saxena, 1995). When they do, they avoid what is considered mainly "women's work" (cooking, cleaning dishes, washing clothes, bathing children, sweeping floors, and so on). The common maxim among men is "Men don't cry, and men don't cook and clean" (Ramu, 1990). The traditional assumption that a wife is in a submissive and a subordinate position in marriage is reflected in the extent to which men exercise control over their wives' income. Working women cannot automatically and unilaterally assume that their earnings are discretionary, and in many instances the husbands appropriate their income. Women's failure to yield to their husbands' authority often results in domestic altercations. The evidence suggests that women often do not retain any control over their income (Ramu, 1989; Mencher, 1988; Mantri, P. Krishnaswamy, and S. Krishnaswamy, 1994; Bannerjee, 1985).

Most working wives do not dare to question conventional assumptions or formulate strategies to use their new resources to alter established beliefs and expectations. This is another instance of the failure of feminist ideology and practices to penetrate the lives of women in India. This failure is especially strong among women who are educated and employed—a constituency that one would have assumed to be the first to respond to feminist ideals. By fulfilling domestic obligations as well as taking on the modern role as co-provider, working women in effect reinforce the patriarchal ideology (Ramu, 1989).

The Impact of Women's Employment on Husbands

Historically, the religious norms, patriarchal values, and cultural assumptions about masculinity and femininity were forcibly articulated within the household. As a result, the husband commanded supreme authority over his wife. She was required to consult him on all matters, attend to all his needs, adjust herself to his personality, and subordinate her wishes and wants to his. This was particularly true for Hindu women, who were expected to be subservient to men at all stages of their lives (Altekar, 1938). While these norms may not be as coercive as they were centuries ago, they continue to be a salient part of the social and ethical ethos of various groups. The self-concept of Indians vis-à-vis domestic life remains based on notions of what it is to be a decent husband-father or wife-mother. Part of being a normal adult man is to be a "good provider" (Bernard, 1981). But traditional forces (e.g., caste status, which often defines one's economic circumstances) do not permit every man to become and remain a good provider. A landless Untouchable man may have no choice but to indenture his labor to upper-caste landowners, and his wife and children may have to seek employment as well. But such economic realities do not necessarily alter the male psyche.

Another important factor to be kept in mind when considering how a wife's work affects her husband is the nature of the links between the world of work and the domestic world of working couples. For example, men are more involved than women in the world of work because they tend to cultivate primary relations at the workplace. Mencher (1988) notes that men in her study would gather in tea or liquor shops after work, and only after some commiseration would they go home for dinner. Likewise a study of factory workers in Bangalore found that even when the husband and wife worked in the same department, at the end of the day the wife returned home by the first bus she could get so that she could cook dinner while her husband went to the union office or coffee shop to spend the evening with friends (Ramu, 1989).

Many urban, middle-class husbands have greeted their wife's employment with ambivalence because, while it undermines their authority at home and their self-image outside the home, it also eases their economic burdens and provides more material comforts (Ramu, 1989; Saxena, 1995). It is significant that Indian men generally do not feel threatened by their wife's paid work. This is because the norms and values of patriarchy are generally shared by both women and men. Most women workers do not disapprove of their husbands for not doing housework or providing child care. Many even encourage the cultivated domestic incompetence of their husbands (Ramu, 1989). Others merely tolerate their husband's dominance over them. In sum, women's employment has brought economic benefits to men, while men's traditional roles have basically remained unchanged.

Nonetheless, many urban Indian men may still have some difficulties in psychologically accommodating their wives' new economic status and what it portends. In sheer egotistical terms, a wife's employment may threaten her husband's self-concept, his sense of masculinity, and his domestic power. Urban men's domestic power, which is key to their sense of well-being and self-esteem, has been drawn largely from their role as good providers as well as from tradition. Now that many men have been forced to share that role with their wives they have to make many concessions and psychological compromises sooner or later. By refusing to share domestic work, they are suggesting that their wives' work does not reflect on what they are as husbands and fathers. Some of them have engaged in coercion and intimidation to retain their domestic authority. Others constantly suspect their wives of immoral conduct, especially when the latter have to work in close proximity with other men (Khanna and Varghese, 1978). In general, however, there is no significant evidence to suggest that husbands of women workers have changed their traditional roles as husbands-fathers.

Women's Employment and Family Life

Taking their cues from many Western studies, most studies of Indian dual-earner households have assessed the negative effects of women's work on family life. Predictably, the findings have suggested, as did Western research, that men in dual-earner households do not help with household tasks when their wives start working. As a result, women work long hours and therefore suffer fatigue, role conflict and self-doubt; the children and aging in-laws are neglected. What is yet to be investigated is the extent to which women's earnings have had an impact on the general welfare of the family members.

The fact is that women's incomes relieve the economic stress that some families would have otherwise experienced, and saves other families from destitution. A comparison of "quality of life" in single- and dual-earner households drawn from various strata and regions of India would be very instructive in this regard. In the meantime, on the basis of a handful of studies, some tentative observations on the relationship between women's employment and family life can be made. First, contemporary Indian society is making legal and political efforts to weaken traditional values and norms that oppress women. But given the predominantly agrarian character of the society, such efforts have yet to yield dramatic results. Nonetheless, changes are occurring rather slowly and unevenly, not only in the lives of men and women and but also within the institution of the family. The difficult question that both men and women confront is how fast they should adopt new values and approaches to life or, alternatively, how soon they can shed traditional modes of thinking and behaving without guilt. For instance, women workers in India have generally succeeded in combining their domestic and work roles.

It is part of their upbringing to adjust to the changing circumstances of their lives. As Blumberg and Dwaraki (1980) note, adjustment has become part of an Indian woman's duty. In their words, "Thus, if the parents refuse to allow her to work, she adjusts; if she goes to live with orthodox in-laws, she adjusts to their ways. In doing so, the woman adopts rationalizations which help her to accept her fate. Adjustment also takes the form of a highly developed sensitivity to the needs and wishes of others" (p. 63). This is not to suggest that working women deliberately embrace servitude. Instead, they develop overt and covert strategies that help them to run their households with a minimum of friction.

Second, most working women attach more importance to their domestic roles than to their jobs. If a woman's in-laws are residing with her, she will make sure that their routine needs are met while she is at work. Working women in Indian extended households have to be sensitive not only to gender-centered problems but also to the intricacies of generational relationships. They are particularly crucial in a culture where failure to care for aged parents is a matter of shame. Since daughters-in-law are the ones who render essential services, most working women try to win their in-laws' support by ensuring that they are cared for one way or another.

Third, although fully cognizant of the value of their wives' earnings, husbands may expect their wives to furnish the same domestic tasks and child care as unemployed wives. Few husbands, however, coerce their wives to provide these domestic services.

Fourth, employed wives have reported higher levels of marital adjustment and happiness (Devi, 1987; Mani, 1987; Ramu, 1989; Mantri, et al., 1994). Such findings do not contradict others stating that women experience role conflict and fatigue. The personal satisfaction women receive from their earnings, the enhanced standard of living of the family, and the increased power in domestic decision-making are factors contributing to the high level of marital satisfaction.

Finally, systematic data on women's earnings as a proportion of men's are not available. However, some case studies of lower-class and unskilled working women have found that women contribute anywhere from 30 to 70% of the total family earnings (Mencher, 1988; Bannerjee, 1985). One urban study reports that women earned

just about as much as their husbands did (Ramu, 1989). Some studies of nutritional intake in rural India have already established that
the caloric intake of children is higher when mothers are employed
(Bidinger, et al., 1986; Walker and Ryan, 1988).

In short, the increasing role of women as co-providers has pro-
foundly altered the internal dynamics of their households in subtle
and unobtrusive ways. For instance, in urban areas dual-earner households tend to be nuclear and smaller than single-earner households
(Khanna and Varghese, 1978; Ramu, 1989). As Bardhan (1985) has
noted, married unskilled workers enjoy greater autonomy than the
nonworkers mainly because of their critical role as "co-providers."
By virtue of this autonomy and the emerging egalitarian ethos in
Indian society (as reflected in democratic elections to village councils, farm lobbies, employees' associations, and so on), working
women are gaining power in domestic decision-making. If the present
trends continue, many Indian women may in fact succeed in enlisting their husbands for domestic work. These positive developments
may not appear profound by comparison to the gains made by working wives in industrialized societies; however, given the burdens of
religious and patriarchal traditions in India, they cannot be dismissed
as marginal.

Married Women and Employment: Implications
for Public Policy

Like many other countries in the world, India does not have a co-
herent family policy. Since its independence in 1947, however, India has made numerous efforts—some through its constitution and
others through direct and indirect policies—to improve the status
of women. Some of these measures have been directed at working
women in particular. Yet it must be acknowledged that these efforts
have yielded mixed results. Legally Indian women (in particular
Hindu women) enjoy equality with men but in reality they continue to be oppressed.

In light of this, as early as 1974 a government-appointed Committee on the Status of Women in India prepared a report entitled
Towards Equality and made a series of recommendations to improve
the social, economic, legal, and political status of women. Twenty
years later, many of these recommendations have yet to be followed.

Lack of resources and political will as well as the ideology of patriarchy, which has percolated into the political, judicial, and administrative systems, have prevented women from gaining equality in all spheres of their lives (see Chatterjji, 1985; K. Sharma, 1985). Also, women workers in India are not organized and do not speak with a united voice, and so there is little public debate on the matter. Other factors that have marginalized women's issues on the national agenda include population pressures, a high unemployment rate, a changing world economic order in which India lacks competitive edge, regional disparities, ethnic and caste stratification, political corruption, and persistent religious fundamentalism. In essence, the condition of ordinary women in India has not improved despite the statutory measures and pressures from women's groups. These basic realities of the general status of women have serious implications for public policy.

In a country where a man is still seen as the "breadwinner" (even when his wife brings in more money), public policy obviously tends to be biased in his favor. The tight labor market abets the discriminatory treatment of women. According to one economist's calculations (Uppal, 1993), India would need to create some 71 million jobs in order to achieve full employment in 1995. Ending unemployment is practically impossible given the new economic policies of the government, which require that the marketplace, not the state, create new jobs. India had a command economy that seldom aided women for nearly four decades, but in 1991 the decision-makers turned to market forces as an alternative strategy to liberate India from its economic woes. As part of these reforms, the public-sector enterprises will be scaled down or sold off, leading to retrenchment of men and certainly women in those industries (e.g., manufacturing and assembling). Consequently there will be more unemployed people in the labor force (see Ghosh, 1994; Ramu, 1995). Under these circumstances it will be more difficult for women to enter the job market as well as demand basic amenities, such as day care for children or extended maternity leave.

Most adult women in India are not in the labor force. Those who are typically perform demanding manual work. Consequently any civilized society that adheres to democratic values and norms should develop and enforce policies to establish equality of opportunity for women in general, and married women in particular. The following is an illustrative list of issues key to upgrading women's economic and domestic roles.

First, because women as individuals are devalued, there is not enough enthusiasm or drive either at the societal or at the family level to provide equal access to education (Mitra, 1979; Chanana, 1988; Karlekar, 1988). In rural areas female children are the last ones to be enrolled in schools and the first ones to be withdrawn. This sustained practice has led to rural women's marginalized position in the labor force. Ironically, the World Bank's report (1991) notes that in 1981 there was an inverse relationship between education and employment among women: The less educated a woman is, the more likely she will be in the labor force. This is not to imply that illiteracy in India ensures employment. Instead, it demonstrates that given the lack of basic skills and training, most women are in jobs that pay low wages and demand more labor. In 1981, 88% of rural and 57% of urban women workers were illiterate. The World Bank's report and the report of the Committee on the Status of Women (1974) have recommended that in addition to providing incentives for parents to enroll their daughters in schools, the government should create programs to train adult women in modern agricultural and entrepreneurial skills.

Second, women's education is critical not only because higher education offers women greater access to skilled and white-collar occupations, but also because it provides them with sufficient strength and independence to question the values and norms that perpetuate subservience. For instance, the reformed inheritance law for Hindus allows a daughter to have the same rights as a son to ancestral property. Yet, in general, women from families with property do not get their share, and this has sustained their dependence on men (Agarwal, 1994).

Third, the vast majority of married working women in India are unorganized, unskilled, and marginal workers. Their wages are not governed by any norms of minimum wages and they enjoy few perks. Most trade unions are dominated by men who pay little or no attention to women's concerns. Therefore, there is a need to build working women's unions so that demands to improve the working conditions can be made collectively.

Finally, there is a need for a well-organized day care system that is funded by the central government. This is important not only as an incentive to join the work force but also as part of improving the condition of married women.

Summary

An attempt has been made in this essay to provide a profile of married working women in the demographic, legal, and social context of India. The information on women workers according to marital status is not available, but it can be assumed that most women workers enumerated in the census are married. About one in four Indian women and one in two men are in the labor force. Discrimination, patriarchal ideology, lack of education and technical skills, and emphasis on women's domestic roles have kept most women away from the labor force. The majority of women workers are unskilled laborers. As in other countries, married women workers in India experience role overload and fatigue. They are pressured by the demands of children, husbands, and in-laws. But the impact of their employment has generally been positive in that it has enabled women to change the domestic balance of power in their favor. Most urban women who have found employment have reported higher levels of marital satisfaction. Additional income has also enabled the dual-earner households to enjoy a better standard of living. There is little, however, to suggest that Indian society has paid serious attention to married working women, and this is evident from the absence of clearly stated policies on family life.

Notes

1.   I am highly indebted to Jude Carlson for her critical reading, which has enhanced the clarity and readability of this chapter.
2.   The population of India in 1981 was over 605 million. At this writing, the 1991 data on the distribution of the population by religion were not available.
3.   The 1991 census data do not include information from the state of Jammu and Kashmir, where enumeration did not take place. It should also be noted that caste is distinct from tribe, and is not a racial or ethnic category. For instance, a tribe in India is a territorial group mainly concentrated in forests and hills and often may not profess Hinduism. If there are internal divisions within a tribe, they are less likely to be on caste criteria. Also, some of the tribal groups in northeastern India follow Christianity and at least one group follows Judaism. Similarly, *varna* or *jati* classifications are not based on racial criteria. True, there are individuals who differ in their skin color, but these differences are not based on their caste origins.

4. The 1991 census data do not include information from the State of Jammu and Kashmir, where no enumeration took place because of political strife. Unless otherwise noted, the data on labor-force participation are drawn from *The Census of India 1991, Series 1, Paper 3 of 1991, Provisional Population Totals: Workers and Their Distribution.*

References

Agarwal, B. (1994). A *field of one's own: Gender and land rights in south Asia.* New Delhi: Cambridge University Press.

Agnes, F. (1992). Maintenance for women: Rhetoric of equality. *Economic and Political Weekly, 27,* 2233–2235.

Agrawal, A.N., Varma, H.O., and Gupta, R.C. (1992). *India: Economic information yearbook, 1991–92.* New Delhi: National Publishing House.

Altekar, A.S. (1938). *The position of women in Hindu civilization.* Delhi: Motilal Banarsidas.

Ambewadikar, R.M. (1986). "Role of development schemes for the scheduled castes and scheduled tribes." In R. Joshi (Ed.), *Untouchables: Voices of the dalit liberation movement* (pp. 49–59). London: Zed Books.

Bannerjee, N. (1985). *Women workers in the unorganized sector.* Hyderabad: Sangam.

Bardhan, K. (1985). Women's work, welfare and status: Forces of tradition and change in India. *Economic and Political Weekly, 20* (51, 52), 2207–2220, 2261–2269.

Bernard, J. (1981). The good-provider role: Its rise and fall. *American Psychologist 36,* 1–12.

Bhatty, Z. (1981). *The economic role and status of women in the beedi industry in Allahabad, India.* Geneva: International Labor Organization.

Bidinger, P., Nag, D.B., and Prabhu, P. (1986). Factors affecting intra-family food distribution in a south Indian village. Unpublished manuscript. Citation from the World Bank, *Gender and poverty in India,* 1991.

Blumberg, R.L. and Dwaraki, L. (1980). *India's educated women: Options and constraints.* Delhi: Hindusthan.

Buhler, G. (1886/1982). *Sacred books of the East—the laws of Manu.* Banaras: Motilal Banarasidas. The 1886 edition was published by the Oxford University Press.

Caplan, P. (1985). *Class and gender in India: Women and their organizations in a south Indian city.* London: Tavistock.

Census of India. (1991). *Provisional population totals: Workers and their distribution.* Paper 3 of 1991. New Delhi: Registrar General of India.

Chakraborrty, K. (1978). *The conflicting worlds of working mothers.* Calcutta: Progressive.

Chanana, K. (1988). Introduction. In K. Chanana (Ed.), *Socialization, education, and women: Explorations in gender identity.* New Delhi: Orient and Longman's.

Chatterjji, J. (1985). *The women's decade, 1975–85: An assessment.* New Delhi: ISPCK.

Chatterji, S.A. (1988). *The Indian women's search for an identity.* Delhi: Vikas.

Committee on the Status of Women. (1974). *Towards equality: Report on the status of women in India.* New Delhi: Department of Social Welfare and the Ministry of Education and Social Welfare.

Desai, N., and Anantram, S. (1985). Middle class women's entry into the world of work. In K. Saradamoni (Ed.), *Women, work, and society—proceedings of the ISI symposium.* Calcutta: Indian Statistical Institute.

Devi, I.M. (1987). *Women, education, employment and family living: A study of emerging Hindu wives in urban India.* Delhi: Gian.

Dube, S.C. (1955). *An Indian village.* London: Routledge and Kegan Paul.

Dunn, D. (1993). Gender inequality in education and employment in the scheduled castes and tribes of India. *Population Research and Policy Review 12,* 53–70.

Ghosh, J. (1994). Gender concerns in macro-economic policy. *Economic and Political Weekly 29* (35), 69–78.

Kakar, S. (1981). *The inner world: A psychoanalytic study of childhood and society in India.* Delhi and New York: Oxford University Press.

Kalpagam, U. (1988). Women in the labor force: An analysis of NSS data. Background paper prepared for the National Commission on Self-Employed Women and Women in the Informal Sector. New Delhi. (Citation from the World Bank, *Gender and poverty in India* 1991.)

Kapur, P. (1970). *Marriage and the working woman in India.* Delhi: Vikas.

Karlekar, M. (1982). *Poverty and women's work: A study of sweeper women in Delhi.* Delhi: Vikas.

Karlekar, M. (1988). Women's nature and access to education. In K. Chanana (Ed.), *Socialization, education, and women: Explorations in gender identity.* New Delhi: Orient and Longman's.

Khanna, G., and Varghese, M.A. (1978). *Indian women today.* Delhi: Vikas.

Mani, G. (1987). Working mothers in Madras City. *Social Welfare* (September 1987), 29–31.

Mantri, P.K., and Krishnaswamy, S. (1994). Sociological correlates of marital adjustment among working women. *International Journal of Sociology of the Family 24* (2), 99–110.

Mehta, R. (1987). *Socio-legal status of women in India.* Delhi: Mittal.

Mencher, J. (1988). Women's work and poverty: Women's contributions to household maintenance in two regions of south India. In J. Bruce and D. Dwyer (Eds.), *A home divided: Women and income control in the third world.* Palo Alto, Calif.: Stanford University Press.

Mies, M. (1980). *Indian women and patriarchy.* New Delhi: Concept.

Mies, M. (1986). *Indian women in subsistence and agricultural labor.* New Delhi: Vistar.

Mitra, A. (1979). *The status of women: Literacy and employment.* Delhi: Indian Council on Social Science Research.

Mitra, A., Pathak, L., and Mukherji, S. (1980). *The status of women—shifts in occupational participation, 1961–71.* New Delhi: Abhinav.

Monteiro, R. (1990). Belief, law and justice for women: Debate on proposed Christian marriage and matrimonial causes bill, 1990. *Economic and Political Weekly, 27,* WS 74–80.

Mulla, D.F. (1970). *The principles of Hindu law.* Bombay: Tripathi.

Nayyar, R. (1987). Female participation rates in rural India. *Economic and Political Weekly, XXII* (51) (December 19), 2207–2216.

Nye, I.F., and Hoffman, L.W. (1963). *The employed mother in America.* Chicago: Rand McNally.

Parashar, A. (1992). *Women and family law reform in India: Uniform civil code and gender equality.* Newbury Park, Calif.: Sage.

Parthasarathi, V. (1988). Socialisation, women and education: An experiment. In K. Chanana (Ed.), *Socialization, women, and education.* New Delhi: Nehru Memorial Museum and Library.

Premi, M.K. (1991). *India's population: Heading towards a billion—an analysis of 1991 census provisional results.* Delhi: B.R.

Ramu, G.N. (1988). *Family structure and fertility: Emerging patterns in an Indian city.* New Delhi, London, and Newbury Park, Calif.: Sage.

Ramu, G.N. (1989). *Women, work and marriage in urban India: A study of dual- and single-earner couples.* New Delhi, London, and Calif.: Sage.

Ramu, G.N. (1989–1990). Men don't cook and men don't cry: A study of housework among urban couples. *Samy Shakti, Annual Journal of the Center for Women's Development Studies, India, IV, V,* 156–174.

Ramu, G.N. (1994). Femininity and maternity: The case of urban Indian women. In J.S. Grewal and H. Johnston (Eds.), *The India-Canada relationship—exploring political, economic and cultural dimensions,* pp. 261–291. New Delhi: Sage.

Ramu, G.N. (1995a). Family system in India. In K. Altergott (Ed.), *International handbook on marriages and families*. Westport, Conn.: Greenwood.

Ramu, G.N. (1995b). Prologue. In G.N. Ramu and V.P. Govitrikar (Eds.), *Liberalization: Indian and Canadian perspectives*, pp. 3–18. New Delhi: Allied.

Rani, K. (1976). *Role conflict in working women*. New Delhi: Chetana.

Rao, R., Ghosh, S., Joshi, G., and Acharya, S. (Eds.) (1994), *Women at work in India—an annotated bibliography, 2*. New Delhi: Sage.

Rath, S. (1987). Working women in Cuttack. *Social Welfare* (April, 1987), 6–9.

Registrar General of India. (1991). *Census of India, 1991, Series 1*. New Delhi: Provisional Population Tables.

Savara, M. (1986). *Changing trends in women's employment: A caste study of the textile industry in Bombay*. Bombay: Himalaya.

Saxena, K. (1995). *Life and status of professional women—a study of Varanasi*. New Delhi: Radiant.

Sharma, K. (1985). *Interaction between policy assumption and rural women's work, occasional paper 1*. New Delhi: Center for Women's Development Studies.

Sharma, K., Hussain, S., and Saharya, A. (1984). *Women in focus: A community in search of equal roles*. Hyderabad: Sangam.

Sharma, R.P. (1988). Men were masters. *The Times of India, Sunday Review*, July 24.

Sharma, U. (1980). *Women, work, and property in northwest India*. London: Tavistock.

Sharma, U. (1986). *Women's work, class and the urban household: A study of Shimla, north India*. London: Tavistock.

Srinivas, M.N. (1962). *Caste in modern India and other essays*. Bombay: Asia Publishing House.

Srinivas, M.N. (1966). *Social change in modern India*. Berkeley: University of California Press.

Standing, H. (1985). Women's employment and the household: Some findings from Calcutta. *Economic and Political Weekly 20* (2), WS23–WS38.

Stern, R.W. (1993). *Changing India*. New Delhi: Cambridge University Press. *Sunday* Staff Reporter. (1994). *Sunday, Weekly News Magazine*, January 22. New Delhi.

Uppal, J.S. (1993). India's new economic policy. *Journal of Economic Development, 18* (2), 23–45.

Wadhera, K. (1976). *The new bread winners*. New Delhi: Viswa Yuvak Kendra.

Walker, T.S., and Ryan, J.G. (1988). *Against the odds: Village and household economies in India's semi-arid tropics*. Manuscript. Cited from the World Bank, *Gender and poverty in India*, 1991.

World Bank. (1991). *Gender and poverty in India—A world bank country study*. Washington, D.C.: World Bank.

Chapter Four
Employed Mothers and Their Families
The Israeli Experience

Ruth Katz

Israeli women receive a double message. They are educated toward modern achievement-oriented values and, at the same time, toward strong family-oriented norms. Israel has an egalitarian educational system and is rapidly developing employment opportunities open equally to men and women, such as advanced communications and high-tech industries. These developments provide many Israeli women a chance for higher achievements and a better standard of living. However, in Israel these advancements are counterbalanced by powerful social factors that encourage universal marriage, marital stability, high fertility, and even the prevalence of extended family ties. Two such factors should be emphasized. While the country as a whole has taken a modern Euro-American direction, the majority of its population are still within, or just one generation away from, their traditional origins. Arabs, Jews of Middle-Eastern or North-African descent, and Orthodox Jews, whatever their country of origin, are committed to family values, norms, and behavior.

Also, family law in Israel is marked by duality: The legal status of women is determined simultaneously by some of the most modern legal approaches as well as by one of the most ancient legal systems in the world. Israel's legal system, which took shape after the establishment of the state in 1948, recognized the right of women to equal opportunity. Israel's declaration of independence is one of the first documents of any legal system to set forth explicitly the notion of equality for women. But this document also establishes the authority of ancient Jewish law, whose source is from Scripture (Raday, 1991). Authority in matters of family law, including marriage and divorce, was incorporated in the respective religious courts: rabbinical courts for Jews, Sharia for Moslems, and so on for other religions, such as Christians and Druze. Consequently, a woman's status among the Jewish and Moslem populations is inferior to that of her husband.

This double message creates a state of anomie: A woman who behaves according to one normative system will be considered deviant in the other. Since both systems of norms are important and central, and have been internalized by the Israeli public, the decision of a mother to seek employment often arouses mixed feelings. The Moslem mother also will face similar ambiguities, if and when the trend develops toward greater participation in the occupational sphere.

This chapter will present a brief historical survey and demographic background of Israeli women, including a characterization of the women's job market. It will also discuss the impact of employment of mothers on their status in the family, on the development of their children, and on their marital life. Lastly, there is a critical review of socioeconomic policy and its impact on women's welfare and gender equality.

Background: Historical, Economic, and Familial

The history of Israeli society is marked by several macrosocial processes: demographic changes in the composition of the population (resulting from waves of immigration that brought together people from a variety of cultures) and economic developments, which took shape at a different pace in various sectors of the society. These processes had a strong impact on family types and on gender roles.

In the fifties, a large influx of émigrés from Middle Eastern countries and from North Africa increased their proportion in the total population from 14% in the late forties to 28% in the sixties. Because of the higher rate of natural increase among emigrants from Asia and Africa, by the early eighties they equalled the population of Euro-American origin. In the fifties the total fertility of women of African-Asian origin was twice that of Euro-American women (5.40 versus 2.53). Despite differences in tradition and varying degrees of exposure to Western influences, the emigrants from Africa and Asia had certain identifiable common characteristics: an extended family with tight interdependence among its members and individuals facing society as representatives of a family in which they invested their resources in exchange for protection and support.

The family played a central role in the immigrant community as an economic, religious, and political framework. The familial patterns that the emigrants from Asia and Africa "imported" to Israel were patriarchal, with authoritarian norms governing intergenerational and intergender relations. Marriages were arranged by parents or relatives, women were wed at a young age, and a premium was placed on high fertility. There was a clear gender division of labor, with emphasis on male leadership and female chastity (Palgi, 1969).

In their countries of origin, most of the women born in Afro-Asia had not taken part in economic activities outside of the home. After immigrating, in the wake of economic constraints, many women turned to the labor market. Given their paucity of relevant skills (a considerable fraction of them arrived without any formal education), most of them entered low-status occupations: housework, labor-intensive industries (food and garment), and agriculture. The status of immigrant women in small-holder settlements is discussed by the anthropologist Shokeid (1987). He notes that with the rise in standards of living among the settlers, the farmers gradually began to manage without the women's labor, and even denied the fact that their wives had ever worked. The traditional norms that had been bent in the early years after immigration were reinstated as the economic situation improved.

As a new generation, born in Israel, began to emerge, a process of convergence between the different ethnic groups set in. Arranged marriages were mostly replaced by individual patterns of courtship. Gender roles became less rigid and more egalitarian. The interethnic gap between age of marriage and fertility narrowed (Peres and Katz, 1981, 1991). The overall fertility rate—approximately 3 children—is similar among native-born mothers, regardless of their parents' origin. This similarity is a result of a marked drop in the fertility of women of African-Asian origin and a small rise in the fertility of women of Euro-American origin. As for non-Jewish ethnic groups, all showed a decline in fertility. However there is great variance in their actual fertility, Moslem women having the highest (4.7), Christian women the lowest (2.1), and Druze women being in between, with a total fertility of 3.8 children (Statistical Abstract of Israel, 1993, Table 3.14). Inter-ethnic marriage (representing approximately 25% of all Jewish couples married in recent years) is another indication of the integration of different ethnicities in the familial sphere.

Toward the end of 1989 a large wave of emigration began from the former Soviet Union, estimated at over half a million people, and a much smaller influx (approximately 50,000) from Ethiopia. This was the second largest wave of emigration, surpassed only by the massive migration in the fifties. The emigrants from the Commonwealth of Independent States (CIS) brought their own patterns of family life. Their family size is below average in Israel, their overall fertility rate being approximately 1.5 children. Their family stability is lower and divorce rate higher that those of the average Israeli. About one-third of the families that emigrated from the CIS are single-parent families resulting from divorce. While the behavior of this group remains that of a first generation, perhaps a process of convergence, similar to that which characterized other ethnic groups, will occur in this case, too, as this wave of immigrants is successfully integrated into Israeli society both economically and culturally; however in this case it is not clear who will do the adapting and who will do the influencing.

Even though differences in fertility rates have narrowed, there is still a considerable gap in participation in the labor force among women from different ethnic backgrounds. Among Jewish women, the highest rate of participation is among native-born (46%), followed by women of Euro-American origin (37%), and lastly women of African-Asian origin (32%). Much of the difference in participation among these categories is explained by differences in schooling, and sometimes also by differences in family status and number of children (Ben-Porath, 1983; Izraeli, 1983).

The economic development that has taken place since the fifties has left a mark on many spheres of life. Israel's current population is primarily urban: Over 90% of the Jewish as well as the Arab population lives in urban communities (Della-Pergola, 1993). The standard of living, as reflected by private consumption per capita, has more than tripled. The percentage of families with home appliances has increased tenfold, and real income per capita has tripled. Housing density has declined rapidly, from 2.4 people per room in the fifties to 1.02 in the nineties (Statistical Abstract of Israel, 1990, Table 11.12). The level of education of the Jewish population has increased from a median of 8 years of schooling in the sixties, to 12 years for men and women alike in 1991. In the Arab sector the picture is different: The median schooling for men is 9.6 and for women 8.3. Here, too, the change was marked, but their starting point, in the fifties, was exceedingly low (Lissak, 1993).

These socioeconomic changes, which brought the standard of living in Israel close to that of several European countries, and which made lifestyle more like that of Western industrialized societies, have had an impact on women's employment, on family life, and on women's interrelationships. I will discuss this impact with respect to three features of the family: the decline in marriage rate, the rise in divorce rate, and the growing eminence of two new family types—single-parent and dual-career families.

In the past Israel's population was characterized by a high tendency to marry, as expressed by a relatively young marriage age and a low percentage of older never-married individuals. Since the mid-seventies there has been a trend toward a decline in the marriage rate, from 9.3 in the early seventies to 6.5 in the early nineties. The age of marriage has been on the rise, and it is now 27 years for men and 24 years for women, for first marriages. The percentage of never-married among 20 to 24 year olds increased from 76.7% for men and 43.8% for women in 1970, to 87.4% and 62.0%, respectively, in 1990. Among women, although not among men, the percentage of never-married among the 45 to 49 cohort is on the rise, from 1.6% in 1970 to 4.1% in 1990. Note that these tendencies occurred in the Jewish majority (Statistical Abstract of Israel, 1993, Table 3.1).

Among the *non-Jewish* populations, in the early seventies a rise was registered in the propensity to marriage, and a further, more gradual rise has been noted in the nineties. The unique combination of modernity and traditionalism under the same roof, in various sectors of Israeli society, can account for these trends. While in the industrialized world the tendency to marry began to drop sharply in the early seventies, plummeting to less than 60%, parallel although less extreme trends are beginning to appear among certain segments of Israeli society.

As for the tendency to divorce, here too one can detect the impact of the duality of norms between modernity and traditionalism. Family stability is declining, as in all developed countries, but in Israel this trend is developing gradually, at a slower pace; Israel possibly has the highest marital stability rate of any industrialized society. There are a variety of indices for measuring divorce rate, although this is not the place to discuss them (for detailed computations regarding Israeli society, see Katz and Peres, 1995). According to the most common index, the crude divorce rate, the figure is 1.4 for Jews and 0.9 for Moslems (Statistical Abstract of Israel, 1993, Table 3.1). Divorce in Israel is more prevalent among secular Jews of Euro-American origin with above-average levels of schooling and income than among other groups in the population. In the Arab sector the divorce rate has also increased, reaching a figure in the nineties comparable to the divorce rate among Jews twenty years earlier. Summing up, the Jewish sector has been following in the wake of the developed Western world. Nevertheless, the change has been slower and more circumspect, indicating conservatism and exceptional stability in the international perspective (Della-Pergola, 1993).

As the divorce rate rises, so does the percentage of single-parent families. An estimated 9.4% of total households with children up to age 17 are single-parent units, with 90% of these headed by divorcées. Two principal reasons can be indicated for the rise in single-parenthood: a rise in women's education, enabling them to earn better and achieve greater economic independence, and a decline in the stigma attached to divorced women. Because of an almost exclusive responsibility for providing for the family, the rate of labor-force participation among single mothers is higher than among mothers from intact families. It is interesting to note that among two emigrant populations—from the CIS and from Ethiopia—single parenthood is far more prevalent than among the veteran Israeli population. In both these groups approximately 30% of the households are single-parent units. This high rate is due, in part, to the immigration process itself, which increases tension and conflict in the family: The spouses may have different bonds to Judaism, and hence differ in motivation to immigrate to Israel; in hastily accomplished migration, as with the wave from Ethiopia, spouses and families often became separated. Adjustment to a new country also poses various challenges for the spouses: earning a living, coping with a decrease in parental authority, and adjusting to increasing dependence on public services in education and welfare. All these are likely to have an adverse effect on marital stability.

A relatively new family structure, which has emerged in the wake of women's entering high-status occupations, is the dual-career family. In such families both spouses are employed full time in positions that enable advancement, require commitment, and are central in the worker's life. It is not easy for Israeli women to embark on such careers, despite the image of Israeli society as allowing full equality between the sexes. This image has drawn heavily on the inspiration of the pioneer women in the early years of Jewish settlement, on women serving in the army, and on the early years of the kibbutz. However, the reality does not match the image, and the entrance of women into high-level positions is proceeding at a snail's pace (see, for example, the article by Izraeli (1988) on women entering managerial positions).

Female Participation in the Labor Force:
Facts and Figures

Since the establishment of the State of Israel, women's participation in the labor force has increased steadily, from 22% in the fifties, to 25% in the sixties, 29% in the seventies, 36% in the eighties, and 43% in the mid-nineties. There is a marked difference between the rate of labor-force participation among Jewish women and non-Jewish women. Looking at the female labor force in these two sectors, we see that in 1992 labor-force participation among Jewish women was 48%, but only 14% among non-Jewish women. The rate of participation among non-Jewish women is far lower, and although there was an impressive rise in the seventies, over the last decade the figure has remained fairly stable. Recently another female population group has been entering the labor force: women emigrants, primarily from the CIS. The longer these women have been in the country, the greater their participation in the labor force. As of 1992, of those women who settled that year, 20% were in the labor force; among those who had settled in 1991, 39%, and among those who had settled in 1990, around 52%.

The general features of the women's labor force in Israel do not differ substantially from those in most industrialized countries. For the total of employed women, 41% generally work part time (as opposed to 11% among men). They work an average of 30 hours per week (in comparison with 41.3 hours for employed men). Women constitute about 43% of the total salaried employees in the economy. The distribution of women's occupations is also quite conventional: forty-five percent of employed women work in public and community services; 34% in scientific, academic, and learned professions; and 14% in industry (in comparison to 19%, 27%, and 20%, respectively, among employed men). As women's level of schooling rises, so does their participation in the labor force. Among women with 16 or more years of schooling, 76% are in the labor force, as among men; whereas among women with only 8 years of schooling, only 16% are in the labor force. The median schooling of employed women is somewhat higher than that of men (12.8 versus 12.1) (Central Bureau of Statistics, 1993).

The conclusion is that schooling is a major factor in women's entry into, and survival in, the labor force. Presumably this selection (which does not operate with respect to men) accounts for the fact that working women are somewhat more educated than working men. As we have seen, there are differences among Jewish women; participation of African-Asian–born women being lower, although far greater than participation of Arab women in the labor force.

Two main processes affect the entry of Arab women into the labor force: modernization and the decline in the amount of agricultural land available to the average rural family. Modernization has affected the traditional family structure, opening new avenues for education and delaying the age of marriage. The decline in the profitability of agriculture and the employment of Arab men as wage earners created a need for additional sources of income, leading Arab women to begin joining the market economy (rising from 6% in the early 1970s to about 14% at present). However the style of their participation in the labor market is influenced by the traditionalism of Arab society. They are unlikely to commute, since social norms and traditions limit their mobility and forbid interaction with men who are not kin. At present, a small fraction of Arab women are employed in agriculture; some hold white-collar or semiprofessional jobs (teaching, nursing) and other service occupations. Most Arab women are confined to their place of residence and are limited to a few occupational positions (Lewin-Epstein and Semyonov, 1992).

Jewish women's participation in the labor force according to marital status breaks down as follows: 66% among divorcées, 49% among married women, and 37% among the never married. It should be noted that mothers' participation in the labor force is greater than all other family statuses. In 1992 about 67% of all mothers of children under age 15 were employed. Their participation in the labor force decreased as the number of children in the family increased, and it increased as the age of the youngest child increased. In fact, 71% of mothers of a single child were in the labor force, in comparison to 44% of mothers of four or more. Some 54% of the mothers whose youngest child was under one year old were in the labor force, in comparison with 73% whose youngest was over ten (Central Bureau of Statistics, 1993).

Comparison across decades indicates a decline in the negative correlation between mothers' participation in the labor force and number of children. In the fifties and sixties there was a sharp decline in labor-force participation beginning with the first child, but since the eighties mothers' participation is noticeably affected from the second child on. Changes have also occurred with respect to the relationship between mothers' participation in the labor force and children's ages. In the sixties the main difference in labor-force participation was between mothers of children under age four and mothers of children over four, whereas in the eighties the difference in participation is between mothers of infants (up to one year) and mothers of children 2 years old and up.

These changes can largely be attributed to the rise in options for preschool education and to the growing tendency of parents to avail themselves of these options. Israel has over 1,000 day care centers, spread over most areas of the country and supported by the Ministry of Welfare as well as women's organizations. The percentage of children attending preschool is 60% for two year olds, 90% for three year olds, and all children four years or older. In the Arab sector, preschool registration is lower: 20% for three year olds, 40% for four year olds, and most for five and up (Safir, 1991). Thus, one could summarize that having many children, especially if some are extremely young, still presents an obstacle to mothers' employment.

The sensitivity to this obstacle has been decreasing over the years, as manifested by the fact that more women are employed despite the presence of young children, and by the fact that the threshold number has increased and the threshold age dropped.

Effects on Children

Of the various consequences of mothers' employment, the public, as well as the mothers themselves, seem to be most sensitive to those consequences affecting the development of their offspring. This sensitivity follows from the assumption of a mother's special commitment and responsibility for the development of her children, which has become institutionalized over many generations. Thus, in child-oriented Israel it is often asked whether mothers' employment, for all its advantages, is not at the expense of children's development.

In a comprehensive study, Peres and Katz (1984) compared intellectual potential (I.Q.) and scholastic achievements of children of employed and nonemployed mothers (N = 739). To measure I.Q. the investigators applied the MILTA test developed by Ortar (1980). Scholastic achievements were assessed by teachers' grades. Teachers were also requested to evaluate pupils' adjustment to school, as well as their sociability. All the comparisons, without exception, indicated some advantage of working mothers' offspring over the children of housewives. However, none of the differences was considerable, and only four of them were significant.

Is this only an ostensible advantage—i.e., one that stems from other background variables? In order to answer this question, the differences found were examined with the relevant background variables controlled. The most likely intervening variable, known for its impact both on the tendency of women to participate in the work force and on the achievement level of offspring, is mothers' schooling. If controlling for this variable would make the significant differences between children of employed mothers and of housewives disappear, then no other variables need be controlled. Indeed, after controlling for the variable of mother's schooling, none of the former differences remained significant. Thus, it turns out that the advantage of children of employed mothers with respect to I.Q. and grades stemmed from differences in education between the two groups of mothers. Nevertheless, note that controlling for mother's schooling did not reverse the direction of differences. In other words, the data did not support the notion that mothers' employment adversely affects offspring's intelligence, scholastic achievements, or behavior.

Mothers' attitudes and conduct are assumed to have an impact on the way children form their notions of gender role and division of labor in the family. Hence many studies examine the impact of mothers' employment on the degree of their children's stereotyping with respect to gender roles. In order to examine this question, children of employed mothers and of housewives were given a list of activities and asked to indicate whether each was appropriate to a woman, a man, or both (Peres and Katz, 1984). Sample activities included cooking, earning money, weeping, being a leader, working hard, and playing with the children. In terms of overall averages, the category most egalitarian in its role perception was daughters of employed mothers (58% on the average responded "appropriate to both"). Next came two groups: sons of employed mothers and daughters of housewives (each responded 52% in the egalitarian pattern). Least flexible in their attitudes were the sons of housewives (46%).

The daughters in this study were also requested to indicate how they view their own future employment in terms of scope (full time, part time, or none at all) and in terms of type of occupation (measured on a prestige scale). The professional aspirations of daughters of working mothers were found to be higher than those of daughters whose mothers did not hold jobs (72.83 versus 67.39; $t = 2.35$ $p \leq 0.005$). This finding supports the idea that the self-perception of daughters of working mothers is less stereotyped. Professions such as pilot, physician, academician, and manager appeared fairly often among them. Thus, it appears that daughters form their decisions on employment, profession, and career via identification with their mothers, who are their major reference figures.

Sons were questioned about their view of the role of their future spouses. As may be expected, sons of housewives had a greater propensity to see their future spouses as housewives, and sons of working mothers were more inclined to view their future spouses as employed. In conclusion, research indicates that children whose mothers have careers of their own hold more gender-equitable views.

Effects on the Mother

Two antithetical approaches have been taken regarding the impact of the woman's dual role as mother and working person on her emotional well-being. Both are empirically supported. The first approach lays emphasis on the tension and conflict between these two roles as a result of several tasks competing for limited resources. This type of role conflict is likely to find expression in physical and emotional attrition. The first approach identifies two types of conflict facing the working mother: first, tension to the point of dysfunction as a result of conflicting demands, as well as suffering from excessive burdens; and second, tension stemming from the clash between contradictory norms and values. Often the spheres of employment and family encourage incompatible patterns of behavior: e.g., self-fulfillment versus family-orientation. In other words, difficulties in dividing her time, handling her task burden, or coping with psychological pressures resulting from conflicting expectations—all these are faced by the woman who combines an occupational role with a familial role. Although it emphasizes the existence of tensions resulting from a dual role, it does not deny the existence of advantages and enrichment.

The second approach also offers advantages for the mother in terms of her economic and psychosocial welfare. The possibility of complementarity and enrichment between the two roles provides the woman with emotional strength, security, and self-fulfillment. A survey of young Israeli families (Marcus and Doron, 1985) found that health, satisfaction, serenity, and good spirits were more prevalent among employed mothers than among housewives.

In another study (Katz, 1989), designed to analyze the impact of mothers' employment on family life, two main questions were addressed: Under what circumstances does role-strain increase in the life of the working mother, and in what situations are the negative consequences outweighed by enrichment and complementary role enhancement? Various aspects of role strain were measured: a sense of burnout, as expressed by high agreement with the statement "I am tired and worn out as a result of the double role"; satisfaction with family life and employment; and a discrepancy between one's self-image at home and at work. To investigate whether resources (schooling, income, occupational prestige) reduce role strain on employed mothers, Katz applied unidirectional analyses of variance while controlling for relevant background variables. Employed mothers with a high level of resources showed fewer indicators of strain than others. Education and occupational prestige were found to have a stronger impact than income on reducing strain and burnout.

A working mother with extensive resources (schooling, income, and occupational prestige) is able to reduce the burden of obligations entailed by a dual task. Such mothers tend to bear fewer children, work shorter hours, and recruit more hired help from outside the family. Another study (Katz and Peres, 1985) found that lessening the task of child-bearing consistently led to a reduction in two indicators of role strain: dissatisfaction at work and a significant gap between self-image at home and at work. Reducing work hours constantly tended to reduce the sense of burnout. Working mothers were able to invest part of their personal income in improving the functioning of the home. This was due not only to the increased size of the family income, but also to the increased say of employed mothers in setting expenditure priorities and determining family consumption.

The findings discussed above are similar to those of Leiblich (1993), who interviewed career women. Her study, too, found that employed women with careers were able to cope with their double roles. Leiblich's study compared successful Israeli and American career women at midlife, however. Her findings are based on two rather small samples (24 American and 24 Israeli women in their early forties). The study found that Israeli women tended to combine family life with career. They were more likely to work in public administration than in business and tended to advance to the rank of second in command. At the same time, Israeli women were not very ambitious about their careers, and viewed past successes without much pride. They worked primarily for individual satisfaction and for economic ends. In addition to her career, the Israeli woman was the main caregiver in her household. She had moderate role conflict, yet was quite satisfied with her combination of career and family life. She obtained support from her husband and parents, rather than from women's groups or organizations. In comparison, Lieblich found that the American career woman of the same age seemed to be struggling with her commitments and choices and had more intense feelings about her achievements and conflicts. Married American subjects seemed less involved in their family than their Israeli counterparts and complained about deep role conflicts. They obtained support both from their husbands and from their ideological women's networks. The author concluded that Israeli women's self-esteem was based, among other things, on having a happy, healthy family, whereas the American woman focused her attention more on her individual achievements than on her family life. These different orientations seem to reflect central cultural values. As a result of a cultural emphasis on family and a concern for national security that brings out the interdependence between men and women, feminism has not taken as firm a hold among women in Israel as it has in the United States (Izraeli and Tabory, 1986).

Mothers' employment has also been found to have an impact on the well-being of single parents. A study comparing the psychological well-being of married women to that of women who were single parents (divorcées or widows) found lower personal well-being among the latter (Katz, 1991). Single mothers executed a wider range of family roles, and many felt overburdened by the need to make decisions alone and to bear the sole responsibility for their children. Most of them go to work out of economic necessity and have insufficient spare time to satisfy their other needs. Notwithstanding attitudes championing devoted motherly care for their children, only a minority managed to achieve an adequate standard of living solely from their earnings. However, a group of single mothers were found whose sense of personal well-being was no worse, and sometimes even better, than that of mothers in two-parent households. These were generally single mothers who had the necessary resources to successfully shoulder the burdens and difficulties described above. The variables that predict a high level of personal well-being include extent of employment, occupational prestige, and income. In addition to greater economic viability, these variables also indicate independent action and social presence. The happiest found expression in performing more roles within the family prior to its dissolution, as well as in working outside the house. In this way, women acquired the skills and flexibility necessary to adapt to life without a spouse.

Effects on the Quality of Marital Life

Two studies investigated the impact of mothers' employment on various aspects of satisfaction: One examined satisfaction with marital life; the other examined general satisfaction, absence of worries, and state of mind. Both studies included spousal satisfaction in the data. The first study (Katz and Briger, 1988) examined the quality of marital life in seven spheres: home-making, child care, finance, standard of living, intimate relations, leisure, and mutual understanding. In each of these spheres, the researchers measured satisfaction with the spousal relationship, rather than overall satisfaction with family life. They found that these seven spheres constitute a unidimensional index of the quality of marriage. Katz and Briger examined further whether the wife's employment affected her own and her spouse's marital satisfaction; they compared the average ratings for quality of marriage among working mothers and housewives and found significant differences. Employed mothers reported greater satisfaction. The same was found among the men: Husbands of working wives reported a higher quality of marital life than husbands of housewives.

Even in the light of this study, the question remains whether the findings reflect the impact of the mother's employment itself on the quality of marital life, or whether what really improves the quality of life is the self-selection of women for work according to the resources available to them, such as schooling, health, and husband's support. Controlling for these variables did not remove the positive correlation between quality of marital life and women's employment, but even strengthened it in certain cases. The most noticeable case of a stronger correlation occurred in comparing a wife's religious to secular orientation. One may presume that religious women who work have passed a more rigorous selection process and that, therefore, they excel in the traits that were found to improve the quality of marital life.

The second study examines the "psychological gain or loss" stemming from mothers' employment (Marcus and Doron, 1985). In all the facets of psychological well-being that were examined—satisfaction from life, absence of worries, and morale—the scores of both spouses were higher among couples in which the wife was employed than among couples in which the wife was not. The authors attributed this to the fact that the employed mother receives various benefits, such as a sense of participation in providing for the family, a sense of responsibility, honor, and independence. The husband's higher psychological well-being was found to stem not only from the economic contribution of his wife's salary, but also from the fact that she was more interesting and became a partner in important decisions, thus reducing the sole responsibility of the man for the family's welfare.

With respect to relations between spouses, Marcus and Doron (1985) examined twelve dimensions of interspouse relations. For five of the dimensions they found a clear and significant trend correlating women's employment with an improvement in relations between spouses. These facets include frequency of conversation on personal problems, enjoyment of each other's company, affectionate behavior, and not "getting on each other's nerves." One inverse relationship was found: When the wife was employed, the spouses' tendencies to criticize one another increased. The researchers presumed that both the "positive" and the "negative" findings stemmed from the wife's becoming a partner with more weight in the interaction between spouses.

Effects on the Division of Labor

Does the mother's work outside the home affect the division of labor between spouses? Is the time and energy a woman invests in her occupation a substitute for or an addition to her burden of mothering and housekeeping? These questions were investigated in a representative nationwide study, comparing 1,000 employed mothers with 500 housewives, all married and with children (Peres and Katz, 1984; Katz, 1989). The subjects were divided into four categories: employed mothers; their husbands; housewives; and their husbands. Combining active time invested on the job and at home shows that the average burden is greatest on working mothers (13.5 hours per day); the least on housewives (9.7 hours), and somewhere in between for husbands in both categories (12.7; 12.8 hours). Husbands do not share significantly in the additional burden arising from their wives' employment. The number of hours they devote to the home and children is about the same, whether or not their wives are employed outside the home. To investigate this constancy in husbands' allocation of time, variances in time allocated to different tasks were compared between men and women. It turns out that husbands' allocation of time to domestic tasks is far more uniform and less flexible than that of wives. In allocation of time to work, the situation is reversed. Here, where men invest most of their time, variance among men was found to be greater than among women. Thus, both husbands and wives allocate their active time in accordance with the need of their principal area of responsibility; a greater variance is found for women at home and for men at work.

The employed women in the first study (Peres and Katz, 1984) were divided into two groups according to their available resources: one group, high in resources (schooling, occupational prestige, and income), and the other, low in these resources. This division was made in order to investigate whether employed mothers with a high level of resources are more capable of enlisting the help of their husbands. No difference was found between either group in the amount of time husbands devoted to home and children. In both cases the fathers allotted about 3 to 3.5 hours, as compared with twice that allotment on the part of the mothers. Significant differences were found between the groups in terms of employing outside help. Women with a high level of resources have a greater tendency to hire help. As might be expected, income had the strongest impact, although schooling and prestige also had significant impacts. In conclusion, the employed mother with a high level of resources has an advantage in obtaining hired help but not in enlisting her husband's assistance. Also, no correlation was found between family size and increased paternal involvement in family work, except when the number of children exceeded 6, which was relatively rare among the Jewish population studied.

Sagi (1982) studied variation in styles of paternal involvement in Israel. It was found that a large number of fathers who were highly involved in child care had working wives, and most of them held full-time jobs. Since this study was not designed to address the issue of maternal employment, it is not clear to what extent the relationship between maternal employment and paternal involvement is associated with factors of circumstance or motivation. In a later article, reviewing the role of fathers in Israel, Sagi notes that one cannot determine whether maternal employment is the antecedent of increased paternal involvement, if it is made possible by increased paternal participation, or if a third variable mediates between the two (Sagi, Koren, and Weinberg, 1987).

Few studies have been made of dual-career families in Israel. The study by Izraeli (1988) on couples where both spouses are doctors compared burnout between the spouses. She found, contrary to her hypothesis, that women did not suffer more burnout than men. The explanation offered by the authors for the absence of a correlation between burnout and job/home conflict among the women studied was that female doctors, a priori, constitute a nontraditional female category that develops normative notions of its own. The attitudes of the female doctors indicated ambivalence. They all believed that men's obligation to care for the children was equal to women's, but less than half of them thought that their careers were as important as or more important than those of their spouses. The most surprising result was in the correlation between burnout and job/home conflict among the male doctors. Their source of burnout had to do with the relations between spouses, especially with the husband's feeling that he had hampered his spouse's career. When a man was married to a woman whose professional level was on a par with, or even higher than, his own, it is hard for him to justify being unresponsive to the expectations that stem from his being a spouse and father. Other studies of dual-career families in different professions and at various stages of married life are likely to indicate whether the findings of this study represent an exception, or whether they indicate that a pattern of more symmetric relations is developing in the wake of symmetry in the professional status of the spouses.

Discussion and Policy Recommendations

The ability of Israeli women to choose their lifestyle vis-à-vis marriage and work must be examined from several points of view: in terms of economic (and socioeconomic) considerations, in terms of equal opportunity in theory and practice, and in terms of social awareness. Participation of women and mothers in the labor force is significant for the economy at large, for women at large, and for each woman as an individual.

The economic significance of women's employment should be discussed. The educational system invests no less in women, and of late even more, than in men. It is hard to imagine that such an investment would not also be put to use for economic needs. Entire sectors of the economy—education, health, electronics, fashion, office work—are based on a work force composed primarily of women. The average monthly expenditure of an Israeli family—about $2,000—could not have come about, were it not based on 1.75 salaries per average family. Recent and anticipated developments in the Israeli economy—such as absorbing half a million emigrants from the CIS, where there is a relatively large minority of single-parent families; changing the balance from a military-defense orientation to a civilian orientation, in the wake of the peace process; and computerizing industry and engineering—all increase supply and demand for women in the work force.

The right to work and enjoy the returns that employment brings (income, prestige, information and support networks) is vested in civil law for women as well as men. However, these laws have become gradually more unequivocal. The legislative changes began with attempts to protect women and prevent their exploitation. For example, prohibiting night work for women, setting an earlier retirement age (60 for women, 65 for men), and labor agreements requiring shorter work hours for mothers of young children. Working mothers at all ranks of employment use a variety of strategies to cope with their double task; they have a high tendency toward part-time work and prefer occupations in which the vacations match those of their children. These strategies result, among other things, in marked differences in the place of men and women in the occupational hierarchy and in the type of occupation and its remuneration (on the average, women in Israel earn 30% less than men). In most instances part-time work prevents women from advancing to senior positions, and the focus of women on occupations that "match" school hours and vacations leads to a drop in the status and returns from these occupations. Thus Izraeli (1992) concludes that the current social policy, instead of encouraging equal opportunity, tends to support a system in which the majority of women are on the "mommy track."

In the eighties the government realized that protective legislation causes more harm than good. Although such legislation grants extra privileges to women, it also deters the rational employer from hiring women and thus further establishes the extra responsibility of the mother for her family and children (Raday, 1991). In 1988 an equal opportunity bill was passed, forbidding advertisement of positions specifically for only one of the sexes and forbidding discrimination on the basis of sex in hiring and firing workers. Retirement age was equalized for men and women, and a restriction was placed on the tendency to lay off women first—since they are generally not the main providers of the family. Rights that in the past had been given to mothers alone were now considered parental rights; i.e., both parents were entitled to a year of leave without pay during the early years of their children's lives and to be absent from work when a child is ill.

Income tax law was also based on the assumption that the man was the main provider, hence income tax files were managed solely under the husband's name, even when the wife had an independent occupation. As a result, husbands had full knowledge of their wives' income and property, whereas the converse was not so. This inequality was especially evident and prejudicial to women's rights in cases of financial litigation between spouses. This distortion has been corrected in part, formally at least, by giving a couple the option of deciding between themselves in whose name their income tax will be filed. To this day, however, the option of each of the heads of the household filing separately does not exist.

In conclusion, the legal system in Israel is extremely progressive in comparison with that of the past and even in comparison with those of other Western countries. However, in Israel, more than in other countries, there is a gap between equality on paper and in practice. Women are concentrated only in a narrow range of hundreds of possible professions (Kraus, 1989), and are conspicuously absent from high-income and high-status positions: out of 120 seats in the Knesset, only 11 are held by women (Izraeli, 1988). Paradoxically, this is exactly the number of women who sat in Israel's first Knesset, elected in the late forties. On the boards of directors of governmental corporations, which in Israel compose entire sectors of the economy (electricity, telecommunications, Dead Sea works, and so on), women's representation is less than 2 percent. There are no women heading any of the local or municipal councils, and Israel's seven universities have, throughout their history, had a total of one female rector. Despite a certain rise in the percentage of women in managerial positions, from 12% in 1973 to 16% in the mideighties, almost total male domination is still evident in this strategic area.

Although the law permits the man to play a greater role in responsibility for the home and the children, these rights are rarely exercised. Although precise data is not available on this, it is rare for a man to take a leave of absence to rear his children or to miss a day of work on account of his children's health. Neither the fathers themselves, nor their employers, are disposed to realize equality of this sort. Given this lag of reality behind egalitarian legislation, women's organizations, as well as the Israeli supreme court, have increased their demands for affirmative action.

The lag in actual realization of the legislation stems primarily from the existence of traditional and patriarchal norms among many sectors of Israeli society. These norms have an impact on two planes: as internalized by both sexes, and as exercised by the mechanisms of social control. For example, an employed father who is in competition with others at the same place of work will be deterred from realizing his parental rights both because he sees himself as less suitable to care for his child, and because he fears the response of his employers and colleagues.

A nationwide study examining the normative values, perceptions, and behavior of the Israeli public with respect to gender roles in the family, at work, and in politics (Zemach and Peled, 1983) found that only among women did the majority hold attitudes favoring egalitarian role division (69% of the women, as opposed to 44% of the men, believed that the role of family provider belonged to both spouses). The man's role outside the home was taken for granted and considered a criterion for his social excellence, whereas the woman's responsibility within the home was perceived as a matter of course. A considerable majority of the subjects considered a well-tended home and children as a criterion of the woman's excellence. Therefore the authors concluded that there is clear gender differentiation on the normative plane among the Israeli population. Izraeli and Tabory (1986) investigated people's perception of the question of equality between the sexes as a social problem and found that discrimination against women's promotion was not perceived as an important social problem among the university student population.

Hence, true equality cannot be achieved simply through legislative means. Changes in the public consciousness and basic cultural assumptions are an integral part of the process of social change. The educational system has an important role to play in bringing about a change in gender roles on the symbolic as well as operational level. It is important that every young person, male or female, be equipped with the skills to perform family-oriented and job-oriented roles. This requirement is justified in view of the relatively long periods of time that a modern adult spends outside the traditional family unit (before marriage, in the event of marriage dissolution, and after the children leave the nest). It is also justified by the need for a less rigid image of men and women, to enable more realization of the needs and characteristics of the individual personality.

References

Ben-Prath, Y. (1983). *Jewish mother goes to work: Trends in the labor force participation of women in Israel 1955–1980*. Jerusalem: Marice Falk Institute for Economic Research in Israel.

Central Bureau of Statistics. (1993). *Statistical abstract of Israel*. Jerusalem.

Della-Pergola, S. (1993). Demographic changes in the state of Israel in the early nineties. In Y. Koff (Ed.), *Allocation of resources to social services 1992–1993* (pp. 63–108). Jerusalem: Center for the Study of Social Policy in Israel. (Hebrew)

Izraeli, D.N. (1983). Israeli women in the work force. *Jerusalem Quarterly, 27*, 59–80.

Izraeli, D.N. (1988). Burning out in medicine: A comparison of husbands and wives in dual career couples. *Journal of Social Behavior and Personality 3*, 329–346.

Izraeli, D.N. (1992). Culture, policy and women in dual-earner families in Israel. In S. Lewis, D.N. Izraeli, and H. Hootsmans (Eds.), *Dual earner families: International perspectives* (pp. 19–45). London: Sage.

Izraeli, D.N., and Tabory, E. (1986). The perception of women's status in Israel as a social problem. *Sex Roles 14*, 663–678.

Katz, R. (1989). Strain and enrichment in the role of employed mothers in Israel. *Marriage and Family Review 14*, 203–218.

Katz, R. (1991). Marital status and well-being: A comparison of widowed, divorced, and married mothers in Israel. *Journal of Divorce and Remarriage 14*, 203–218.

Katz, R., and Briger, R. (1988). Modernity and the quality of marriage in Israel: The impact of socio-cultural factors on marital satisfaction. *Journal of Comparative Family Studies 19*, 371–380.

Katz, R., and Peres, Y. (1985). Is resource theory equally applicable to wives and hus-
    bands? *Journal of Comparative Family Studies 16*, 1–10.
Katz, R., and Peres, Y. (1996). Marital crisis and therapy in their social context. *Contem-
    porary Family Therapy.*
Kraus, V. (1989). Ethnic, gender and the process of status attainment in Israel. *Re-
    search in Inequality and Social Conflict 1*, 193–217.
Leiblich, A. (1993). Preliminary comparison of Israeli and American successful career
    women at mid-life. In Y. Azmon and D.N. Izraeli (Eds.), *Women in Israel* (pp. 195–
    208). New Brunswick: Transaction.
Lewin-Epstein, N., and Semyonov, M. (1992). Modernization and subordination: Arab
    women in the Israeli labour-force. *European Sociological Review 8*, 39–51.
Lissak, M. (1993). Social characteristics—Changes and implications. In Y. Koff (Ed.),
    Allocation of resources to social services 1992–1993 (pp. 109–152). Jerusalem:
    Center for the Study of Social Policy in Israel. (Hebrew)
Marcus, Y., and Doron, N. (1985). Is womens' employment worthwhile? *Society and
    Welfare 6*, 222–231. (Hebrew)
Ortar, G. (1980). *M.I.L.T.A. tests.* Jerusalem: Ministry of Education.
Palgi, P. (1969). Family types in Israel. In R. Bar-Yosef and E. Shelah (Eds.), *The family
    in Israel* (pp. 115–124). Jerusalem: Academon. (Hebrew)
Peres, Y., and Katz, R. (1981). Stability and centrality: The nuclear family in modern
    Israel. *Social Forces 59*, 687–704.
Peres, Y., and Katz, R. (1984). *The Employed Mother and Her Family.* Research report
    presented to the Ministry of Labour and Welfare. Jerusalem: Modiin Ezrachi.
    (Hebrew)
Peres, Y., and Katz, R. (1991) The family in Israel: Change and continuity. In L.
    Shamgar-Handelman and R. Bar-Yosef (Eds.), *Families in Israel* (pp. 9–32). Jerusa-
    lem: Academon. (Hebrew)
Raday, F. (1991). Women in the Israeli Law. In B. Swirsky and M.P. Safir (Eds.), *Calling
    the equality bluff: Women in Israel* (pp. 178–187). New York: Pergamon Press.
Safir, M.P. (1991). Tradition and public policy give family first priority. In B. Swirsky and
    M.P. Safir (Eds.), *Calling the equality bluff: Women in Israel* (pp. 57–66). New
    York: Pergamon Press.
Sagi, A. (1982). Antecedents and consequences of various degrees of paternal involve-
    ment in child rearing: The Israeli project. In M.E. Lamb (Ed.), *Non-traditional fami-
    lies: Parenting and child development* (pp. 205–232). Hillsdale, N.J.: Lawrence
    Erlbaum.
Sagi, A., Koren, N., and Weinberg, M. (1987). Fathers in Israel. In M.E. Lamb (Ed.), *The
    father's role: Cross-cultural perspectives* (pp. 197–226). Hillsdale, N.J.: Lawrence
    Erlbaum.
Shokeid, M. (1987). Implications of immigration on family life of Moroccan Jews in
    Israel. *Society and Welfare 8*, 3–14. (Hebrew)
Zemach, T., and Peled, Z. (1983). *The Public Image of the Status of Women.* Research
    report submitted to the Office of the Prime Minister's Advisor on the Status of
    Women. Jerusalem: Israel Institute of Applied Social Research. (Hebrew)

Chapter Five
Maternal Employment and Family Patterns
Mexican Women in the Maquiladora Industry

Elsa O. Valdez

During the past three decades, Mexican women have entered the labor market in unprecedented numbers, working in both the formal industrial and service sectors. The history of the Border Industrialization Program underscores this dramatic change in women's roles and in adjustment of the cultural attitudes. Conventional beliefs that women's employment destroys the family by interfering with their reproductive roles are giving way to new views of wage work as a means for women to help support their households. A pivotal study by Tiano (1994) suggests that there has been an "erosion of normative proscriptions to women's employment" (p. 222) similar to that of other industrially developing nations.

The focus of this chapter is to examine the effects of maternal employment on children; mother's mental health, personal autonomy, social identity, and the importance of family; conjugal relationships; and family structure. It will be argued that patriarchal relations of production and reproduction uniquely affect women such that they enter the labor market from a doubly disadvantaged position because of class and gender. Furthermore, these employed mothers utilize a "set of strategies" that grow out of their roles as wives, mothers, and workers to cope with difficult working conditions and family life in general. This set of strategies includes material resources as well as emotional support from the extended family and fictive kinship. This implies that women are active agents who engage in some level of self-determination. Thus, "although women's wide-scale labor participation has not eroded patriarchy at a systemic level, Mexican women have achieved some personally liberating gains such as more control and autonomy over their lives," as suggested by Tiano (p. 233). This study is significant because it (a) adds to the body of literature on Third World families "that has placed little emphasis on the dynamics of the household and its connection with wider socioeconomic processes—showing the arbitrariness and insufficiency of analyzing the two areas separately" (Beneria and Roldan, 1987, p. 5); (b) provides a feminist basis for dealing with gender and class issues, such as examining how women's roles at work are conditioned by dynamics set up at the household level; and (c) challenges ethnocentric assumptions and stereotypes about Third World women, such as Latinas being passive and not capable of engaging in active resistance and self-determination.

The data for this analysis is drawn from my own study, as reported in this chapter, of intensive interviews of women employed in an electronics maquila in San Luis Rio Colorado, Sonora. Subsequently, while these findings cannot be generalized to the larger maquila worker industry, they do provide an in-depth portrait of working-class women's lives. They live in an urban border town and take part in daily struggles on a personal or collective level to improve their lives as well as those of their families and community. In order to examine the impact of employment on mothers and families, one must first understand the sweeping changes in the Mexican economy.

The Mexican Economy

Between 1950 and 1974 Mexico underwent high rates of economic growth: Social welfare and general standards of living improved substantially over these two decades (Steele, 1992). There were also improvements in public education: between 1950 and 1980, primary education increased from 17.6% to 79.8%; nationally the number of schools tripled; and school enrollment increased sevenfold. However, the Mexican economy experienced one of several serious crises in 1982. Steele notes that:

Since 1982, an economic crisis has existed in Mexico. The crisis, caused by rising interest rates and falling oil prices, has caused severe hardships for the poor, and many of the gains of the previous two decades have been threatened. Real wages have declined by 40 percent and social sector spending has declined from 20 percent of total government expenditures in 1982 to around 12 percent in 1991 (p. 340).

One major obstacle to Mexican economic recovery and investor confidence has been Mexico's large foreign debt of $107 billion, the second largest debt in the developing world (Clement, Jenner, Ganster, and Setran, 1989).

According to Beneria and Roldan (1987), industrialization in Mexico has been geared toward import substitution, especially of consumption products. However, the highly uneven distribution of income and lack of development of the rural sector have placed limits on the growth of the domestic market and on this industrialization. Households are very poor. The income distribution in Mexico is very unequal—in fact, the most unequal in Latin America (Selby, Murphy, and Lorenzen, 1990). World Bank figures show the ratio of income between that earned by the top 20% of Mexicans and that earned by the bottom 20% with the top quintile of the income distribution earning 20 or more times the amount of the bottom quintile. This is compared with 11 times in the United States and six times in the United Kingdom (p. 85). Furthermore, "the purchasing power of incomes has deteriorated sharply since 1982, with economists estimating a loss of 40 percent from 1982 to 1987 in individual incomes." (Selby, et al., 1990, p. 85).

The Maquiladora Industry

Maquiladoras began in 1965 when the Border Industrialization Program was established by the Mexican government, allowing wholly owned subsidiaries of foreign companies to operate in Mexico (Arreola and Curtis, 1993). About 90% of the maquiladoras are located in the north of Mexico bordering the states of California, Arizona, New Mexico, and Texas (Clement, et al., 1989). Border towns such as San Luis Rio Colorado, Mexicali, and Tijuana supply cheap labor, small overhead, close proximity to the United States, and favorable reductions in duties primarily for American industry, but also for Japanese investors. Early maquiladoras were initially small operations using converted old buildings and requiring little capital investment in facilities (Arreola and Curtis, 1993). The trend today is for large, elaborate maquiladora industrial parks usually located on the outskirts of towns.

In the early stages of maquiladora development in border communities, approximately 90% of the workers hired consisted of single

young women, 16 to 24 years old (Warner, 1990). Although the
proportion of men in the industry has been steadily rising in the
1980s, there are still many more women on the maquila shop floor
than men (Sklair, 1993). In 1992, men represented only 40.4% of
the national maquiladora work force (p. 241). Maquiladora managers claim that they prefer to hire women for tasks such as assembly
work because they have greater dexterity and visual acuity and are
more patient than men (Warner, 1990). Stoddard (1987) argues that
women score higher on maquila dexterity screening tests because
the test is designed to measure female dexterity or gender-specific
ability (cited in Warner, p. 188). Tiano (1994) notes that some
changes in hiring practices have occurred within the electronics
maquilas, the more "restrictive" employer, in the last few years. For
example, the managers she interviewed indicated that they were now
more willing to hire older women, partnered women, and women
with children. She attributes this shift in hiring practices to the
maquila industry's reluctance to increase wages. Her analysis showed
that young unencumbered women who resided with their family
and had at least 6 or more years of education could afford to shop
around for better-paying jobs.

In fact, many of these young women eventually went into the
service sector, which paid more money. As the pool of available workers in the electronics industry has shrunk, maquiladora managers
have had to adjust their ideology of "maquila grade" women. That
is, rather than raising wages to keep the young, single, maquila-grade
workers, employers have opted to hire women that ten years ago
were considered unsuitable. She also notes that, in contrast, the garment industry has historically hired older, partnered, and single
mothers; but she attributes this to the fact that wages and educational requirements in this industry have always been lower than in
the electronics industry. Very rough data from INEGI (Instituto
Nacional de Estadistica, Geografia e Informatica) for May 1992 indicate that average weekly wages are about U.S. $52 for maquila
operatives, $140 for technicians, and $215 for staff (Sklair, 1993).

The Mexican maquiladora program produces a wide range of
products and performs a variety of services (Clement, et al., 1989).
INEGI also reports that, in 1988, Baja California had the largest
concentration of maquiladoras in the area of electronics (29.4%),

followed by apparel (14.8%) and other products (15.2%). Workplace facilities such as safety provisions, child care, subsidized meals, and recreation tend to be a function of plant size and sector rather than ownership (Sklair, 1993).

Women and Working Conditions in the Maquiladora Industry

Research on the occupational effects on women's health and well-being in the maquila industry tends to be highly controversial and mixed. Several studies, cited in Guendelman's and Silberg's 1993 review of the literature, found that adverse working conditions such as poor ventilation, few rest periods, excessive noise levels, unsafe machinery, long hours of microscopic assembly work, and exposure to toxic chemicals and carcinogens were reported by maquila workers. But in their own study, Guendelman and Silberg collected data on 480 Mexican women and compared health problems across four groups—electronics, garment, services, and housewives/students—and found "that maquiladora workers were not worse off than service employees or non-wage earners" (p. 43). In fact, the results suggest that with respect to functional impediments (i.e., health problems that prevent the performance of daily activities) and nervousness, maquiladora workers' health—particularly among women in electronics—was better than that of service workers. Sklair (1993) suggests that some newer revisionist studies suggest that female maquila workers do not suffer more health hazards than other groups of women in Mexico.

Theoretical Frameworks for Examining Women in the Maquiladora Industry

A few previous studies have documented maquila workers' household arrangements or assessed the links between women's domestic status and their employment (Tiano, 1994). However, two current works on the household and work have added a wealth of information, some of it conflictive, to this body of research. For example, Tiano notes that "an employed woman typically performs the lion's share of domestic tasks in addition to her job" (p. 121) but paid employment has liberated women in terms of personal autonomy and control over their lives. In contrast, Beneria's and Roldan's study

(1987) of Mexican women engaged in industrial homework "did not find that women's control over their incomes empowered them significantly in the bargaining of gender relations within the home" (p. 165).

Additionally, until recently much of the literature on female export-manufacturing workers in Third World countries emphasized women's docility and passivity (Lopez, 1970; Baerresen, 1970; Van Waas, 1981; Nash and Safa, 1985; Leacock and Safa, 1986). Lim (1990) critiques these and other studies that have perpetuated the stereotype of female export processors. She maintains that while these negative images were appropriate during the initial development of the export-manufacturing industry, this conventional image does not apply as these programs mature. Thus, Lim concludes that negative stereotypes of female assembly workers are a result of the data that was collected during the 1970s when export factories were in their initial developmental stages. More recent studies challenge the myth that women who work in export manufacturing are "docile and downtrodden."

Tiano (1994) maintains that female maquila workers actually are "active agents taking responsibility for their lives within the parameters of their structural and cultural conditions" (p. 221). Young (1987) notes that researchers need to be careful about making generalizations about female export-manufacturing workers as a group. The data indicate, to the contrary, not only that some maquila workers depart from the female stereotype but also that they are far from unorganizable. Along the same vein, Pena (1987) laments that "there has been no major sociological research on work stoppages, sabotage, or informal counterplanning as practiced by Third World women workers" (p. 130). Her study of shop floor struggles in Mexico's maquiladora industry challenges the "prognosis of maquila workers as women lacking the ability or motivation to engage in struggle" (p. 131).

The exploitation view is consistent with socialist feminist analyses of women's roles in capitalist societies (Tiano, 1994). Scholars such as Eisenstein argue that women are subordinated because "preexisting patriarchal relations create a gender-stratified labor force" of which capitalism takes advantage (cited in Tiano, 1994, p. 40). Women are less likely to gain the training for skilled positions and are penalized by discriminatory hiring that reserves the better-paying jobs for men, who are assumed to support a family (Warner, 1990). Consequently, women's primary roles as wives and mothers are disadvantageous for participation in the labor market; hence, the maquiladora industry does not provide stable work opportunities for Mexican women.

In contrast, proponents of the "integrative" perspective view the export-manufacturing industry in a more positive light since it assumes that women's liberation will occur with their integration into Mexico's political economy. That is, maquila jobs provide women with stable employment, income, fringe benefits, assembly skills that can be used to be competitive in the labor market, occupational mobility, and options to early marriage and lower fertility rates. Scholars such as Stoddard (1987) believe that maquila jobs offer a significant improvement over other employment options available to women such as steady wages at or above a minimum wage. Furthermore, export-processing work enables women in Mexico to become more autonomous and self-reliant and to challenge patriarchal relations at home and in the larger society. Subsequently, maquila workers can gain material sources that enable them to negotiate effectively with male household members.

The theoretical framework that will be used to guide this analysis will be somewhat connected to the integration approach; but, more specifically it will be linked to feminist scholarship emanating from exploitation theory because of its focus on the interaction of patriarchal relations of production and reproduction, and women's doubly subordinate position based on class and gender. Additionally, a third approach—symbolic interaction—will provide us with valuable insights of micro-level processes, which is where interaction and exploitation theory may fall short. Proponents of symbolic interaction examine how socially constructed abstracts such as norms, values, and ideas operate to influence people's behaviors and ideologies. For example, how does maquila employment ideology—such as the idea that women are well suited for maquila work because it consists of repetitive tasks that require patience and nimble finger—affect women's orientation toward their jobs, wage-earning roles, and domestic roles? Or, does paid work lead to a change in women's consciousness and perception of themselves? In short, the three perspectives—interaction, exploitation, and symbolic interaction—will enable us to uncover the processes of creation and re-creation of class and gender relations that occur simultaneously and entail both material and ideological dimensions.

Valdez Study
Site of the Study

San Luis Rio Colorado, Sonora, is located on the Eastern margin of the Colorado River delta where Sonora, Arizona, Baja California, and California intersect. Records indicate that the initial settlement of San Luis Rio Colorado occurred around 1915—with its border counterpart San Luis, Arizona—when the Yuma Valley Railroad was extended south from its junction with the Southern Pacific Railroad. In 1917, the official founding date, the governor of Sonora ordered soldiers to establish a military garrison in San Luis Rio Colorado. Later it became the center of government-sponsored agricultural developments. Today, San Luis Rio Colorado is a major service center for cotton- and sorghum-farming hinterland (Arreola and Curtis, 1993).

The Censo General (General Census) of 1990 indicates that significant population growth has occurred in this border town: from 28,545 in 1960 to 111,508 in 1990. In 1990, the ratio of men to women in all occupations for San Luis Rio Colorado was 77 to 23%. The *Twin Plant News,* cited in Arreola and Curtis, notes that in 1990 there were 1,564 maquiladoras in the various border cities, which employed 357,641 workers; and in San Luis Rio Colorado, twelve maquilas employed 3,000 workers. However, when this data was collected in September of 1994, the president of the local maquila association reported that the number of maquilas had grown to approximately 22.

Unlike most maquiladoras, which are located in an industrial park on the periphery of the city, the maquila in this study is situated near several large apartment complexes and neighborhoods where many of the workers live. There are approximately 450 employees who assemble electronic components for automobiles. According to the manager of the plant, the male to female ratio is about 50/50; but they are an exception. For example, another maquila that is located about a mile from this one specializes in producing women's lingerie; there, 99% of the employees are women. Mothers reported working one of three shifts, and they are usually rotated every three months.

The maquila is large and modern, with eating facilities for employees. Maquila operatives at this plant work six days a week, eight hours a day, and earn about U.S. $55 to $65 a week depending on length of time employed. Employees are required to have a secundaria education (equivalent to high school in the United States). Labor turnover is not a problem at this maquila, and the manager attributes this to the fact that most people who live in San Luis Rio Colorado tend to be permanent residents, unlike the situation in Tijuana or other border cities, where people migrate from the interior of Mexico and tend to be less stable.

Sample and Data Collection Procedure

Intensive interviews of ten working mothers with children were conducted in the women's homes over a period of three weeks. Each interview lasted about 45 minutes and was administered in Spanish. The intensive interview method was determined to be the most appropriate design, since this made it possible to assess women's subjective experiences. The author had had previous contact with one of the women who worked in the maquila, and the subsequent participants were contacted through this informant. The questionnaire included open-ended questions about working conditions, housework, child care arrangements, and conjugal relations. Additionally, there were semistructured questions related to the importance of family, women's perceptions of themselves at home, at work, and in the larger society, attitudes toward gender roles, and whether they had felt depressed the previous week.

The mothers' ages ranged from 23 to 38. Six of the women had been married from 2 to 8 years, the other four from 10 to 15 years. Four of the participants had three children between 4 months and 12 years old; five had two children ranging in age from 2 to 14 years; one had one child who was 5 years old. All of the ten mothers lived within three to four miles of the maquila site. Eight of the women were currently working the night shift (5:00 P.M. to 1:30 A.M.), and two mothers were on the day shift. They normally worked 48 hours per week and earned between U.S. $56 to $70 per week. Three of the women had been employed at the electronics maquila for at least one year, four had been employed for at least three years, and the other three reported being employed for five years. All of the women had previously held lower paying service-type jobs before coming to work at this particular maquila. Family weekly incomes varied from about U.S. $112 to $200. All ten mothers were operatives and had at least nine years of education.

Findings

Effects of Maternal Employment on Children

The most consistent trend of the effects of mother's work on the family was that, because of working conditions such as shift work, working 48 hours per week, and the exhaustive nature of maquila work, there was little time or energy for the children. Some mothers were visibly upset about having to spend so much time away from their children and leaving them in the care of other family members or neighbors. For example, Lucia has three children, ages 1, 7, and 8 years, and had been married for 10 years. She stayed home for the first five years of her marriage and subsequently, because of financial necessity, was forced to work full time. By the time the last child came along she realized how fortunate she had been to have been able to stay home during the formative years of her first two children. During the interview Lucia became very emotional as she explained how work affected her children and her parenting roles:

I am not so happy with this arrangement. Even though my sister-in-law takes good care of my children, I wish I didn't have to work so I could stay home full time with the baby and be home when the other two come home from school. Because this is such a major regret for me, there are times at night when I cry because I feel bad. I tell my husband, why can't I stay home and care for the baby? When other people care for your children it's not the same. The children can't be mischievous like normal children, they have to be quiet . . . they're not as free to move about.

Maribel, who is 23, married for seven years, with two children ages 2 and 6, also reported feeling that her work put additional burdens and stresses on her children's lives:

Well, I get up at the crack of dawn and by the time I come home I'm exhausted and in no mood to attend to anyone. All I want to do is rest. . . . Before I go to work I fix lunches, and when I come home I have to make dinner, bathe the children and tidy up the house. It's hard on my kids. I've lost my sense of humor and I don't play with them anymore. I can tell that my kids feel sad because Mama is always too tired to do anything.

Andrea, a 27-year-old mother of a 5-year-old daughter, married for 5 years, feels that her rotating work schedule causes a lot of disruption in her daughter's life:

I would like to spend a lot more time with my daughter . . . attend to her needs better. But it's impossible with this horrible work shift. We need the money so I can't quit. When I can, I try to dedicate some time to my daughter . . . but it never seems like enough time.

In contrast, other parents found effective ways to cope with the negative effects on the family of mother's work. Rosa, who has been married for ten years and is 27 years old, commented that since she and her husband started working different shifts—so that one parent was always caring for the two children (3 and 8 years old)—things have improved. The children get their needs met and seem to be happier. Before this current child care arrangement existed, Rosa's mother-in-law and later a neighbor cared for the children. According to Rosa, the children were a lot quieter, but now she has noticed an improvement in their communication skills with both herself and their father:

Even though I feel tired when I get home from work, I feel good knowing that my children are happy and well cared for. My husband gives them their dinner and puts them to bed. When I come home I talk to them about different things and so does their father.

Lety, a 38-year-old mother who has been married for 15 years and has two sons, 8 and 14 years old, saw work as having some positive effects on her children. Although she does not get a lot of help from her husband, she has a large extended family that is available to lend a hand when she needs it:

My mother takes care of my boys until I get home. By then she has already given them their dinner and so I mostly have to help them with homework. If I need help around the house I can ask one of my younger sisters to come over and help me. I also have my sons do chores so they don't grow up thinking that housework is only women's work. I think that because I work, my sons are better off. . . . I can buy things for them. . . . I get to talk to people at work and I feel good about myself. . . . I think my kids pick up on this. Also, my husband and sons seem to appreciate my efforts.

Georgina, 24 years old, is in her second marriage. Her two children are 4 and 6, and currently she and her husband are living with her parents because he is between jobs. She admits that it's difficult to go back home and live with one's parents, but it does make things easier when it comes to child care. Presently, she is working the night shift. Her mother does not work and cares for her children while she is at work. Also, she doesn't have to worry about housework or preparing meals. Georgina and her family plan to live there long enough to save up some money so they can perhaps eventually purchase a small lot near her parents and build their own home. This way, she can continue to work without having to sacrifice her children's well-being in the process:

I think my kids are fine as long as my mother cares for them. Some of my friends at work don't have it so good. They have to leave their kids with neighbors and in these times you have to be careful where you leave your children. I spend a lot of time with them because I don't have to worry about doing housework.

However mothers felt about the effects of work on their children, all ten families appeared to be very child-centered. Even in the poorest households it is clear that families value their children's well-being. For example, Georgina's parents live in a small, two-bedroom wooden structure that by U.S. standards would be deemed uninhabitable. The two children were wearing clothes that didn't fit well, even though clean and mended. As the interview was in progress, the children played with their toys and would periodically attempt to get their mother's attention. She was very patient with them, but eventually asked their grandmother to come and occupy them so that we could finish the interview. For Georgina and her family, the income from her job at the maquila provides a means of survival, especially as her husband is temporarily unemployed. And with material and emotional assistance from her family, Georgina is able to cope with the demands and stresses that work puts on her children's well-being.

Effects of Employment on Mother's Mental Health

Work appeared to affect mothers in a variety of ways. Respondents were asked to explain how their job at the maquila affected their lives in general. For the most part, the women reported that everything was fine and overall their job did not seem to affect their lives. Yet their responses to the questions assessing whether they suffered from depression the past week revealed that all three had felt very depressed the past week. Furthermore, when asked to explain why they felt this way, all three responded that it had to do with their "double shift" responsibilities. For example, Rosa, who shares child care with her husband and had earlier reported that things had improved at home for her children, later added:

Yes I felt depressed last week. It was hard to concentrate. One of my children was having exams at school and he needed help, but I had to go to work. At work I kept thinking that he would not remember what we had reviewed and I couldn't concentrate. I didn't sleep well either. I got home from work and slept until about six o'clock . . . then I took the older child to school, gave the younger one breakfast, and then it was time to go pick up the older one from school. Then it was time to get ready for work. I was upset because I couldn't help my son with his exam questions and also the little one is taking medication, and I couldn't be around to do that either.

The other mothers also contended that they felt depressed and at times had no appetite. Several of them attributed this to the fact that they felt torn between helping provide for their families and fulfilling their responsibilities at home; others blamed family and economic problems for their depression. Overall, all ten participants indicated some level of role overload and role conflict, which subsequently appeared to exacerbate levels of depression.

Personal Freedom and Self-Direction

Respondents were also asked to comment on whether work has enabled them to acquire more personal autonomy and control over their lives and, if so, in what ways. The general consensus was overwhelmingly "yes." As one mother put it:

I don't have to ask my husband for money to buy things such as personal items or I can give my parents a few extra pesos when they really need it. Also, when we decide how we are going to spend our income, I feel that my input is just as important as his. Occasionally, I get a bonus at work and I will take the children to see a movie or get something to eat without having to ask him. Also, since we both know that my income is necessary, I've noticed that he is somewhat less controlling now than before I started working.

Self-Image/Social Identity

The effects of work on mother's self-image or social identity were also examined. Women were asked to describe what they considered good qualities in themselves and whether they felt important or special, and were subsequently identified as either family oriented, family/work oriented, or work oriented. Eight of the participants based their social identity on the basis of whether their children, husbands, family, or close friends had conveyed or acknowledged that they had good qualities or were important or special:

I feel I have many good qualities because my husband, children, and family make me see this. If I feel important it's because of what I can do for my family and my kids. Also, I'm proud of the fact that although I married young, I have a good marriage. . . . My good qualities come from being a good mother. I know a few mothers who don't worry about their children's education or don't give them good advice about things. I worry about every aspect of their lives. I've had people compliment me on my mothering skills.

In contrast, for two of the mothers both work and family were important elements with respect to their self-image or social identity. Lucia summed up her perception of herself as follows:

Yes, I feel I have a lot of good qualities . . . especially as a mother. I feel that during the time I have been a mother I have done it well. For my children and husband I am very important. . . . they have told me so. My work is also important to me. Three days ago my supervisor told me I was one of their best workers and he gave me high marks on my job performance evaluation. I felt really good about myself.

Along the same vein, Alice, who is 27 years old, with three children, ages 1, 7, and 8, evaluates herself based on her parenting skills as well as her work roles. She commented, "I'm proud of my skills as a mother and as a wage earner. My income helps us to get ahead. As for any special qualities or if I'm important or special you'd have to ask my family or friends."

Importance of Family

The findings on the effects of maternal employment on the importance of family indicates that overall most of the respondents felt that although family comes first, it is also good to be independent, and that at times it is better to confide in friends than in family. The concept "to be independent" was interpreted by the participants to mean being able to stand on one's own feet so that parents don't worry. A recurring theme was that it's not right to burden one's extended family with personal or economic problems frequently; but in cases of extreme financial or emotional crisis the family could always be counted on to lend a hand:

Since I've started working I find that I have started to rely more and more on my friends, but still whenever I'm dealing with a major crisis my mother and sisters are the first people I turn to. For example, just last month I went to the doctor and he told me I needed a biopsy because he had found a lump in my breast. I was so scared . . . I thought I was going to die. I immediately went down to my mother's home and they helped me by reassuring me that it was in God's hands and that I would be fine. It turned out the lump was benign. Thank God.

And if extended family members couldn't help, fictive kin such as *compadres* (godparents) or close friends from work could be called upon for help:

My comadre is the best. You see my husband and I have been having some marital problems. We argue a lot over his going out with his friends to a local bar. I get upset because we barely have enough money to survive and we can't afford any extra expenses. So my comadre suggested that I have him pay the household bills for a month so that he could see how much his drinking habit costs us. Well after the first two weeks he was amazed at how much money we could set aside if he gave up his weekly visits to the bar, and so now he invites his friends over to the house and asks them to bring a few beers with them.

In sum, maternal employment has not altered the importance of family and community for these families. That is, these mothers are traditional in their views of the importance of family, while simultaneously acknowledging the value of fictive kinship and friendship networks.

Effects of Maternal Employment on Marital Relationship

When mothers were asked to describe how work affected their conjugal relationship, the most frequently cited response was that, because of the many demands in their lives, intimate relations and spending time alone were often a problem.

Yes, work does affect our marital relationship because at the end of the day we are both tired. When we work different shifts there are times when we hardly see one another. Consequently, intimate relations are infrequent and besides it is often impossible to spend time alone.

In addition, several of the women commented that their husbands felt somewhat threatened with any contact they might have with male co-workers:

My working affects our relationship quite a bit. In the beginning we both agreed that we needed a second income and so he helped me find this job. When I got out real late he would come and pick me up from work and on several occasions he became enraged because I was talking to a male co-worker. I finally told him that if he didn't stop being so jealous I would quit my job. I felt that his accusations were unjust, especially with all the sacrifices I was making. He finally stopped, but not until I put my foot down.

Selby, et al. (1990) also examined the impact of the economic crisis on Mexican urban households in several large cities and found the following:

Male dignity has been so assaulted by unemployment and the necessity of relying on women for the substance that men formerly provided, that men have taken it out on their wives, and domestic violence has increased. But there is another side to the picture. Never have men needed their women more than right now; not just to cook, keep house, mend the clothes, and look after the children, but to earn the income that makes it possible to survive. It is too optimistic, not to say simplistic, to suggest that the survivors of the crisis are creating a whole new form of Mexican family life, more democratic, more shared, and more tranquil. But it is not too much to say that survival these days requires a wholly new concept of family life, as well as a new conception of the kinds of sacrifices required just to survive (p. 176).

For these families as well, economic survival has required the husband's acceptance, albeit reluctant, of the necessity for his wife to work.

Effects of Maternal Employment on Family Structure
The effects of work on family structure illustrate the interactive relationship between production and reproduction as proposed by exploitation theorists. In all of the families, mothers tended to be highly

egalitarian in their views of male and female roles, and were rather positive toward feminism. However, when asked to describe the domestic division of labor, all of the families exhibited a traditional structure: Mothers performed the bulk of household chores and child care. One mother agreed that women should be able to work outside the home, but then added, "It's fine as long as she continues to attend to the needs of her husband and children." She appreciated the fact that her husband occasionally fixed breakfast on Sundays. Upon further probing, several of the mothers admitted that they would like for their husbands to help out more with the housework and child care:

I do everything, he has never wanted to do anything around the house. It's not like I want him to do everything. I just wish he would cooperate and help out once in a while. Also, he thinks that providing for the children economically or giving them money is enough to make him a good father. I haven't been able to make him understand that children also need to have an emotional relationship with their father. I don't think it's fair that I work and take care of everything. I've tried talking to him . . . repeatedly. But it seems that all I do is talk. . . . He tells me that I make sense, but everything stays the same . . . nothing changes. I want him to make an effort to be a friend to his children. . . . He needs to make them feel that they can talk to him about anything.

Then mothers were asked "Do you know other families in which husbands and wives share domestic tasks?" The general response was that everyone they knew had a similar arrangement. This comparable "frame of reference" makes it less likely that women will initiate change in the domestic division of labor in the near future. However, when it comes to decision-making between husbands and wives, respondents reported that in issues involving important matters such as the children or economic issues, both tended to be involved:

I feel that both husband and wife should work together when it comes to making important decisions regarding the well-being of the family. It's important that there be a consensus . . . that they both discuss the problem at hand. For example, when we got married we discussed how many children we wanted. We both agreed that we wanted two and that's how many we had. We also talked about birth control methods and we decided that after the birth of our second child, he would get a vasectomy. I wasn't sure if he would actually do it, but he did and so now I don't have to worry about getting pregnant.

Therefore, although the women in this study exhibit egalitarian views toward gender roles and were generally favorable toward feminism, their ideology did not fit with the actual division of labor practiced at home. Conventional family structures also affected mothers by limiting their upward mobility. That is, the ten participants said that they preferred the night shift because it made it easier to get things done at home and they would often choose that shift over an earlier shift if given a choice. Since the night shift was so physically and emotionally draining, any opportunity for promotion was usually not an option. Therefore, although management offered training that could lead to promotion for some of its workers, the women in this study were routinely unable to take advantage of this opportunity because it interfered with their responsibilities at home.

Discussion

The effects of maternal employment on children, mothers, fathers, and family structure are multifaceted and complex. The commonalities and divergences of the three sociological perspectives—symbolic interaction, integration, and exploitation—provide a useful theoretical basis for a qualitatively grounded analysis of the effects of mothers' work on family patterns and the interactive effects of the patriarchal relations of production and reproduction.

A recurring theme is that women are creative agents who endeavor to remake and redefine existing roles rather than being passive, conforming, unreflective actors as proposed by exploitation theorists. Williams (1990) notes, "The definition of one's 'self' and one's 'mind' emerges out of interaction with others, and the meaning that husbands and wives attach to objects and other persons is likewise a result of ongoing interaction with these. From the standpoint of symbolic interactionism, there are no truly 'isolated' human beings; how persons define themselves and others is a product of ongoing interaction with others" (p. 140). In addition to the "social self" or social/personal identity, Williams also emphasizes the "social mind." She contends that "the social mind engages in complex social calculations. . . . Through a variety of social calculations, which often are interwoven with such emotions as empathy, we are able to take the roles of others" (pp. 142–143). As we have seen, while the women in this analysis appeared to define themselves primarily in terms of parental roles rather than work roles, they nonetheless exhibited ongoing social calculations and in most cases do not fit the stereotype of docile or compliant workers and wives.

Integration theorists contend that work empowers and liberates women so that they are able to negotiate effectively within the labor market and household. As a result, maquila work (a) brings about positive changes in family structure such as inciting the relaxation of traditional gender roles, (b) enables women to develop assembly skills that they can use for upward mobility, (c) gives women options such as postponing marriage and reducing the number of offspring and (d) enhances their general well-being. While these mothers have not been able to get their husbands to do more housework or child care tasks, and are routinely unable to apply for promotions at work, they have achieved significant levels of decision-making power within the household. They have acquired some degree of personal autonomy and self-determination as a result of waged work.

The exploitation approach, in contrast, emphasizes how capitalism takes advantage of patriarchal relations of production and reproduction. That is, traditional gender roles found at home are easily replicated in the workplace since patriarchy is entrenched at a systematic level. Consequently, work does little to empower or liberate women. The findings support the exploitation approach. These mothers did work out of necessity; their primary roles as mothers and wives limited their chances of upward mobility; and their wage earnings had not enabled them to change the traditional domestic division of labor. Additionally, the low wages that they earn makes it rather difficult for them to strike out on their own in the event, for example, that they may be involved in an abusive relationship. All had experienced bouts of depression due to role overload and role conflict related to their working conditions, as suggested by exploitation theorists.

All three perspectives concur that female maquila workers are employed out of necessity, and the gender division of labor in the job market and within the household limits their employment options and power. Yet they disagree with the notion that work improves women's lives. Tiano (1994) notes that we need to consider "the varying consequences of labor-force participation according to women's class position, education, and life-cycle stage" (p. 41). Employment may be more liberating for young, relatively well educated women than for their older, unskilled counterparts. She concludes that the various perspectives "describe a particular aspect of women's experiences" (p. 41).

Social Policy Implications

While maquiladoras have brought about employment alternatives for women and expanded their potential for economic participation, they have also generated social tensions and painful dilemmas (Fernandez-Kelly, 1983). Tiano (1994) summarized the plight of these women. Working-class women enter the labor market from a doubly subordinated position because of their gender as well as their class. The ideology of reproduction that defines women in terms of their roles as wives and mothers, the gender division of labor that doubly burdens women with unpaid domestic duties as well as wage work, and the gender segregation in the occupational sphere that confines women to a narrow range of "female" jobs drastically restricts the terms of women's labor-force participation to keep them in a subordinate position in the labor market.

What can be recommended to deal with the highly exploitative situation that employed maquila women encounter? Tiano (1994) suggests the possibility of the creation of some type of collective organization to improve the working conditions and secure a higher legal minimum wage with improved fringe benefits. Currently, maquiladora employees lack trade union representation, yet maquiladora owners' interests are protected by a strong maquiladora association. According to one informant, as recently as two years ago one of the local assembly plants experienced a workers' strike organized by the women themselves. They were on strike for two weeks and, unfortunately, the management fired all of the women and replaced them within a couple of days. This resulted in squashing any further strikes among the entire maquila industry in San Luis Rio Colorado for fear of retaliation from maquila management. If workers were to succeed in organizing to demand better working conditions and higher wages, they may be able to transform the work environment to make it more appealing to women, including those with the best employment options in the labor market. Simultaneously, women's bargaining power and well-being would be enhanced.

Beneria and Roldan (1987) recommend government implementation of decision-making policies and actions that are inherent in feminism: a democratic process that would express goals and objectives from the bottom up; that is, the inclusion of women's needs, as expressed by the women themselves, in any program for change. These would include a network of interdependent objectives such as changes in ownership and control of the means of production; improvement of the educational background of women and the upgrading of their skills; the design of employment strategies; changes in socialization processes affecting the formation of gender traits; equal sharing by men and women in child care and domestic work or the setting up of more socialized facilities for day care and other domestic services; and improved services for birth control and family planning.

Conclusion

Despite the exploitative nature of the patriarchal relations between production and reproduction inherent in maquiladora employment and the difficulties of improving the situation, it is not concluded that, from the perspective of the women themselves, their employment in the electronics maquila is totally negative. According to the mothers, their income, no matter how low, can be used to secure at least a minimal level of personal autonomy and control over their lives; persuade husbands to share more equally in decision-making, and perhaps housework and child care; and improve their self-image, social identity, and "social mind," which is often damaged by economic dependency on their husbands. As a group, the mothers in this study expressed optimism for the future based on their religious faith and—equally as important—on their belief that they can make a difference for themselves, their families, and their community.

References

Arreola, D.D., and Curtis, J.R. (1993). *The Mexican border cities: Landscape anatomy and place personality.* Tucson: University of Arizona Press.

Baerresen, D. (1970). *The border industrialization program of Mexico.* Lexington: Heath-Lexington.

Beneria, L., and Roldan, M. (1987). *The crossroads of class and gender: Industrial homework, subcontracting, and household dynamics in Mexico City.* Chicago: University of Chicago Press.

Clement, N.C., Jenner, S.R., Ganster, P., and Setran, A. (1989). *Maquiladora resource guide.* San Diego: Institute for Regional Studies of the Californias.

Fernandez-Kelly, M.P. (1983). *For we are sold: I and my people.* Albany: SUNY Press.

Guendelman, S., and Silberg, M.J. (1993). The health consequences of maquiladora work: women on the U.S.-Mexican border. *American Journal of Public Health 83,* 37–44.

Leacock, E., and Safa, H.I. (1986). *Women's work: Development and the division of labor by gender.* Westport, Massachusetts: Bergin and Garvey.

Lim, L. (1990). Women's work in export factories: The politics of cause. In I. Tinder (Ed.), *Persistent inequalities* (pp. 101–119). New York: Oxford University Press.

Lopez, D. (1970). Low wages lures south of the border. *American Federationist 77* (June), 10–12.

Nash, J., and Safa, H.I. (1985). *Women and change in Latin America.* Westport, Massachusetts: Bergin and Garvey.

Pena, D. (1987). Tortuosidad: Shop floor struggles of female maquiladora workers. In V. Ruiz and S. Tiano (Eds.), *Women on the U.S.-Mexico border: Responses to change* (pp. 129–154). Boston: Allen and Unwin.

Ruiz, V., and Tiano, S. (1987). *Women on the U.S.-Mexico border: Responses to change.* Boston: Allen and Unwin.

Selby, H.A., Murphy, A.D., and Lorenzen, S.A., with Cabrera, I., Castaneda, I., and Love, I.R. (1990). *The Mexican urban household: Organizing for self-defense.* Austin: University of Texas Press.

Sklair, L. (1993). *Assembling for development: The maquila industry in Mexico and the United States.* San Diego: Center for U.S.-Mexican Studies.

Steele, D. (1992). Women's participation decision and earnings in Mexico. In G. Psacharopoulos and Z. Tzannatos (Eds.), *Case studies on women's employment and pay in Latin America* (pp. 323–348). Washington, D.C.: World Bank.

Stoddard, E. (1987). *Maquila: assembly plants in northern Mexico.* El Paso: Texas Western.

Tiano, S. (1994). *Patriarchy on the line: Labor, gender, and ideology in the Mexican maquila industry.* Philadelphia: Temple University Press.

Van Waas, M. (1981). *The multinationals' strategy for labor: Foreign assemby plants in Mexico's border industrialization program.* Ph.D. dissertation, University of California at Berkeley.

Warner, J.A. (1990). The sociological impact of the maquiladoras. In K. Fatemi (Ed.), *The maquiladora industry: Economic solution or problem?* (pp. 183–197). New York: Praeger.

Williams, N. (1990). *The Mexican American family: Tradition and change.* New York: General Hall.

Young, G. (1987). Gender identification and working-class solidarity among maquila workers in Ciudad Juarez: Stereotypes and realities. In V. Ruiz and S. Tiano (Eds.), *Women on the U.S.-Mexico border: Responses to change* (pp. 105–127). Boston: Allen and Unwin.

Chapter Six
Effects of Employment on the Families of African Working Mothers
The Case of Nigeria

Justin A. Odulana

In 1975 the United Nations adopted a world plan of action for a "decade of the woman." A declaration was proclaimed that national efforts should be made to achieve equality for women by including them in national developments and in the peace process (United Nations, 1980). Undoubtedly, many nations gracefully endorsed and ratified the spirit of the declaration. Others, especially the less affluent nations, saw the declaration as another attempt by industrialized nations to perpetrate and impose a nuclear lifestyle on them. They feared that such imposition may lead ultimately to the breakup of the family systems in their countries. Irrespective of the rationality of such fears, the goals and objectives of the declaration, nonetheless, remain relevant today. They constitute the basis by which national activities and efforts to empower and liberate women, especially in Africa, can be measured.

The issue of inequality that affects women globally is closely related, in Africa, to two broad assumptions. The first is that of African male domination of the social, economic, and political spectrum of society. The second is the perpetuation of the problem of underdevelopment in the continent occasioned by unfair international economic, social, and political relations.

The intent of the United Nations decade of the woman, and all post-decade activities, however, recognized that the status of women needs to be improved in the economic, political, social, cultural, and other dimensions of human life. The declaration encouraged improvement in women's lives within the family, and at local and national levels. It directed that the status and role of women should be an integral part of national development, which should attempt to establish a new national and international order based on equity,

sovereignty, equality, interdependence, common interest, and cooperation (United Nations, 1980). Nigeria, the tenth largest producer
of crude oil in the world (Hargreaves, Eden-Green, and Devaney,
1994), with nearly twice the size of any other African country, a
population of over 100 million people, and a fertility rate of over
3% per annum (Federal Office of Statistics, 1992) presents an excit-
ing modern case study of how the decade and post-decade accomplishments of women have impacted their status in employment,
and the influence of such impact on working mothers and on their
families.

Present Demographics

Since Nigeria gained independence in 1960, there has been a paucity of reliable population and demographic data at the local, regional, and national level from which meaningful assessments of its
progress could be made. Vital registration data are virtually nonex-
istent, and many of the data available are outdated. This lack of data
is a result of the inherent difficulties of data collection in a country
so culturally diverse, and so superstitiously and politically sensitive
to any form of head count (Federal Office of Statistics, 1992). Compounded with these factors is the political instability in the country,
heralded in with its independence from Britain.

Situated on the Gulf of Guinea in West Africa, Nigeria is
bounded by Niger on the north, Cameroon to the east, and Benin
on the west. It covers an area of about 356,669 square miles, or
923,768 square kilometers, and had an estimated population in 1991
of 112,258,100 persons, with a characteristic gender distribution of
61,874,660 men, and 50,383,440 women. The country is the largest in Africa, and by far the most populous in the continent (Federal
Office of Statistics, 1992).

The many ethnolinguistic groups that make up Nigeria existed
as separate and autonomous political, cultural, and economic enti-
ties long before 1914, when the country was merged into a British
Colonial territory. Nigeria repossessed her independence from England on October 1, 1960, and three years later became a republic.
In 1967, the country was divided into 12 states. The number of
states increased to 19 in 1976, and to 21 in 1988. Nine more states
were formed in 1991, bringing the total number to 30, plus Abuja,

which became the Federal Capital Territory when the capital was relocated from Lagos (Hargreaves, et al., 1994).

In addition to religion and ethnicity, both language and education affect the status and role of women in Nigeria. Although Islam and Christianity are the two main religions of the country, an important segment of the population follow the indigenous traditional religion. There are about 380 ethnic groups in the country, the majority groups being Edo, Efik, Fulani, Hausa, Igbo, Kanuri, Tiv, Urhobo, and Yoruba. Most ethnic groups are concentrated in different parts of the country. The Hausa, Kanuri, and Fulani live primarily in the north; the Yoruba inhabit the southwest; the Igbo and Efik are found in the southeast; the Tiv live in the midsection of the country; and the Edo and Urhobo reside in the Niger River delta (Federal Office of Statistics, 1992).

Internal migration, especially from rural to urban areas, has been one of the important demographic themes of modern Nigeria. With the transfer of the federation capital from Lagos to Abuja, high rates of migration and natural increase produced an urban population that grew from between 3 and 4 million residents in 1950 to nearly 17 million in 1980 (Federal Office of Statistics, 1992). While still predominantly rural, the population of Nigeria has become more urbanized.

Historical Roles of African Women

The African continent has experienced profound changes since the early nineteenth century. These changes undoubtedly affected all aspects of life, especially the political, social and economic systems of the continent. African societies changed from precapitalist to capitalist systems, from political domination to political independence, from women's subjugation to women's emancipation, and from rural to urban settings. These changes have directly and indirectly influenced the lives of African women, and most especially the lives of Nigerian women and members of their extended families.

In precolonial traditional Africa, the main source of livelihood for the family was subsistence farming. During that period, the division of labor in hunting and gathering were evidenced in household systems. Such systems were consistent with the extended family structure that were the foundations of most socioeconomic units in Africa.

Historical division of labor in traditional Africa required women to produce, prepare, and store food; to manufacture baskets, mats, and clothing; to provide care for the sick and for children, and to perform a range of personal and domestic chores for children and men, usually their husbands. Conversely, men were required to herd the cattle, clear the field for cultivation, and protect the land in all its economic, religious, and political dimensions (Brydon and Chant, 1989; Asabere, 1994).

Extended Family System

In Nigeria, the extended family system provides a safety net against most socioeconomic pressures, including old age, assurances of smooth rights of passage, and other life crises. Among the Nigerian communities where adherence to the practice of extended family system is loyal to its broader sense, the system remains a state of mind rather than a particular kind of structure or set of household arrangements. The system has no anticipating value as to whether or not generations live together. It cannot be described with kinship diagrams, family size, or pedigree. What really distinguishes the Nigerian extended family from most other African family structures is the relative ease with which anyone can become a member. In spite of many Western researchers' overlapping description of polygamy/polyandry with the extended family structure, the classical extended family in Nigeria mostly consists of a group of persons who may be bound together by blood, marriage, religion, cohabitation, language, tribe, heritage, customs, practice, or geography. The structure accepts monogamous, polygamous, and polyandrous marriages, and some loosely tied cenogamy. Families could be patriarchal or matriarchal, but every person who belongs to that family is obligated to the other members within that extended family, and each family, based on the customs of its tribe, has well defined customary lines of authority and practices that ensure the guardianship, upkeep or custody of less fortunate members of the tribe, such as fatherless children, the disabled, the sick, the unemployed and the older members of the family.

The Nigerian extended family system, as such, is unlike those found in other cultures, which Stanton (1995) described as a corporate economic or political unit based on kinship. The system encourages its members to retain affinity with members of their families of procreation, and at the same time establish membership with a family of orientation.

Hay and Stichter (1984) and Qunta (1987) argued that the changes African communities experienced and continue to experience have brought about new gender relations and even strengthened some existing ones. Other scholars agree that colonialism restructured Africa's traditional economic and social heritages and that these changes had significant impacts on the economic, political, and social lives of African women. There are, however, conflicting opinions among scholars on the effects of the decade of women on African women, especially Nigerian women.

Literacy of Nigerian Women

There is widespread agreement that the education of girls is one of the most important investments that any developing nation can make for its own future. With the cultural, ethnic, and linguistic diversity in the nation, two questions are particularly relevant in the area of female education in the country. The first is: Has the decade of the woman impacted the pattern of the general education of Nigerian women? The second question is: Which aspect of life, if any, has the decade of the woman affected most among Nigerian women, and to what level?

Although the first question is far beyond the scope of this chapter, even at a cursory level, there are trends that address the question. According to the United Nations Children Fund (1994), 51% of Nigerian girls reach at least grade 5 of primary school, which compared very favorably with reports from other nonindustrialized countries. Table 1, below, suggests also that ten years into the decade of the woman, almost half of the children in secondary schools in Nigeria were female.

Table 1 Nigerian Secondary-School Enrollment, for Academic Years 1975–76 and 1985–86.

Academic Year	Men	Women	Total	% Women
1975–1976	692,361	53,356	745,717	7.2
1985–1986	1,758,866	1,329,845	3,088,711	43.1

Source: Federal Ministry of Education, Lagos, Nigeria

Unlike the high percentages of Nigerian girl children in secondary schools, postsecondary school enrollments of Nigerian women have not made similar gains. Table 2 suggests that except for technical colleges, which recorded a gain from 4.5% in the 1984–85 academic year to 15% in 1987–88, there were no significant increases in the number of girls enrolled at polytechnics, and only a marginal increase at the university level.

Table 2 Enrollments in Nigeria Post-Secondary Schools.

Institutions	Men	Women	Total	% Women
Polytechnics				
1984–1985	48,466	12,117	60,583	20.0
1987–1988	N.A	N.A.	55,569	20.0
Technical Colleges				
1984–1985	47,400	2,256	49,656	4.5
1987–1988	52,772	9,329	62,101	15.0
Universities				
1984–1985	97,546	28,739	126,285	22.8
1987–1988	119,236	41,531	160,767	29.8

N.A. = Not available.
Sources: National Universities Commission of Nigeria, Nigerian National Board for Technical Education, and courtesy of Dr. D. Osisanya, University of Lagos, Nigeria

Economy

Nigeria has a mixed economy in which petroleum plays a key role. During the late seventies, the nation ranked as the sixth largest producer of crude oil in the world, and the second largest in Africa. During that period, petroleum accounted for about 90% of Nigerian exports and 80% of government revenue. Economic growth soared as the country enjoyed the high price of oil on the world market and experienced a massive inflow of foreign exchange. The boom in oil prices of the seventies sparked considerable rural to urban migration, resulting in a decline in the agricultural sector (Federal Office of Statistics, 1992).

Bell and Reich (1988) reported that Nigeria profited tremendously from the oil boom, that oil revenues boosted domestic income and prices in the country, and that the low exchange rate of Nigerian currency made foreign imported goods relatively cheaper, shifting consumption of foods from local to imported food stuffs.

Following the orgy of local consumption financed by the petroleum boom and unregulated construction projects in a new federal capital in Abuja, the beginning of the 1980s marked a downturn in the economy of the country. The decline led to an unprecedented reduction in living standards and devastating income decline (Wilson and Lewis, 1990). In the mid-eighties, the federal government in Nigeria finally accepted the terms of the Structural Adjustment Program (SAP) developed by the World Bank, and at the same time launched a War Against Indiscipline (WAR) in the country (Lubeck, 1992). One of the consequences of SAP was a nosedive of the Nigerian currency (the Naira) to about $0.35 (from about $1.50 in 1982). By June 1990 the Naira reached an all-time low of $0.10, according to the Economist Intelligence Unit (1990).

Many African countries experienced military regimes before, during, and after the decade of the woman—with varying dimensions of authoritarianism or repression against the country; in most cases, it was the mothers who bore the brunt.

Nigerian Women in the Professions

Irrespective of the country's economic situation, Nigerian women, either in the rural or urban setting, have traditionally played important roles in the economy of the nation. At the rural level, Nigerian women are well reputed for their artistry in the preparation of food products and consumer goods such as earthenware, cloth weaving, and soap from palm oil for local consumption and export markets (United Nations Department of International Economic and Social Affairs, 1986). Nigerian women not only account for a significant share of the entrepreneurial drive and initiative in the small-scale sector, their roles are also very strong in other enterprises, such as the restaurant and hotel industries, where they outnumbered men by almost two to one (Table 3).

Women have also made their marks in the formal sector of employment. Taking into account the great disparities and unevenness in available distribution of work force in Nigeria during the pre-decade era, Table 4 suggested that within the decade, the Nigerian Civil Service marginally mobilized and integrated women into its administrative occupations. Professional women's share in the federal civil service at the eighth to eleventh levels appeared to be sig-

Table 3 Economically Active Population in Nigeria among People
Aged 14 Years and Over, September 1986 (in thousands).

Industry	Men	Women	Total
Agriculture, hunting, forestry, and fishing	9,800.6	3,458.4	13,259.0
Mining and quarrying	6.8	0	6.8
Manufacturing	806.4	457.3	1,263.7
Electricity, gas, and water	127.0	3.4	130.4
Construction	545.6	0	545.6
Trade, restaurants, and hotels	2,676.6	4,740.8	7,417.4
Transport, storage, and communications	1,094.7	17.2	1,111.9
Financing, insurance, real estate, and business services	109.8	10.3	120.1
Community, social, and personal services	3,939.5	962.6	4,902.1
Activities inadequately defined	597.1	147.8	744.9
Total Employed	19,704.1	9,797.8	29,501.9

Source: International Labor Organization Year Book 1986

nificant for the decade, especially in light of the background of military rule in the country.

The significance of these achievements for the Nigerian woman and for her family are both transformational and multifarious. The social and economic changes that accrued have transformed the Nigerian woman and her family structure. The Federal Office of Statistics (1992) reported that the increasing number of women accepting paid employment outside their traditional role of homemaking has rapidly multiplied the number of single-headed households and made female-headed households more common in urban areas, especially in the southern states.

The pivotal question, then, is this: How have all these changes impacted the families of Nigerian working mothers? In the next section of this chapter, such impacts on her child, on the working mother herself, on the father, the family structure, and the effects on government and businesses in the country are addressed.

Table 4 Distribution of Women Staff in Management/Executive
Positions in the Nigerian Civil Service, 1984 and 1988.

Level	1984			1988		
	Men	Women	% Women	Men	Women	% Women
Dir. Gen	0	0	0	40	6	15.0
17	41	0	0	85	8	9.4
16	74	11	14.9	253	17	6.7
15	157	15	9.6	475	51	10.7
14	206	21	10.2	891	93	10.7
13	195	33	16.9	1,435	202	14.1
12	717	106	14.8	2,289	376	16.4
11	1,149	74	6.4	3,918	848	21.6
10	1,413	134	9.5	5,354	1,236	23.1
*08–09	3,922	357	9.1	7,620	1,851	24.3
05–07	13,385	1,621	12.1	79,873	8,810	11.0
03–04	69,239	7,773	11.2	99,791	12,524	12.6
01–02	19,618	1,833	9.3	23,590	7,583	32.1

*Levels 8 and above required the incumbents to possess a college level education.
Source: Federal Civil Service Commission of Nigeria

Effects of Mother's Employment on the Child

One of the benefits of the Nigerian extended family system used to
be the abundance of people within the family who were favorable
disposed to providing mothercare to infant children of the family.
The entry of Nigerian mothers into the labor market created both a
conflict and an opportunity for the child. The conflict was that it
adversely affected the supply of members of the extended family to
provide mothercare, and the opportunity was that it widened the
field of employment opportunities for other women. Taking up
employment by the mother ultimately exposes the child to foster
care, provided mostly by domestic servants from neighboring countries. Consequently, most of the children of working mothers in
Nigeria have some form of substitute care through those employed
domestic servants, but lack mothers' care.

Evidence that women's employment opportunities conflict with
the practice of breastfeeding in the country included data presented
in the Nigeria Demographic and Health Survey for 1990. The data
demonstrated that many of the Nigerian mothers who have wage

jobs were unable to breast-feed their babies during the day. According to the data, about 97% of Nigerian children were normally breast-fed for some period of time, but by the time the children were two months old, only 2% were fed breast milk exclusively. Most of the children (57%) under two months of age were given water in addition to breast milk. The survey also reported that as many as 38% of newborns in Nigeria (newborn to one month of age) were already being given supplements (including bottle and teat/nipple) other than plain water. By the time the children were two to three months old, supplements had been introduced to 57%. By age four to five months, one-third of breast-feeding children had had food introduced into their diets (Federal Office of Statistics, 1992). In 1993, only three maternity hospitals in the country met the ten steps to successful breast-feeding being promoted by WHO/UNICEF (UNICEF, 1994).

Nigeria has one of the highest mortality rates in the continent for children under the age of five years. Neither mother's education nor her employment has impacted this rate in any positive way. Nearly one in five children born in Nigeria dies before age five. Of every 1,000 babies born, 87 die during their first year of life. There has been little improvement in infant and child mortality during the past 15 years. Undernutrition and diarrhea (which exacerbates the problem of undernutrition) remain the two major contributing factors to childhood mortality in the country. Over 40% of Nigerian children under five are chronically undernourished (Federal Office of Statistics, 1992; UNICEF, 1994; Keyfitz and Flieger, 1994), and childhood diarrhea affects as many as 18% of all the children among this age group (PRB Chartbook, 1992). Mothers taking up employment thus has important health implications and effects on neonates and on the vulnerability of young children to infections in the country. The lack of exclusive breastfeeding by working mothers denies Nigerian babies the essential immunity to disease, through the mother's antibodies, that is essential in the first few months of life.

Effects of Employment on the Mother

The news that 500,000 women die each year in childbirth and that 99% of those women are in nonindustrialized countries shocked participants at the Safe Motherhood Conference in Nairobi in 1987

(Koblinsky, Campbell, and Harlow, 1993). What was not so apparent, at that time, was the fact that at least 10% of the worldwide 500,000 maternal deaths occur in Nigeria (MotherCare Working Paper: 17B, 1993).

According to researchers in several parts of the country, the major causes of maternal death among Nigerian women, both employed and homemakers, included eclampsia (Ekwempu, 1982; Akpala and Ozumba, 1991); hemorrhage (Akinkugbe and Ajibayo, 1966; Wakile, 1984); obstructed labor (Kulkarni, Kyari, and Basumallik, 1983); and abortion-related sepsis (Akingha, 1975; Ogunniyi, Makinde, and Dare, 1991). The World Health Organization (WHO) classification of countries in which "mothers will risk death to give life" places Nigeria among the top on the list (WHO, 1993).

Research results indicate that a critical interplay exists between employment patterns of women in general and their reproductive roles, family size, family health, family structure, and other demographic issues such as migration (International Labor Office/United Nations Institute for Training and Research, 1983; United Nations, 1986).

Before the decade, just 1% of Nigerian women were using a modern family-planning method. That figure, after the decade, was 6% (3.5% using a modern method, and 2.5% using traditional methods). Periodic abstinence (rhythm method), the pill, IUD, and injection became the most popular methods among married couples after the decade, compared with herbs or exclusive breast-feeding before the decade (Federal Office of Statistics, 1992).

Oppong and Abu (1987) argue that education in Africa opened some opportunities for Africans. Employment opportunities for Nigerian mothers was instrumental in relaxing some customary constraints, which had potential effects on various aspects of their individualism. Employment made it possible for Nigerian mothers to acquire new types of knowledge through on-the-job training and provided them with the ability to understand a range of views. This situation enhanced and affected participation in a variety of activities including family life. Employment impacted parental knowledge and provided the ability to be familiar with health issues such as family planning and the use of contraceptives.

Employment provides the opportunity for mothers to become economically independent. The salary or profit the mothers earn means that they do not have to depend on their husbands, and being financially capable means that they can be self-reliant and independent and can enjoy a high standard of living. Success in their work increases their prestige and self-esteem, which is usually not possible for unemployed mothers. Mothers with occupational skills can more easily find new jobs, and they are able to earn larger incomes. Thus, Nigerian mothers enhance their personal resources and their autonomy, which in turn impacts other aspects and roles in their domestic and parental spheres.

Several studies argue that the effects of employment on women are in the areas of family size, health care, and child care (Federal Office of Statistics, 1992), self-esteem, and economic independence (Sudarkasa 1986). Separating work and home, however, creates the possibility of other conflicts. While education has been influential in changing the familial roles of Nigerian women, employment has also impacted their independence and their conjugal relationships. Gross and Bingham (1982) gave an example of a Nigerian woman who moved to the city after her husband divorced her because she was not able to have children. In the city this woman became a prominent trader and was highly honored in her community. Women who achieve material self-sufficiency through employment and combine such achievement with motherhood become role models for other Nigerian women. Employment remains the predominant indicator or determinant of equality of the sexes in Nigeria, and motherhood implies an assurance of companionship, comfort, support, and decent living in old age.

Effects of Mothers' Employment on Husbands

The Nigerian mother has been studied from many angles, especially because of her fecundity. The Nigerian father, however, still remains an empirically understudied social enigma. It could be argued that employment of Nigerian mothers has impacted Nigerian husbands in three important, interrelated ways. First, it has softened Nigerian husbands' attitudes toward the use of contraceptives. Before the decade, administrative practices regarding spousal consent for the supply and use of contraceptives varied from state to state but generally supported the obtaining of consent, which is frequently denied by the husbands (Odulana, 1978). In

1990 data from the Nigeria demographic and health survey indicated that 43% of Nigerian women said that their husbands approved of family planning. Married women (as well as their husbands) who lived in urban areas and were better educated were more likely than other women to approve of the use of family planning (Federal Office of Statistics, 1992).

Second, the absence of wives from the home has accentuated the practice of polygamy among Nigerian husbands. In one study, 41 percent of currently married women were in a polygamous union, and it was not uncommon for a woman to have two or more co-wives (Federal Office of Statistics, 1992).

A third impact of mothers' employment on fathers is in the area of migration. Formerly, migrants, especially in West African countries, were men who moved from rural to urban areas to seek employment. West African women made short migrations to join their husbands. With the relocation of the federal capital to Abuja, husbands of employed mothers who were transferred to the new capital followed their wives. Nigerian mothers in both the private and public sectors also migrate to neighboring countries such as Ghana, and they take their husbands with them. In the 1980s, the Yoruba adult population in Ghana consisted of 44% women, and 33 percent of the Hausa were women (Njoku, 1980).

Odulana (1995) conducted an informal telephone survey regarding the effects on Nigerian fathers in households where the wives worked outside the home. Eight Nigerian husbands surveyed in the United States, four in Lagos, and two in Ibadan were unanimous in pointing to the fact that Nigerian fathers were increasingly sharing in child care and other household responsibilities, especially in urban, educated, and monogamous families in which wives were employed.

Effects of Women's Employment on Family Structure

The family in Nigeria is regarded as the foundation of Nigerian society. Nigerian women are considered heroes and harbingers of social reconstruction, while the mother in the family is considered the intermediary between her family and their gods. The effects of Nigerian working mothers' employment on their family structure should be seen in the light of the social, economic, and military realities in the country. The powerbrokers in Nigeria have argued that the devaluation of the currency led to the deindustrialization of Nigeria. Estimates have been suggested that 20 to 30% of manufacturers went under, and that industrial capacity varied from 30 to 45%. More concretely, however, the devaluation of the nation's currency meant that a top-of-the-line senior civil servant or university professor whose salary was worth $45,000 before devaluation in 1985 earned less than $6,000 a year, and the minimum wage in the country fell from about $200 a month to less than $15.

The circumstances created by SAP had important consequences on the working mother and her family structure. Family systems, as they were known in the country, disintegrated. Many professionals and skilled workers left the country. Expenditures on medical, educational, and social services in the country were reduced, and the standards of living of the Nigerian family eroded. Despite the assault on their family's structure, economic rights, and material living standards, Nigerian working mothers did not passively accept their fate. A number of riots organized against the Nigerian military regime, its local agents, and international collaborators were supported by working mothers. Olukoshi (1990) reported that working mothers supported lawyers who boycotted courts and led strikes of over 14,000 lawyers, and Lubeck (1992) reported that similar actions organized by doctors and journalists in the country won popular support.

Crises, however, have their ways of creating solutions that would have been unthinkable in a noncrisis situation. SAP and devaluation of the economy combined together to offer the Nigerian working mother an opportunity to influence policy-making in government and business. The point here is that the SAP and the outrage by various professionals, working mothers, and students generated organizational activities that affected not only government and business but also the working mothers themselves. We now turn our attention to these effects.

Effects of Working Mothers on Governmental and Business Policies

Innovations forced by the structural adjustment programs in Nigeria created a new demand for internal produce to substitute for imported goods. SAP led to a boom in agriculture in the country. It accelerated demand for both food and raw material production, and created corporate, commercial, and small-holder farmers. Consumers competed for the limited supply of maize, which forced the price up by over 300% because of the devaluation. In addition, there was competition in other primary industries that were traditionally "manned" by women in Nigeria. National responses to increase locally produced foods provided Nigerian mothers with the awareness of their newly enhanced political and economic weight (Watts, 1987). Andrae and Beckman (1987) reported that some authorities in Nigeria even attempted to contract peasant working mothers to produce industrial raw materials that had formerly been imported.

The windfall benefits from SAP enhanced the status of working mothers in the country. It heralded a period in which mothers started enjoying paid maternity leave (Odulana, 1978) and car and housing allowances similar to those enjoyed by men.

Summary

Inevitably, a summary of this type of study, especially in a patrilineal system, will be expected to contain some major caveats. Such caveats will be expected to suggest that the effects of employment on Nigerian working mothers and their children will depend largely on their education, their husbands' education, and the tribes from which both or either hail. The type of marriage contract entered into, which subsequently should dictate the terms of her legal entitlement under custody, maintenance, and inheritance laws, will shape the effects of her employment on her husband and her family structure. The impact on employers and on the nation's policies will depend on where working mothers live and work, and on whether their employment is in the public, private, or independent sector. Such caveats have, however, been substantially dealt with by other scholars of the Nigerian scene. While their work is beyond the scope of this chapter, the reader is referred to them as described in the following paragraph.

Berry (1985) studied the patrilineal system of the extended Yoruba community as it affects work and the accumulation of wealth. Waterman (1982), among others, provided a compelling social essay on division and unity among Nigerian workers. Leith-Ross (1978) studied Ibo women from a more distinct gender perspective. Talbot

(1968) presented some powerful insights on the mysteries of the Ibibios. Apter (1992) discussed the balance of power between Yoruba men and women. Callaway (1987) illustrated the constraints of the Muslim religion on Kano women. Lubeck (1986) presented profiles of the Muslim working class in northern Nigeria, and Aina (1990) depicted the distinctive elements of shantytown economy in Lagos.

The recurring problems experienced by the approach in this chapter could then be summarized under two categories: First, the existing and accessible literatures upon which this study is based are uneven in terms of the subject, its perspective, and the depth of the descriptive and analytical content of the effect of employment on Nigerian working mothers. Second, available data on working mothers for most countries in the Third World are notoriously incomplete, unreliable, and in some cases just not available. Consequently, selectivity is necessary in drawing some general conclusions on the effect of employment on the families of working mothers in Nigeria.

This chapter does not claim to offer an exhaustive coverage of all the inherent factors that might influence employment of Nigerian mothers, or of how those influences could impact the various constituencies of the mother. The perspectives presented in this chapter may not, therefore, be the dominant view about working mothers in Nigeria. In this chapter, an attempt has been made to examine the basic outline of what employment has done to the Nigerian working mothers, their husbands, and their family structure. The discourse is based on the position that the impact, the dynamics, and the relationships that constitute those impacts cannot be viewed independently of the linkages with the wider issues affecting Nigerian women in general.

The one strong point that emerges from this chapter is that the time has come for broader regional studies on the effect of employment on working mothers. There is a need for more detailed, long-term, cross-cultural studies of such themes that are central to the employment of mothers, and how this employment impacts the children, the mothers, their husbands, the family structure, and the nation. Such studies need to be developed within the context of a theoretical framework that is critical and holistic.

References

Aina, T.A. (1990). Shanty town economy: The case of metropolitan Lagos, Nigeria. In
S. Datta (Ed.), *Third world urbanization: Reappraisals and new perspective.*
Stockholm: Swedish Council for Research in the Humanities and Social Sci-
ences.

Akingha, J.B. (1975). Abortion, maternity, and other health problems in Nigeria. *Nigerian Medical Journal* 7(4), 465–471.

Akinkugbe, A., and Ajibayo, A. (1966). Auto-transfusion as a life-saving measure in
ruptured ectopic pregnancy. *Journal of the Nigerian Medical Association* 3(3),
379–382.

Akpala, C.O., and Ozumba, B.C. (1991). Maternal mortality in a rural community in
northern Nigeria. *Orient Journal of Medicine* 3(3), 168–171.

Andrae, G., and Beckman, B. (1987). *Industry goes farming.* Report No. 80. Uppsala:
Scandinavian Institute of African Studies.

Apter, A. (1992). *Black critics and kings: The hermeneutics of power in Yoruba society.*
Chicago and London: University of Chicago Press.

Asabere, P.K. (1994). Public policy and the emergent African land tenure system: The
case of Ghana. *Journal of Black Studies 24,* 281–289.

Bell, D.E., and Reich, M.R. (1988). *Health nutrition and economic crisis approaches to
policy in the third world.* Dover: Auburn.

Berry, S. (1985). *Fathers work for their sons: Accumulation, mobility, and class formation in an extended Yoruba community.* Berkeley, Calif.: University of California
Press.

Brydon, L., and Chant, S. (1989). *Women in the third world.* New Brunswick, N.J.:
Rutgers University Press.

Callaway, B. (1987). *Muslim Hausa women in Nigeria: Tradition and change.* Syracuse,
N.Y.: Syracuse University Press.

Economist. (1990). *Economist Intelligence Unit (EIU).* London: Economist.

Ekwempu, C.C. (1982). Maternal mortality in eclampsis in the Guinea Savannah region
of Nigeria. Clinical and experimental hypertention, part B. *Hypertension in Pregnancy 81*(4), 531–537.

Federal Office of Statistics of Nigeria. (1992). *Demographic and health survey, Nigeria*
(DHS). Lagos, Nigeria: Federal Office of Statistics of Nigeria.

Gross, S.H., and Bingham, M.W. (1982). *Women in Africa of the sub-Sahara.* Hudson,
Wisconsin: Gary and McCuen.

Hargreaves, D., Eden-Green, M., and Devaney, J. (1994). *World index of resources and
population.* Brookfield, Vt.: Dartmouth.

Hay, M.J., and Stichter, S. (1984). *African women south of the Sahara.* London and
New York: Longman.

Hay, M.J., and Wright, M. (1982). *African women and the law: Historical perspectives.*
Boston: Boston University Press.

International Labor Office/United Nations Institute for Training and Research (1983).
*Seminar on women and demographic issues, Tashkent, October 11–19, 1983,
Conclusions.* Geneva: ILO.

International Labor Organization (1986). *Year book of labor statistics.* Geneva: International Labor Office.

Keyfitz, N., and Flieger, W. (1994). *World population growth and aging.* Chicago: University of Chicago Press.

Koblinsky, M.A., Campbell, O.M.R., and Harlow, S.D. (1993). Mother and more: A
broader perspective on women's health. In M. Koblinsky, J. Timyan, and J. Gay,
(Eds.), *The health of women: A global perspective.* Boulder and San Francisco:
Westview.

Kulkarni, R., Kyari, O.A., and Basumallik, M.K. (1983). An analytical study of obstructed
labor. *Nigerian Medical Practitioner 5*(1), 11–18.

Leith-Ross, S. (1978). *African women: A study of the Ibo of Nigeria*. London: Routledge and Kegan Paul.

Lubeck, P. (1986). *Islam and urban labor in Northern Nigeria: The making of a Muslim working class*. Cambridge: Cambridge University Press.

Lubeck, P. (1992). Restructuring Nigeria's urban-industrial sector within the West African Region: The interplay of crisis, linkages and population resistance. *International Journal of Urban and Regional Research 16*(1), 6–23.

MotherCare Working Paper 17B. (1993). *Mothercare Nigeria maternal healthcare project qualitative research*. Arlington, Va.: John Snow.

Njoku, J.E.E. (1980). *The world of the African woman*. London: Scarecrow Press.

Odulana, J.A. (1978). *Family welfare laws in ten African countries: Report of the Africa Regional Law Panel field trips, 1977/78, 1*. Nairobi, Kenya: International Planned Parenthood Federation, African Region.

Ogunniyi, S.O., Makinde, O.O., and Dare, O.F. (1991). Abortion-related deaths in Ile Ife, Nigeria: A 12-year review. *African Journal of Medicine and Medical Science 19*, 271–274.

Olukoshi, B. (1990). *Associational life during the Nigerian transition to civilian rule*. Paper presented at the conference on Democratic Transition and Structural Adjustment in Nigeria. Palo Alto, Calif.: Stanford University Press.

Oppong, C., and Abu, K. (1987). *Seven roles of women: Impact of education, migration and employment on Ghanian mothers*. Geneva: International Labor Office.

Population Reference Bureau. (1992). *Chartbook: Africa demographic and health surveys*. Washington, D.C.: Population Reference Bureau.

Qunta, C. (1987). *Women in Southern Africa*. Worcester, UK: Billing and Sons.

Stanton, M.E. (1995). Patterns of kinship and residence. In B.B. Ingoldsby and S. Smith (Eds.), *Families in multicultural perspective*, 97–116. New York: Guilford.

Sudarkasa, N. (1986). The status of women in indigenous African societies. *Feminist Studies 12*(1), 91–103.

Talbot, D.A. (1968). *Women's mysteries of a primitive people: The Ibibios of southern Nigeria*. Frank Cass.

UNICEF. (1994). *The progress of nations*. New York: UNICEF.

United Nations. (1980). *Report of the world conference of the United Nations Decade for Women: Equality, development and peace*. Copenhagen: United Nations.

United Nations. (1986). *World survey on the role of women in development*. New York: United Nations.

United Nations Department of International Economic and Social Affairs (1986). *World Survey of the role of women in development*. New York: United Nations.

Wakile, D.E. (1984). Maternal mortality in Lagos University Teaching Hospital—A three year review. *Nigerian Medical Practitioner 7*(5), 147–150.

Ware, H. (Ed.) (1981). *Women, education and modernization of the family in West Africa*. Australia: Australian National University Press.

Waterman, P. (1982). *Division and unity among Nigerian workers: Lagos Trade-Unionism 1940s–1960s*. The Hague: State Sociological Institute.

Watts, M. (Ed.) (1987). *State, oil and agriculture in Nigeria*. Berkeley, Calif.: University of California Press.

Wilson, E., and Lewis, P. (1990). *Public private sector relations under the transition: Promises and pitfalls of privatization*. Paper delivered at the Conference on Democratic Transition and Structural Adjustment in Nigeria. Palo Alto, Calif.: Stanford University Press.

World Health Organization. (1993). *Maternal mortality: A global factbook, 1991*. Geneva: WHO Division of Family Health.

Chapter Seven
Filipino Maternal Employment
Its Impact on Self, Husband, and Children

Teresita Paed Pedrajas

The Philippines is an archipelago of 7,100 islands, composed of thirteen regions and one national capital region. As of 1995, it a population of about 65 million. Mananzan (1985) described the country as blessed by nature, with rich forest and marine resources, a tropical climate, and a strategic location. The Philippines is an agricultural-marine-forest setting, with a communal society that is diverse and open. Hence, its people are less rigid and hierarchical than those in the West, the Middle East, or even Asia.

Marriage and the Family in the Philippines

In the Philippines, marriage is still considered as the indispensable starting point of the family. At the turn of the century, most marriages were contracted fairly early; however, more and more single people today are delaying marriage. As of 1973, the average age at first marriage was approximately 23 years for women and 25 years for men; in 1991 it was 25 years and 27 years, respectively. Urban dwellers marry about three years later than their rural counterparts (NEDA-NCSO, 1975, 1993, *National Demographic Surveys, 1968 and 1973*, as cited in Castillo, 1976).

It is the Filipino custom and tradition for the married couple to be monogamous. Sex is limited to conjugal partners, who will not separate its unitive and procreation purposes. Both husband and wife are economically active. Wives are often college-educated, and take to their own occupations or professions, or are involved in entrepreneurial ventures as they supervise the household chores, assisted by their relatives or hired live-in maids. While grandparents, aunts, or uncles are typically the substitute caretakers of children when mothers work outside the home, husbands also take an active role in family responsibilities. Researchers have found that older children are often observed to be assigned the caretaker role, particularly around ages 5 to 7 (Whiting, 1966; Concepcion and Cagigon, 1978). In another study, Domingo (1977) found that mothers teach preschool children to be nurturant toward younger siblings; in turn, the younger ones are expected to respect and obey their older siblings, specifically the older sister who assumes the mother's role in the latter's absence. Bouiler (1976) and Cabanero (1978) concluded that children's participation in child care responsibilities is a considerable contribution to efficient household functioning.

Researchers have explored the roles assumed by the husband and wife in the Filipino family. Sevilla (1982) observed that each spouse has a particular area of influence in which decisions are made. Likewise, Licuanan and Gonzalez (1976) found that, among the lower classes, women exercise influence over household chores, child care, discipline of female children, and family finances; the men's sphere of influence includes his livelihood and discipline of male children.

Porio, Lynch, and Hollnsteiner (1975) completed a cross-class study of the Filipino family and found that both husband and wife make decisions regarding the children's discipline, school, and family investments.

Children in the Filipino Family

As pointed out by Concepcion and Cagigon (1978), children are considered to be the seal of marriage bonds, and the first child usually arrives between nine and 24 months after the wedding. There is great diversity in family size, from small (2–3 members) to large (5–8 members), across the whole range of income levels. Sociologists view the Filipino family as the child's developmental environment—the earliest physical and social setting, which provides nourishment, sustenance, support, security, guidance, and inspiration to learn about the world. Of all the socializing institutions, the family is the first and most influential in shaping the personality, character, and human potential in all aspects of life that build a self-reliant, dynamic, progressive, and humane society. All members of the Filipino family lend support for this process, and in 1987 the Philippine constitution specified that the state shall strengthen the family as a basic social institution. The new civil code provides guiding principles that sustain the solidarity of the family through the courts and administrative offices. In the Philippines, it is expected that the rearing of youth for civic efficiency and development of moral character should be equally shared between parents and government.

In order to offset the high cost of living, especially in metropolitan Manila, all of the family members cooperate to support the family. Participation by grandparents is more than strictly custodial. For example, Domingo (1977) observed that grandparents' opinions were sought after and seriously considered by the parents. Dover (1967) claimed that grandparent-child relationships were more affectionate and less structured (restrictive) than parent-child relationships, which are formal and authority-oriented. However, as Flores (1970) pointed out, grandmothers can be a drawback in child care if they are too permissive, thereby spoiling the children. Corpuz and Nunez (1982) found that grandmothers often act as secondary caretakers of children and are thus significant persons, when they are present in the household. They observed that fathers usually take the role of caretaker in the absence of a grandmother.

Kin Groups and Urbanization

Medina (1991) explored the changes in the Philippine society from the traditional agricultural to the modern industrial type, and how these changes have affected the family and the larger kin group. While the characteristic solidarity of the Filipino kin group still persists, the urbanization of society has brought up questions about traditional relationships, age and gender roles, and patterns of authority. The growth of industrial centers, migration to cities, separation of family members due to work, education, travel, decrease in contact, and more limited reciprocal ties have combined to make the individual more independent of the family and kin group. Even so, the vital importance of the kin group is still the basis of the Filipino family, and is especially apparent at weddings, deaths, birthdays, special anniversaries, election campaigns, and during crisis situations, when the more fortunate relatives rush to the aid of the needy ones. The larger kin group of the Filipino consists not only of the consanguineal kin (those related by blood), but also the affinal kin (those related by marriage). The rituals of baptism, confirmation, and weddings expand the kinship structure because the family sponsors acquire kinlike relationships with the family of the sponsored. Among the sponsors, it is common practice to give annual Christmas and birthday gifts and become involved as consultants, advisers, or even financiers in the context of whatever crisis or concerns their sponsored children are undergoing. At times, they may also support education, travel, and so on if the parents are in dire need of help due to poverty and disability.

It is a typical gesture of all married Filipinos to give care, assistance, help, and comfort to their parents, especially those who are very old. Also, assistance is given to brothers and sisters if they are helpless, young, or unfortunate. Some married couples extend support to their kin for education, housing, and allowance as a way to express their gratitude to their parents or relatives. In-laws and other relatives in the first, second, and third degrees in consanguinity frequently stay in working mothers' residences as they stop over in metropolitan Manila. Filipino families typically accommodate these visitors for free, or on a low-cost basis. These visitors may stay for short or long periods for purposes of personal visiting or to seek work opportunities, education, or cultural activities. They are considered members of the extended family, and show their appreciation for the host family by helping with the household chores.

Medina (1991) observed that there appears to be a trend toward the nuclearization of the household. While the Filipino household may be nuclear (composed of the husband, wife, and children) the family is bilaterally extended to include both maternal and paternal relatives. The Filipino family is characterized as the traditionally consanguineal. This means that blood ties with both husband and wife are considered very important, so that relationships with the first, second, and third degrees with cousins, aunts, and uncles are recognized. The kinsmen, though they do not share the same household, identify with and assist one another, participate in joint activities, pool resources, share responsibilities, and maintain expressive and emotional relations among all family members.

Medina (1991) also observed that there are larger extended-family households in the urban areas more often than in the rural areas. This appears to be the result of the gravitation by rural residents toward more affluent relatives in urban areas, and the general trend toward urbanization, which affects the availability of adequate housing. Besides the nuclear and extended households, there are also some 13% of households that are headed by single parents, according to De Guzman (1990). Most of these households are headed by women, with about two-thirds of them widows; one-fifth were married women whose spouses were temporarily away, and about one-tenth were separated from their spouses.

A Study of Filipino Women

For this discussion, 500 Filipino women who lived in Metropolitan Manila were studied. These women responded to a questionnaire that asked how they perceived the effects of their employment on themselves, their husbands, and their children. However, some background information on Filipino women and the Filipino family will be helpful preceding a discussion of the study.

Through the years, Filipino women have displayed the steely courage and toughness needed to overcome crises that have continuously beset the country. Aleta, Silva, and Eleazar (1977) gave a very interesting historical perspective of Filipino women:

The equality between men and women in the Philippines dates back to the ancient Malay tradition. Historians on pre-Spanish Philippines note that our Filipino women ancestors held a privileged position in society. She had equal inheritance and property rights, a respectable position of authority in the family, social, and political life. The effect of Spanish colonization was to demote the Filipino woman to a minor social status. She was mainly sheltered from everyday affairs and prevented from participating in business, political, educational and social affairs. (78)

However, during the Spanish period, several women worked for the revolution and have been recognized by historians. Today, the efforts of Filipino women are well recognized in the country. Former President Corazon C. Aquino issued Proclamation 224 declaring the first week of March every year as Women's Week, and March 8 as Women's Rights and International Peace Day. From 1986 through 1992, First Lady President Aquino emphasized how Filipino women are active agents of change.

Some outstanding Filipinas, who were noted mainly for peaceful educational and political reforms, were described by the *Times Journal*, July 5, 1975, in an article entitled "The Gutsy Dozen." For example, Librada Avelino (1873–1934), an educator, was not convinced that "reading, writing, arithmetic" were enough education for girls. She introduced the concept of girls taking active interest in the government. She founded the Centro Escolar de Senoritas, which emphasized practical lessons in citizenship. In the early 1900s, Margarita Roxas founded La Concordia Girls' School, and Francisca Benitez established the Philippine Women's University. Fausta Labrador opened a hospital for the poor and a school for poor children. Jacinta Zaera de Cailles, a philanthropist, was one of the country's leading feminists, who organized scholarships for poor but bright students and led the National League of Women in the National Federation of Women's Clubs when Filipino women clamored for and won the right to vote in 1937. Maria Ylagan Orosa pioneered in the fields of nutrition and home economics, giving lectures and demonstrations in several areas. By 1941, she had organized 537 rural improvement clubs throughout the country.

Roles of Filipino Women

Filipino women have complex, varied roles, and have made important contributions on local, national, and international levels. The introduction of mass media in the twentieth century opened new opportunities to Filipino women to expand their roles and areas of accomplishment. Through more educational exposure, women increased their political awareness, and lobbied the congress for various rights. For example, women lobbied to get themselves elected to office, to hold property in their own names, and to dispose of it freely, as well as to receive equal pay for equal work. They started forming groups such as the Philippine Association of University Women, the League of Women Voters, and the National Federation of Women's Clubs. As a result, 325 women were elected to public office, mostly as heads of towns or provinces. The passage of the Paraphernal Law in 1932 allowed the wife to dispose of her paraphernal property without her husband's consent.

While Filipino women have established many roles for themselves, perhaps their most important role is that of religious teacher in the family as well as in the larger society. Some international manifestations of their religiosity and spirituality were the People Power EDSA Peaceful Revolution in 1986 and the tremendous welcome and farewell attendance to the Pontifical Mass with Pope John Paul II during the X World Youth Day in Manila, January 11–15, 1995. Mothers teach family members to develop an interpersonal relationship with a personal God who provides love, life, sustenance, and joy. In the home, they are thought of as co-creators with God, nurturers, and responsible for forming values in the young, as well as overseeing housekeeping and financial aspects of home management.

In their role as teacher of morals, they are supported and assisted by their husbands, parents, in-laws, or other trusted relatives. Outside the home, they are productive workers in the economy, as managers or entrepreneurs. In the workplace, they are supported through educational and child care programs. They are leaders with their own realms of responsibility in politics, religion, and in nongovernmental organizations. All of these roles make contributions to national progress and development. In fact, De Leon (1994) described the role of Filipino women in nation building as having positive effects in every field of endeavor—business, the professions, the arts, education, civic work, and public service.

Filipino Working Women and the Family

According to the National Statistics Office of the Philippines (1992), women constitute nearly 40% of the Filipino work force. Filipino women have varied skills (see Figures 1 and 2) and are hired in all corners of the globe. Many of them rise through the ranks by taking advantage of staff-development programs. Some female employees are sent to institutions to earn graduate degrees on scholarships or funding programs, while others attend graduate school on their own. Asian working women see their employment both as a way to develop themselves as total persons, and as a major assistance to their husbands in meeting the family's financial demands. They also see that their efforts are appreciated by all family members.

Various research studies have been conducted about Asian working women in general, and Filipino working women in particular. Quisumbing and Lazarus (1985) found that there are several reasons why Asian women work. Some of these reasons are (a) economic necessity; (b) preparation for a time when a woman might have to support herself fully; (c) increased level of self-esteem; (d) establishment of a good career in order to become a better marriage prospect; and (e) smaller family size, enabling women increased opportunities to make contributions to the larger society. According to these authors, Asian women work to improve themselves intellectually, and make use of their potentials. In fact, many of these women are deeply committed to a highly skilled professional occupation (e.g., as law, medicine, education, fine arts, or journalism). It was also noted that these women are motivated by the need for social interactions with and intellectual stimulation from like-minded people.

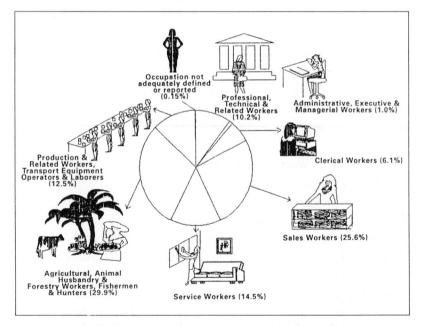

Figure 1. Employed Filipino women by major occupations (in thousands) as of October 1991. Source: National Statistics Office.

Castillo (1976) completed a study of the working wife that analyzed the mass of existing information from census reports and labor force surveys, national demographic surveys, graduate student theses, and both published and unpublished research reports. She made a comprehensive profile of Filipino women, and found many dimensions, including matrimonial risk-taker, child-bearer, adolescent recipient of education, migrant, member of the labor force, working wife, decision-maker and participant in politics, informal organizations and church activities.

Method

This was an empirical research study of 500 Filipino working mothers in Metro Manila, and their perspectives as to the effects of their employment on themselves, their husbands, and their children. The Metro Manila region is known as the business, industrial, political, cultural, educational, and religious center of the Philippines. Ages ranged from 31 to 45 years, with a median age of approximately 38 years. The length of time these mothers had worked outside the family ranged from 10 to 25 years, with the median being approximately 20 years. Respondents were generally well educated, with 55% employed as professionals, 28% in administrative positions, 14% clerical, 2% in service occupations, and 1% in technical jobs.

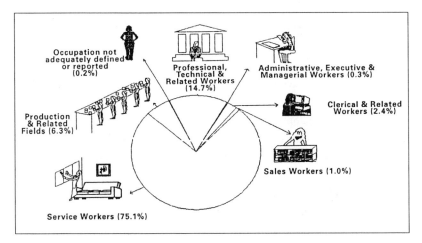

Figure 2. Female Filipino overseas contract workers as of October 1991. Source: National Statistics Office.

Annual income ranged from 1,000 pesos (US $40) to 50,000 pesos (US $2,000). Approximately 70% of the respondents earned from 1,000 to 10,000 pesos (US $40 to $400), and 30% earned from 10,500 to 50,000 pesos (US $420 to $2,000). As of 1994, the average annual income in the Philippines was 3,575 pesos (US $143).

The research questions were the following:

1. What are the effects of the working mother on herself, her husband, and her children? Effects were studied in terms of the following areas: (a) physical; (b) social; (c) emotional; (d) intellectual; (e) economic; (f) moral; and (g) spiritual.

2. What are working mothers' feelings about their employment outside the family?

3. What are the existing governmental laws and policies that protect and support working mothers?

A set of questionnaires was constructed to assess the working mothers' perspectives about their employment and its effect on themselves, their husbands, and their children. These perspectives were compared with existing literature based on previous research. The questionnaire consisted of 66 questions, with each question ranked on a scale of 1 to 6 in importance. Questions included the following categories and subcategories:

1. Effects of Maternal Employment on Self:
   a. Physical
   b. Social
   c. Emotional
   d. Intellectual
   e. Economic
   f. Moral
   g. Spiritual
2. Effects of Maternal Employment on Husband
3. Effects of Maternal Employment on Children

Results

Respondents perceived that there was more than one effect in any one of the following areas that resulted from working outside the home; therefore, percentages will add up to more than 100%. In general, working mothers felt positive about their employment. For example, the following feelings were reported: fulfilled (92%); compensated (78%); challenged (72%); enriched (47%); and happy (37%). However, some women felt strained (15%) and tired (12%).

Effects on Mother

Physical Effects. In general, 50% acknowledged that their physical time, intended for family life, had been taken away by their employment. The highest number of respondents (87%) reported that working outside the family home made them feel more conscious of their body and physical appearance. In addition, 67% said they were more conscious of health habits; 57% were more aware of food intake; 57% were concerned with health in general; and 22% said they were more conscious of clothing and jewelry.

Social Effects. Socially, the women felt that working outside the home had positive effects. Some 84% saw that they were better able to develop harmonious relationships with children; 83% found that they could accept others better; 72% said they had more contact with varied personalities; 57% reported improved relationships with husbands; 40% said they were more able to develop harmonious relationships with in-laws; 26% found that their relationships with close friends and relatives had improved; and 24% said that relations with others, in general, had improved.

Emotional Effects. Working mothers perceived their employment to aid them in their awareness and acceptance of their feelings and the feelings of others. In fact, 94% reported being better able to adjust to varied personality types; 88% became more aware of their own feelings, and 69% were more aware of others' feelings; 72% reported greater flexibility in adjusting to life situations; 47% described themselves as more able to accept their own feelings; and 37% said they could better accept others' feelings.

Intellectual Effects. In general, working women found that their intellectual growth had been enhanced by working outside the home. For example, 71% had developed their decision-making skills; 70% felt they had a broader understanding of life's realities; 48% responded that their professional skills had improved; 37% said they could now practice the career for which they had prepared; and 26% found improved academic preparation by joining the work force.

Economic Effects. There was unanimous agreement among the women that their working outside the home was necessary to assist their husband in meeting basic family needs (100%). Also, 69% said that they found working gave them a sense of security and stability to better cope with life's realities; 48% found that they could afford some luxuries; and 47% said they received adequate compensation.

Moral Effects. In general, the women reported that working outside the home made them feel as if they were assuming co-responsibility for the formation of the family (92%). In addition, 87% said they worked to help support their own family's needs; 70% reported that they worked to help support their own parents, brothers, and sisters; 12% saw that their working left the responsibility for developing moral formation of the children to husbands, parents, and in-laws; and 8% said they worked to help in the moral formation of others under their care.

Spiritual Effects. Working mothers found that their employment had some positive spiritual effects. For example, 76% reported feeling that their employment enhanced their role as co-creators of God on earth; 70% said their employment gave them chances to pray fervently for blessings; 53% said they found they could improve their talents, gifts, and skills of personhood; and 45% voiced concern for husbands' and children's spirituality, as well as that of other people in their lives.

Effects on Husband

Generally, working mothers perceived their employment as favorable to their husbands, because of their husbands' feeling of their wives' cooperation to meet life's demands (93%). Also, 81% said that their husbands were supportive of their assuming employment tasks; 73% reported that their husbands felt a commonality of purpose in bringing up the family; 53% described their husbands as willing to do household chores; and 45% said their husbands gave them consideration. However, 13% reported that their employment caused physical and intellectual tiredness that affected their sexual relationship; and 12% of the respondents claimed that their employment caused a feeling of competition between them and their husbands.

Effects on Children

Working mothers perceived that their employment had a significant effect on their children. For example, many claimed that there was less time spent with children (92%). However, these mothers perceived that their children felt secure that their mother was helping to support the children (72%); 70% said that mothers' work was the children's source of inspiration to work for a living, too; 59% perceived that their children were proud that their mothers worked; 58% felt as though they could better understand their children's psychological needs; 44% reported spending quality time with their children; 37% said that they thought they were giving their children more quality guidance; and 50% responded that their children had learned to be understanding about the demands of their working mother's job.

Discussion

In general, Filipino mothers found their employment to be fulfilling, especially in the context of their multiple roles. For example, women in this study perceived themselves as fulfilling their role of spiritual and moral teacher for the children by showing them the example of working to help support the whole family, often including in-laws, brothers, and sisters. A majority of the women found that there were generally positive effects on their physical health and appearance through heightened awareness about these issues, while a minority found that their employment caused them to feel tired and strained (which had a negative effect on their sexual relationship). However, women who reported feeling tired and strained may have been involved in routine, mechanical tasks that do not include mental stimulation, as well as those who have not been adequately compensated or are waiting to be retired due to old age. Working mothers perceived that their employment was a significant factor in their physical health. Excellent health was perceived as synonymous with regular work, high performance, and stability—on the job, at home, and in the community. This health factor was supported in the workplace, since many employers offered physical fitness programs. Other research agrees with this finding (Quisumbing and Lazarus, 1985).

Conclusions

Working mothers in this study perceived their employment as a significant factor in their development as total persons in various aspects of life: physical, social, emotional, intellectual, economic, spiritual, and moral. These aspects are interrelated to their relationships with their children, husbands, colleagues, in-laws, and other relatives. These mothers perceived their employment as a concrete manifestation of genuine partnership with their husbands. Thus, they perceived their husbands as supportive of them in their assumption of employment tasks, and reported that their husbands gave consideration to them, as the husbands took part in domestic tasks and child care. These mothers perceived that their employment had favorable effects on their children. Specifically, they recognized that less time was spent with their children, but also claimed that they spent quality time for better guidance and expressed feeling more understanding of their children's psychological needs. Thus, the working mothers perceived their children to feel secure and proud of them and that the children saw their mothers as a source of inspiration to work, also, when they reached adulthood. Working mothers who were professionals and career women experienced fulfillment in their jobs, as they felt compensated, challenged, enriched, and happy. Their husbands and children were reported to be supportive, contributing to the household tasks and roles of working mothers. In addition to support from the family, the Philippine constitution of 1987 gave fundamental equality between women and men in terms of employment, opportunities for promotion, practices of a profession, the acquisition, control, and disposition of property, and so on. Further, the constitution gives special concern to working women in terms of safe and healthful working conditions, facilities, maternity leave benefits, family planning services, and physical fitness programs.

The Cooperation of the Entire Filipino Family

An important conclusion of this study was that the Filipino family members all cooperate. Specifically, the children, father, hired domestic help, or relatives take over the working mother's responsibilities for the benefit of everyone. Family members see it as their moral responsibility to assume tasks at home, as the highest motives in life. In this way, the working mother is able to fulfill her multiple roles, and family members can all contribute to the family's support. Older children were found to be especially helpful to their working mothers, as other researchers also found (Whiting, 1966; Concepcion and Cagigon, 1978; Domingo, 1977; Boulier, 1976, Cabanero, 1978).

Another conclusion of this study was that the main reason that most Filipino women work outside the home is to assist with the family's financial demands, often including the needs of in-laws and other kin. Engaging in an occupation for the lower-class Filipina is mainly perceived as an extension of her traditional homemaker role as co-creator and co-provider for the family. Husbands and children accepted the mother's work outside the family as necessary to meet financial needs and appreciated her efforts, as other research has also found (Sevilla, 1982; Pedrajas, 1994a; Pedrajas, 1994b). Women from the middle- and upper-income levels reported additional reasons for working: to apply one's education or training, love of the particular work involved, social stimulation, and self-development. All of these motives were understood by the husbands and children. Husbands of working mothers recognized that their wives' employment fostered their wives' broader outlook on life in general, and family life in particular. Wives utilized what they learned in office work to improve their family's lifestyle and atmosphere, and became resourceful in tapping the talents of friends or co-workers for family needs. While most working mothers felt supported by their husbands, a minority of them reported feeling a sense of competition with their husbands, which other research has found (Porio, et al., 1975).

Women perceived that even though less time was spent with them, their children seemed to understand the need for their employment, and that their work was appreciated as a vital ingredient of the whole family's economic well-being. Since working women perceived that they had support from extended family members, they felt that their important role of spiritual teacher to the children was being shared by kin, and therefore fulfilled. Working mothers had learned to manage their time well, and had ways of discovering, checking, and monitoring their children's needs and feelings, behavior, attitudes, skills, and values in life via planned, open communication, projects, or family outings. The women also felt as though they had improved their understanding of their children's psychological needs, thereby enhancing the quality of time spent with children. Children perceived that their working mothers had helped them have a broader understanding about life in general, and family life in particular. Another study by Pedrajas (1994b) found that children of working mothers perceived their mothers as their inspiration to strive in attaining happiness through work, and seemed to assume they would join the work force in adult life, whether or not they married. Working mothers were perceived as spiritual teachers by their children (Quisumbing and Lazarus, 1985).

Another important conclusion of this study was that the Filipinos, especially women, are deeply religious people. They maintain an intimate interpersonal relationship with God. For example, the women reported that as they work they invoke God's blessings for their children, husband, parents, relatives, friends' spirituality, security, happiness, and success, as well as asking for blessings for other people. Working women are aware of their responsibility to develop their talents, and maximize the use of their gifts and skills of personhood, as a manifestation of their intimate friendship with God. The working women in this study perceived that their husbands and children appreciated them for their spiritual teaching and moral guidance. Other research has also found this to be the case (Pedrajas, 1994a; Pedrajas, 1994b).

Summary

In the Philippines, the family, kinship ties, and religion are of utmost importance. While most rural households are nuclear, the higher cost of living in urban areas has resulted in more households consisting of the extended family. Wives typically assume multiple roles as co-creators with their husbands, forming an egalitarian marital relationship. Both husband and wife share in decision-making, child care, and financial support. When Filipino women work outside the family, the other family members cooperate with child care and household chores. Henc:, working women feel supported in their efforts to improve their families' quality of life. Even though they spend less time with their husbands and children, the time they do spend is of a higher quality.

Working wives have found that their employment results in better health and a better understanding of people—which in turn improves their relationships with their husbands and children. Filipino working women see their employment as a way to fulfill their vital role as the spiritual and moral teacher for the family. As they work, they ask for God's blessing for their husbands, children, and kin. They are supported in their efforts by the entire family. Grandmothers are especially important in sharing child care, as are husbands and older siblings.

In addition to working women being supported by their families, they are also assisted by various governmental regulations. The Philippine constitution of 1987 was structured to strengthen the family as a basic social institution. The new civil code lays down general principles that sustain the solidarity of the family. The constitution also gives recognition to the role of women in the task of nation-building. Many articles in the constitution explicitly protect working women, stating, "The State shall protect working women by providing safe and healthful working conditions . . . that will enhance their welfare and enable them to realize their full potential in the service of the nation." Women are also prohibited from doing night work, except in agricultural work and then only when given at least nine consecutive hours of rest. Exceptions to this are during national emergencies, or when the special skill or dexterity of women is required, or when women are in management positions. Through the constitution, the secretary of labor is charged with the responsibility of requiring employers to provide for a dressing room for women as well as a nursery at the workplace. Maternity leave with pay is to be provided, as well as leave and financial assistance for miscarriages and abortions. Longer paid leave is provided for caesarian delivery or complications of pregnancy and childbirth, and comprehensive family planning is also available for free in organizations that maintain a clinic or infirmary. Family planning services include education and free contraceptives such as birth control pills and intrauterine devices.

Implications

While the constitution states that "men and women are fundamentally equal," men continue to dominate positions of responsibility and authority. Therefore, there is a need for more active support of women's rights through the Filipino government. Elena Masilungan (1991) presented five positive steps that would uphold the rights and welfare of these women, as follows:

1. Promulgation of the Family Code of the Philippines, which eliminated many of the discriminatory provisions that were legacies of the Spanish period.

2. In the senate, the creation of a Committee on Women and Family Relations that is responsible for legislation concerning women.

3. The National Commission on the Role of Filipino Women was established in 1975 and needs to continue its efforts to review, evaluate, and recommend measures to ensure the full integration of women in economics, social, political, cultural and family life at all levels, on an equal basis with men.

4. New government agencies can be more helpful to women—such as the Bureau of Women and Young Workers under the Department of Labor and Employment, the Agricultural Training Institute of the Department of Agriculture, and the Bureau of Women under the Department of Social Welfare and Development.

5. The Philippine Development Plan for Women (PDPW) has defined objectives, policies, and major programs in the various sectors regarding women's development, including the following: (a) the economic sector; (b) the social sector, and (c) the special concerns sector. The economic sector includes agriculture, agrarian reform, environment and natural resources, industry, trade, industrial relations, and services. The social sector includes education and training, health, nutrition and family planning, housing, social welfare, and community development. The special concerns sector includes women and migration, production, violence against women, media, arts, and culture.

It is noteworthy that the PDPW's task of integrating women's concerns at all levels of developmental planning is a multidimensional approach. Issues included are: national commitment and political will, relevant and effective policies and programs, provision of adequate resources, efficient monitoring, and women's participation. The PDPW addresses the concerns of women for equality and development in various ways, such as individual concerns, family concerns, sociocultural concerns, economic concerns, and legal and political concerns.

Recommendations for Further Study

While this study included 500 working mothers in the Metro Manila area, a similar study could be completed assessing the perceptions of working mothers toward employment in all major cities and provinces of the country. In addition to other geographic areas being studied, data could be gathered about other occupation sectors. Other research could include a comprehensive study on the interrelatedness of perceptions among the working mothers toward employment on the self, the perceptions of their husbands, and perceptions of their children. Financial support for such research could come from funding agencies that are concerned with women's welfare and development. Research on the effects of employment on working mothers, their husbands, and children could be utilized to improve, support, and underscore the varied needs and concerns of working mothers— which could improve Filipino family life. In addition, a study on how the implementation of governmental or nongovernmental programs affects working mothers may be the source of good baseline data for making further decisions that affect this special sector.

References

Aleta, I.R., Silva, T.L. and Eleazar, C.P. (1977). *A profile of Filipino women, their status and role*. Manila, Philippines: Capital.

Boulier, B.L. (1976). *Children and household economic activity in Laguna, Philippines.* University of the Philippines School of Economics Institute of Economic Development and Research. Quezon City, Philippines.

Cabanero, T. (1978). The shadow price of children in Laguna households. *Philippine Economic Journal 36,* 17.

Castillo, G.T. (1976). *The Filipino woman as manpower: The image and empirical reality.* Los Banos, Laguna, Philippines: University of the Philippines.

Concepcion, M.B., and Cagigon, J.V. (1978). *Selected demographic and socioeconomic characteristics of households in central Luzon and metro Manila.* 1977 area fertility survey. Manila, Philippines: University of the Philippines Population Institute.

Corpus, A., and Nunez, D. (1982). *Early childhood enrichment program: Final research report, National Economic Development Authority.* UNICEF Country Programming Project.

De Guzman, E.A. (1990). *Family households in the Philippines: Current perspectives and future prospects.* Proposed as Part of the Family in the late '80s. University of the Philippines Associations Project on the State of the Nation.

De Leon, H.S. (1994). *Textbook on the Philippine constitution.* Manila, Philippines: Rex Bookstore.

Domingo, M.F.A. (1977). *Child rearing practices in Barrio Cruz na Ligao.* Master's thesis. Quezon City, Philippines: University of the Philippines.

Dover, E. (1967). *Kalinga of Northern Luzon.* New York: Holt, Rinehart and Winston.

Flores, P.M. (1970). *Career women and motherhood in a changing society: sociopsychological development of Filipino children.* Manila, Philippines: Regal.

The gutsy dozen. *Times Journal,* (1975, July 5) Manila, Philippines.

Licuanan, P.B., and Gonzales, A.M. (1976). *Filipino women in development.* Quezon City, Philippines: Institute of Philippine Culture, Ateneo de Manila University.

Mananzan, M.J., OSB. (1987). *Essays on Woman.* Manila, Philippines: St. Scholastica College.

Masilungan, E. (1991). *Institutionalizing women power development.* Special Report by the Development Plan for Women Philippine Development, 18, No. 6, January–February 1991. National Economic Development Authority.

Medina, B.T.G. (1991). *The Filipino family: A text with selected readings.* Quezon City, Philippines: University of the Philippines Press.

National Statistics Office. (1992). *Statistics on the Filipino women.* In cooperation with the National Commission on the Role of Filipino Women. Manila, Philippines.

Pedrajas, T.P. (1994a). *Survey of husbands' perceptions on working wives in some aspects of life.* Manila, Philippines: San Beda College, Mendiola.

Pedrajas, T.P. (1994b). *Survey of childrens' perceptions on working mothers in some aspects of life.* Manila, Philippines: San Beda College, Mendiola.

Porio, E., Lynch, F., and Hollnsteiner, M. (1975). *The Filipino family, community and nation: The same yesterday, today and tomorrow.* Quezon City, Philippines: Institute of Philippine Culture, Ateneo de Manila University.

Quisumbing, L.R., and Lazarus, B.R. (1985). *Women and work in Asia, A call for Asia.* Manila, Philippines: Commission on Women and Work, Asian Women's Institute.

Sevilla, J.C.A. (1982). *Research on the Filipino family: Review and prospects.* Metro Manila, Philippines: Research for Development Department, Development Academy of the Philippines, Pasig.

Whiting, B. (1966). *Six Cultures: Vol. VI.* New York: John Wiley and Sons.

Chapter Eight
Work and Family Situations of Women in Top Management in Puerto Rico

Eileen M. Colberg Luciano and Evelyn Ramos Marcano

Puerto Rico is a relatively small (3,435-square-miles), densely populated Caribbean island with 3.6 million inhabitants. After four centuries of Spanish colonization, the island became a U.S. territory in 1898 as a result of the Spanish-American War. Puerto Rican society has undergone dramatic changes during the twentieth century. Recent decades have witnessed a rapid transition from rural, agrarian society to a more urban, industrial, and commercial economic structure.

Literature on the traditional Puerto Rican family stresses that the place for women is at home. Puerto Rican women are taught to value very highly their roles as mothers and housekeepers. The power of the female lies in her position as housekeeper, mother, and teacher of the next generation. The socialization process usually reinforces in women dependency, stability, obedience, responsibility, and submission. The place of the man as head of the household affords him a superior position of power, authority, and privilege, in contrast to the inferior, subordinate, and restricted status of the female (Colberg and Burgos, 1988; Rodriquez, 1984; Burgos, 1986).

The role of mother and wife ascribed to women presupposes that they will not have to worry about supporting themselves or their families, since this is the man's role. Yet the majority of employed women are married. In 1980, 62% (169,000) of employed women were married (Departamento del Trabajo y Recursos Humanos, 1983a); in 1993, 60% were married (Departamento del Trabajo y Recursos Humanos, 1993). Also, the rate of divorced women in 1970 was 38 for every 1,000; in 1980 it was 72 for every 1,000; and in 1990 it increased to 93 for every 1,000 women (Junta de Planificación, 1993).

According to census data, the proportion of families headed by single mothers increased from 15% in 1970 to 18% in 1980. The 1990 census revealed that 23.2% of the families in Puerto Rico are headed by single mothers (Junta de Planificación, 1993). This becomes even more complicated by unemployment. In 1980, 17% of the unemployed women were single mothers (Departamento del Trabajo y Recursos Humanos, 1983b). Many of these families headed by single women are under the poverty level (Colón, García and Alegría, 1986). The Commission for the Betterment of Women's Rights maintains that Puerto Rican girls are socialized to become housekeepers, mothers, and wives. Boys are trained for future roles of wage earners, providers, and leaders. The commission concludes that these assumptions lead to discriminatory educational practices, limited occupational opportunities, and a psychological predisposition to an image of females as inferior and helpless (Wagenheim, 1975). Therefore, there are confusing contradictions between the socialization of women in Puerto Rico and the hard reality they face when working outside the home, whether they are married or not. The multiplicity of roles becomes overbearing when it clashes with fairy-tale expectations of men being the caretakers of and sole providers for their households (Ramos Marcano, 1994b; Colberg and Burgos, 1988).

Although more and more women have joined the world of employment and participate in a variety of roles previously assigned to men, discourses of female subordination are still embedded in the Puerto Rican culture. The traditional values of the Puerto Ricans are important, but one should remember Wagenheim's warning (1975) against the risk of reinforcing stereotypes in defining the culture of a people, or as Pacheco (1981) describes it, listing their official values.

Historical Background of Employed Women in Puerto Rico

Before the twentieth century, women stayed home to take care of household, family, and agricultural tasks. In addition, Rivera Quintero (1980) describes them as picking coffee and performing the roles of wash maids, seamstresses, and servants. With the development of capitalism came the separation of work, where paid work is assigned to men and domestic work to women. In 1889, the invasion by the United States accelerated the capitalist system in Puerto Rico, which in turn accelerated the incorporation of women into the job market on the bases of inequality and sexism. The Spanish colonization also preached inequality between genders, reproduced mainly through educational systems. However, not until the invasion by the United States was there a marked separation between public and domestic boundaries and a rearticulation of the sexual division of labor (Rivera Quintero, 1987). This was evidenced by a greater amount of men than women appearing in the work force (Colón, Mergal, and Torres, 1986). The family was no longer a unit of production. Women's work did not receive monetary compensation or recognition. Devaluation of their work intensified the image of women as inferior and subordinate (Colón, et al., 1986; Rivera Quintero, 1980).

The number of women in the work force increased dramatically after 1889. Women were recruited in large numbers for tobacco stripping, home needlework, and fabrication of straw hats (Rivera Quintero, 1980). World War I brought about a large home needlework industry when North America stopped importing European embroidery. In 1955, manufacturing surpassed agriculture as a generator of income (Wagenheim, 1975). With the growth of industrialization and the decline of tobacco and needlework, women entered manufacturing and professional services, ensuring their own role in the Puerto Rican economy (Picó, 1988).

In 1910, female participation in the work force was 9.9% (Cristía, 1988); in 1970, it was 24.5%, and in 1980 it increased to 29% (Junta de Planificación, 1993). According to Gali Bras (1989), in 1988, four out of every 10 employed persons were women. Although in 1990 the proportion of employed women was reported to be 37.2%, during the last 33 years the economy generated 446,000 jobs, with 59.6% of these jobs held by women (Junta de Planificación, 1993; Departamento del Trabajo y Recursos Humanos, 1993). The Junta de Planificación of Puerto Rico projects that by the year 2000, 53% of the work force will be female (De los Reyes, 1987).

Women's concentration in the service fields is viewed as an extension of their domestic role. Teaching became one of the main occupations of middle- and upper-class women and gradually became a "female" profession. By 1930, 74.5% of all teachers were female (Picó, 1976). In 1980, the distribution of women in the following occupations was office work (26.9%), professionals (18.7%), machine operators (16.8 %), nondomestic work (14.4%), and executives, managers, and administrators (6%). The majority of the female executives, managers, and administrators were located in public administration, which was the sector that employed the most women (Acevedo, 1987; Departamento del Trabajo y Recursos Humanos, 1983b; Junta de Planificación, 1987).

Historically, the opportunities of paid work for women revolved around jobs that required less preparation and offered lower salaries. Picó (1976) found a distinct segregation by sex. Women are teachers, nurses, service employees, and factory operators. Their proportion in technical and professional fields has decreased since World War II. In 1940, women represented 50.7 percent of all technical and professional workers, but in 1970 they constituted 48.3 percent of these workers. These statistics show women holding a small portion of such high-status professional occupations as lawyers (11.4 percent), scientists (13.3 percent), and engineers (2.2 percent).

In earlier times, women were discriminated against by being cloistered in the home; now discrimination is expressed through lower salaries, absence of participation in administrative positions (Azize, 1987), and the multiplicity of tasks of employed work and housework (Colón, et al., 1986). Although women have advanced educationally and professionally, the patriarchal ideology still permeates Puerto Rican society and organizations. During the past 33 years, women have increased their participation in office and professional work, occupying more than half of these positions. In 1960, 36% of women were in office and professional work; in 1990 it increased to more than 50%. While in 1960, 28% were machine operators and seamstresses, in 1990 that figure was 17%, and in 1993 it decreased to 14%. Although women occupy more professional positions than men and have more academic preparation than men, they still hold fewer administrative positions than men (Departamento del Trabajo y Recursos Humanos, 1993).

Women occupy only 30% of the following professions: accountants, architects, engineers, lawyers and judges, medical doctors, dentists, managers, and administrators. In the Puerto Rican social context, these are precisely the occupations with the most prestige and highest pay. On the other hand, women occupy 80% of the following professions: librarians, graduate nurses, therapists, health technologists and technicians, office clerks, secretaries, receptionists and typists (Junta de Planificación, 1987). Women occupy professions traditionally considered "feminine," which offer lower salaries and less prestige.

The occupations available for Puerto Rican women have changed in recent years. They have diversified and increased in number and scope, but women still do not have the same opportunities as men. The number of women in positions of highest prestige and better compensation is still low in comparison to men. However, women in Puerto Rico have received more formal education than men in the past 25 years (Departamento del Trabajo y Recursos Humanos, 1993; Pacheco, 1981). Rivera (1987) presents statistics revealing that since 1942 there has been an equal or larger number of women registered in the principal university of the island, the University of Puerto Rico, with the exception of only one not very significant period with fewer women, between 1954 and 1960. Since 1969, women have reached a majority that has continued to increase. In a statistical analysis of higher education institutions in Puerto Rico from 1992 to 1993, the Council of Higher Education of Puerto Rico (1993) reports that three-fifths of the university student body are women, while men are still predominant in the faculty.

The Workplace as a Reproducer of Social Construction of Gender

The social construction of the workplace is a replica of society in general, which is based on opposites and differences such as race, religion, nationality, age, and gender. Central to this structural ideology is the idea of dominance, where one group or conceptualization is deemed to be superior to and dominant over others (Astin and Leland, 1991): for example, leaders over subordinates, whites over blacks, heterosexuals over homosexuals, men over women, one religion and one nation over others. This is known in society as the hierarchical model of domination, in organized formal work structures as bureaucracy (Ferguson, 1984) and in family structures as patriarchy (Muñoz and Fernández, 1980).

The social construction of gender is a product of social historical processes that occur in the structure of interpersonal relations of groups. The position that people occupy in that social structure will influence those conceptions. Organizations construct, validate, and transmit discourses on gender. Typically, men occupy social positions of more power and prestige than women. These circumstances set the genders to live in different worlds, at a conceptual and concrete level. The subordination of women is constructed within this system of dominance, where they are perceived as weak and less prepared to function in positions that require leadership and competition. Women are perceived to be dependent on men. Women's limited independence is subject to what the patriarchal system dictates. Table 1 illustrates the similarities between the patriarchal structure in the family and the bureaucratic structure in the workplace. In both structures, women occupy a position subordinate to that of men.

Puerto Rican Women and Hierarchical Work Structures

Upper-level positions in the organizations are still reserved for men. This was the general consensus of speakers and human resource administrators interviewed by Sagardía (1992). This author believes it is due to gender stereotypes and prejudices. The situation of unequal power among women and men in organizations is reinforced through the traditional discourses of society about how women should behave. According to García and Muñoz (1993), women have a 15% chance of occupying lower-level managerial positions, but only a 5% chance of occupying positions in middle management, and a 1% chance in upper management. In addition to not advancing as high as men, women do not obtain as much job security in the organization.

According to Carreras (1985), the prevailing situation of unequal power between men and women in organizations is reinforced through the traditional conceptions of what constitutes female behavior and the corresponding positions for women. These conceptions are still firmly fixed in the minds of those who have the power to change the possibilities for improvement and development of women in the organizations. Coria (1985) explains women's subordination as it applies to Latin women. She states that the reality of

Table 1 Comparison of the models of patriarchy and bureaucracy and its impact on gender.

Principles	Patriarchy	Bureaucracy
Direct supervision	Father to mother, parents to children	Management to employees
Specialization and division of labor	Women: house, children, reproduction Men: main provider Children: apprentices	Tasks, professions
Hierarchy of authority	Father to mother Mother to children Elders to minors	Board of directors to president, Management to employees
Values	Children's discipline to become good citizens	Discipline to ensure efficiency and production

Note: Adapted and translated from table prepared by Colberg Luciano in "La construcción social del género y la subjetividad: Educación y trabajo [The social construction of gender and subjectivity: Education and work]" by Bravo, Colberg, Martínez, Martínez, Méndez, and Seijo, 1994, *Género y mujeres puertorriqueñas*, Río Piedras: Universidad de Puerto Rico, Centro de Investigaciones Sociales. Adapted with permission.

women is constructed in the economic subordination of dependency, which includes social, emotional, and psychological subordination.

Acevedo (1987) mentions three factors that characterize women's participation in the work force: occupational segregation, salary differences, and displacement due to advances in technology resulting in a decreased need for employees. It is clear that women's participation in the work force depends on the dominant ideology that determines their entrance in the job market and the specific occupations they can occupy.

Masculine and Feminine Characteristics of Work Styles

At present, women in Puerto Rico have diverse roles, opportunities, and expectations. This results in a variety of pressures and tensions. Women develop skills to be able to work in the men's domain, the world of remunerated work. When they adapt their skills to their new work environment, these skills are considered masculine.

Schein (1973) conducted a study in the United States to determine the relationship between gender-stereotyped roles and the managerial styles of women. Successful managers perceived themselves as possessing characteristics associated with men. Also, the relationship between gender-stereotyped roles and characteristics form an image of women as being less qualified than men for managerial positions. Results such as these suggest that accepting stereotyped masculine characteristics as a basis for success in management could become a requirement for women in the present organizational climate.

Research in the United States by Heilman, Block, Simon, and Martell (1989) indicates that the vision of a successful manager is more congruent with the characteristics attributed to men than those attributed to women. These findings concur with those of Schein (1973), indicating little change in the pattern of these descriptions during more than a decade. Likewise, a comparative study of the characteristics and managerial styles of female and male managers in Puerto Rico by García and Muñoz (1993) revealed that the managers who participated in the study displayed characteristics socially ascribed to men much more often than characteristics ascribed to

Table 2 Characteristics of traditional masculine and feminine work styles.

Masculine Style	Feminine Style
unlimited space	limited space
economic independence	economic dependency
control of emotions	lack of control of emotions
delineated time	continuous time
strategic planning	spontaneity
lineal thinking	holistic thinking
quick decisions	decisions with time
assertiveness	submissiveness
management of big money	management of small money
priority to work	priority to family

Note: Adapted and translated from table prepared by Colberg Luciano in "La construcción social del género y la subjetividad: Educación y trabajo [The social construction of gender and subjectivity: Education and work]" by Bravo et al., 1994, *Género y mujeres puertorriqueñas*. Adapted with permission.

women, concurring with studies in the United States (Schein, 1973, 1975; Heilman, 1989).

Pereira and Rivera (1989) conducted a study of the determinants and antecedents of achievement of women in upper management in Puerto Rico. They found that the majority of the women in the sample were influenced by supportive parents who did not reinforce stereotyped feminine characteristics. These women also believe that their partners' support was vital in order to successfully comply with their roles as professionals, wives, and mothers. The authors conclude that women's professional success is due to the interaction of upbringing, education, personal characteristics, personal vision of their life and goals, and a strong support network. Yet work structures, originated by men for men, demand certain characteristics of personality traditionally ascribed to men, not women. Work style characteristics ascribed to gender are socially constructed, not biologically assigned. These characteristics are listed in Table 2.

At present, there are few studies about Puerto Rican women that describe gender processes or discuss how the multiple factors of work and family affect women who are in top management positions in Puerto Rico. Therefore, this study was a timely examination of this topic. The following paragraphs describe the method used in this study. For the purpose of this study, the characteristics studied were defined in the following section, based on Coria (1985).

Definition of Terms
Limited—Unlimited Space
Men, in their primary role of main provider of the family, are socialized to move in a wider scope or space of action than women. Men are permitted more mobility to explore the environment. Women, because of their primary role of household and family caretaker, are limited to a smaller space, the home and its surroundings.

Big Money—Small Money
Big money is generally administered by business owners and administrators, and used for making transcendental decisions. It provides the one who manages it with security, solvency, and power. Big money is generally administered by men. Small money is the petty cash used

daily, for which one must account. It does not provide the one who manages it with security, solvency, or power. Small money is generally administered by nonhierarchical personnel, who are usually women.

Reason—Emotion

Some scholars have stated that emotions are a feminine characteristic, while reason is a characteristic of men. This epistemological trap has consolidated the belief that reasoning is a masculine privilege.

Work—Family Priority

Women are socialized so that their roles as wife and mother become the priorities of their lives. Men, on the other hand, are to give priority to their role as providers.

Strategic Planning—Spontaneity

Women are socialized to be spontaneous, to act with an absence of strategic planning, while men are trained to plan strategically.

Assertiveness—Inhibition

Assertiveness is defined as insisting on one's right to legitimize ideas, sentiments, and needs. When women insist on their rights, they are often thought of as aggressive, which is not acceptable for their gender. Therefore, women behave in a more inhibited or submissive way, not insisting on their rights.

Method

Data for this study was collected by conducting in-depth interviews with eleven women in top management positions in Puerto Rico, using a semistructured interview guide. The first part of the interview guide consisted of demographic questions and questions related to work, family, and social factors. The second part consisted of critical incidents related to work and family situations. While one main interviewer asked the questions, the other took notes and also participated in the interview in a flexible, naturalistic manner. This method is suggested for studies of men and women when exploring, discovering, and understanding the construction of gender (Berger and Luckman, 1967). It provides the necessary flexibility to generate additional information that was not anticipated.

Selection and Description of the Sample

The sample consisted of women in top management positions from various organizations in Puerto Rico. They were selected from *Perfil de Negocios*, a section announcing recent promotions that appears in a local newspaper, *El Nuevo Día*. A preliminary list consisted of 110 women who were promoted in 1991, and included their organizations and positions. For a final selection of the sample, the organizations and positions were classified as masculine or feminine. Organizations and positions classified as masculine were those that traditionally were designated to men, such as manufacturing and the banking industries. Positions included presidents and corporate officers. The organizations and positions classified as feminine were those traditionally assigned to women, mostly those related to service organizations such as hospitals, hotels, or educational institutions. Positions included administrative assistants, public relations workers, and human resource directors.

Once the organizations and the positions were classified as masculine and feminine, a selection of women whose positions and organizations were classified as masculine was made. The sample size was reduced to 32 women in "masculine" positions and organizations. The researchers contacted the 32 women by telephone to coordinate interviews. Finally, 11 women were interviewed for the study. The positions they had been promoted to were distributed as follows: one president, two associates, three directors, two managers, and one consultant. Their work experience in their present positions ranged from one to two years because of the method used for the selection of population. Their ages ranged from 25 to 49 years, with only one participant over 50. Four of the participants were married and seven were single. Five participants had children and six participants did not. Three participants earned less than $40,000 annually; one participant earned from $40,000 to $60,000, and seven earned more than $61,000. Each of the women interviewed had a bachelor's degree.

Description of Research Instruments

To collect the information for the research, an interview guide was designed. The interview guide consisted of two sections; questions and critical incidents or potential scenarios, as shown in Table 3. The

questions addressed demographics about the women and their partners or husbands, if appropriate. In addition, the questions asked for
information about the women's multiple roles, time for self, and social
and support networks. The critical incidents were presented orally to
the women as potential scenarios, and the women were asked to indicate how they would respond in these scenarios. Critical incident categories included work—family priority; limited—unlimited space;
assertiveness—inhibition; reason—emotion; big money—small
money; organization—improvisation; and strategic planning—spontaneity. These categories (with the exception of strategic planning—
spontaneity, organization—spontaneity, and assertiveness—inhibition)
appear in a study by Coria (1985) on women in Argentina. Participants' responses to the critical incidents provide a fuller picture of the
socially constructed reality of these women.

Results

The demographic data reveal that 64% of the women in the sample
were single and did not have children. This surpasses the data by
Long (1988), which found 45% of his sample had never been married or were divorced and 50% had no children. Both studies con-
firm the assertion by Muñoz and Fernández (1980) that there do
not exist social infrastructures that permit women to simultaneously
assume their employee-wife-mother roles. Therefore, employed
women, especially those in top management, have to give priority to
one role over the other.

It was found that 100% of the women in the sample worked
more than eight hours daily and worked on Saturdays and Sundays.
Of the eleven women interviewed, five had children between 3 and
26 years of age. All of the mothers delegated child care to others, to
either relatives, employees, or educational institutions. Five of the
women had employees in charge of cooking; eight had employees in
charge of cleaning and washing and ironing. Therefore, 80% delegated household chores and 100% of the mothers delegated child
care responsibilities while they worked. This data indicates that these
women gave more priority to their remunerated work than to their
family and household, if this is measured by the amount of time
dedicated to their different roles. This also indicates the difficulty of
combining both priorities while maintaining a high professional rank

Table 3 Interview guide.

Part I	Questions
Demographic data of participants	1–9
Demographic data of husbands/partners	10–12
Mother role	13–14
Caretaker role or support network	15–19
Housekeeper role or support network	20–21
Paid work role and time investment	22–27
Time for self	28–29
Social network	30–37

Part II	Critical Incidents
Work—Family Priority	1, 6
Limited—Unlimited Space	2, 3, 4
Assertiveness—Inhibition	7
Reason—Emotion	8
Big Money—Small Money	9
Organization—Improvisation	10
Strategic Planning—Spontaneity	5, 11

demanding long work hours.

The majority of the participants had from four to nine close friends, and nine participants believed they had received support from these friends for their careers. In addition, ten of the participants found career support from relatives, and eight found this support from co-workers.

Results of Critical Incidents

The participants were asked to answer how they would react to the following critical incidents (or potential scenarios), presented to them orally. The results were classified and tabulated. Some of the outstanding comments the women made have been included in order to provide rich information that would have been obscured if only presented numerically.

Critical Incident 1: Work—Family Priority

Particpants were asked how they would respond to the following scenario: "You are presenting a report to top management at a meeting programmed two months ago. You receive a message that your child is sick at school and must be picked up."

Work: Participant chooses to stay at business meeting   n=2
Family: Participant leaves meeting business meeting   n=6
           Participant has no children   n=3

Respondents' comments included:

"I am never absent."

"If my son is sick while I am working, I make arrangements for my domestic employee to take charge. Unless of course it is something serious. I avoid being absent from work as much as possible."

"The responsibility of my family is not negotiable; it is just as important or even more than my job."

"I'd leave the meeting only if it's a serious condition."

These answers indicate that family held priority over work for these women. This could be due to the fact that the situation presented a health emergency situation. Therefore, the majority chose to leave the meeting and attend to their family. On the other hand, on critical incident 6, where the participants had to choose between a birthday celebration and a business meeting, the majority gave priority to work.

Critical Incident 2: Limited—Unlimited Space
Participants were asked how they would respond in the following scenario: "You are offered the opportunity to travel within two days to the United States (with a male co-worker) to observe the implementation of a new program."

Unlimited Space: Participant goes on business trip   n=11
Limited Space: Participant decides not to go on trip   n=0

Respondents' comments included:

"Of course."

"No problem."

"I'm used to traveling."

Critical incident 2 shows that 100% of the sample were willing to travel with short notice to comply with their career demands, indicating that these women had unlimited space in this type of situation.

Critical Incident 3: Limited—Unlimited Space
Participants were asked how they would respond in the following

scenario: "Your organization offers you a much higher position if you relocate outside the island. Your salary would be three times more, plus they would pay relocation expenses."

Unlimited Space:	Participant accepts offer	n=4
Limited Space:	Participant rejects offer or decision depends on others	n=7

Respondents' comments included:

"When I was single I would relocate easily, but now we (referring to her boyfriend) would both determine what is most convenient for both. My happiness is worth more than money."

"Short trips, no problem. Relocation, no. My roots are here."

"No, I can't leave my family alone." (This participant was not married.)

The results of critical incident 3 indicate that only four of the eleven women considered it possible to relocate to another country to further their career opportunities; the other seven considered their spouses, children, or other relationships first. Therefore, the majority's space was limited when considering relocation for an extended period, and they gave priority to their relationships.

Critical Incident 4: Limited—Unlimited Space
(For married women or with partner) Respondents were asked how they would respond in the following scenario: "Your husband is offered an opportunity to work in the United States."

Unlimited Space:	Participant refuses to relocate	n=2
Limited Space:	Participant decides to relocate	n=3
	Not applicable (no partner)	n=6

Respondents' comments included:

"If it's important for him, I'd go. I can go anywhere. I've always had a job and I always will. If there is no position for me, they'll make one for me. And if I have to start at the bottom, I am willing to do so because I will rise."

Critical incident 4 did not establish if women were more willing to relocate for the benefit of their partner's careers than for their own careers because the majority did not have a partner. Those who considered it a possibility to relocate to benefit their partner's career were confident they'd have no problem getting a job in the new location.

Critical Incident 5: Strategic Planning—Spontaneity

Respondents were asked what they would decide in the following scenario: "You are offered an administrative assistant. He is an intelligent, assertive, and ambitious man."

Accepted Assistant   n=11

Respondents' comments included:

"I would accept him. I would not feel threatened by him."

"I would keep my eye on him."

"I would accept him only if he's very efficient."

"I would accept him with caution. One always sees competition because it's a man's world."

Originally the answers were to be categorized as follows. If the woman accepted the assistant, it was to be interpreted as spontaneity. If the woman refused the assistant because she anticipated his becoming competition it was to be interpreted as strategic planning. However, the answers to this question indicated that it did not measure what was intended. All the women answered they would accept the male assistant. They did not consider him a threat because they were very sure of themselves. Therefore, these answers could not be interpreted necessarily as lack of strategic planning, but could be an indication of a well-established reputation and a high level of confidence in their capacities.

Critical Incident 6: Work—Family Priority (for Women with Children)

Participants were asked how they would respond to the following scenario: "It is your daughter's or son's birthday and the birthday party is scheduled to begin at 7 P.M. It is 6:30 P.M. and you are at a very important meeting that most probably will last for at least two more hours."

Work: Participant chooses to stay at business meeting   n=4

Family: Participant leaves for birthday celebration   n=2

        Participant decides, depending on meeting   n=1
        and birthday

Respondents' comments included:

"I'd give instructions for my mother and my domestic employee to begin with the activity until my arrival."

"I'm so organized, I plan everything ahead of time. This situation would not happen." In critical incident 6, where the participants had to choose between a birthday celebration and a business meeting, the majority gave priority to work over their child's birthday party. This contrasts with incident 1, in which a child's illness took priority over work.

Critical Incident 7: Assertiveness—Inhibition

"You've worked hard on a special project with a male co-worker. During the oral report in front of your supervisors, he gave the impression that he had done all the work."

| Assertiveness: | Participant chooses to assert herself in a difficult situation | n=7 |
| Inhibition: | Participant avoids confrontation | n=4 |

Respondents' comments included:

"I would not permit such a thing. I'd immediately clarify."

"It would bother me, but I'd stay quiet."

"That actually happened to me once. I immediately called my supervisor and denounced the situation in public."

Critical incident 7, which measures assertiveness, indicates that the majority of these managers were assertive. Even the four whose answers were classified as "unassertive" when using the definitions pre-established for the categories could be considered "assertive" based on the more complete information provided by the oral histories. They indicated that they would not assert themselves in the specific situation presented (a co-worker taking credit for their work in public) because their established reputation provided the needed security in themselves and their merits at work. Two respondents just simply did not accept that a co-worker would dare to do such a thing to them, indicating the type of respect they motivated in others.

Critical Incident 8: Reason—Emotion

Participants were asked what they would decide to do in the following scenario: "Your secretary has been working with you for four years. During this past year, she has been constantly late, has made lots of mistakes, and hasn't met deadlines. You have called her attention to the problem several times. You know she has been going through a crisis after her divorce and has economic problems."

| Reason: | Participant fires employee | n=8 |
| Emotion: | Participant does not fire employee | n=3 |

Respondents' comments included:

"If my secretary is not doing her job and I already have called her attention to the problem various times, I would fire her. Personal problems affect everybody, but the responsibility of the business is not negotiable."

"If I've given her various opportunities and she doesn't improve, I would definitely fire her. I'm nice and I love you, but your home is your home, work is work."

"I had that situation once, but since she normally was an excellent secretary, I was very understanding. I let her have a flexible schedule and delegated work to the other secretary until she was able to solve her situation."

The results of critical incident 8 suggest that reason prevailed over emotions when these women made this type of decision. Only three participants out of eleven chose not to fire their employee in this scenario.

Critical Incident 9: Big Money—Small Money

Respondents were asked what they would do in the following scenario: "Your immediate boss is on a business trip and out of reach. Something important has come up. If you make the correct decision, the company will gain a lot of money; if you make the wrong decision it could lose a lot of money."

| Big Money: | Participant makes decision and assumes responsibility | n=10 |
| Small Money: | Participant delegates or avoids decision | n=1 |

Respondents' comments included the following:

"I'm used to making decisions that move a lot of money."

"I would consult with other managers, but would assume the responsibility for the final decision."

"My boss respects my decisions."

The answers to critical incident 9 establish that 99% of the women in the sample made decisions in which big money was involved in a potential scenario, and that they were, in reality, responsible for the management of big money.

Critical Incident 10: Organization—Improvisation

Respondents were asked how they would handle the following scenario: "You have a lot of correspondence on your desk that needs to be answered. You have two telephone calls on hold and a meeting in 15 minutes."

Organization: Participant delineates preestablished   n=11
                 plan

Improvisation: Participant has no preestablished plan   n=0

Respondents' comments included:

"Being organized is very important; it saves time. And time is money."

"I'm extremely organized."

Responses to critical incident 10 indicated that 100% of the respondents worked in a highly organized manner. They all described a preestablished plan to complete their work.

Critical Incident 11: Strategic Planning—Spontaneity

Respondents were asked how they would approach the following scenario: "The position you aspire to in the future has been traditionally assigned to men. You have already identified your competitor. What strategies would you use to demonstrate you are the best candidate?"

Strategic Planning: Participant delineates plan   n=3

Spontaneity: Participant lets things happen,   n=8
                does not plan

Respondents' comments included:

"I have never worked for a position. I work for money and satisfaction."

"I work like a man."

"I'm proud of being a woman. What a woman can't achieve, no one can."

"Sometimes I feel like Cinderella. The rapidness of my promotions scares me. "

"I have not experienced discrimination for being a women because I don't permit it."

The preestablished categorizing of the responses for critical incident 11 supposedly indicate a lack of strategic career planning for achieving promotions in eight of the participants. Yet, the other information collected during the interviews indicates that dedication to their work and their excellent work performance were the factors that strategically geared these women through their careers, rather than premeditated plans to obtain higher positions.

Discussion, Conclusions, and Implications

Our study examined the social construction of gender in the employment setting and its effect on women and their families. The respondents' answers to questions, and their approaches to critical incidents (potential scenarios) about work and family situations offered the following information.

Effects of Employment on Women, Family, and Organizations

The traditional social construction of gender is being deconstructed (Berger and Luckman, 1967; Berger and Kellner, 1970). There exist other constructions more integrative to explain the phenomena, not of gender, but of people in the organized work and family environments. For example, in the family and work environments, we should be looking for other forms of relating that depart from the traditional, exploitative manner in which we relate to each other. As Frankel (1993) suggests in her introduction, a reevaluation of the responsibility for housework and parenting is necessary. Roles have changed; organizations must transform also. The hunger for power over the other, as strengthened by the scientific and pragmatic paradigm of the differences, only isolates us and creates the appropriate climate for struggling work environments. Resources are limited if we limit them for some and not for others. We base our evaluations of persons under different circumstances, with different access to resources and more or less submitted to the rules and norms of our patriarchal model, on socially validated illusions that create our reality and by which we are programmed without our total conscious knowing.

Are there other forms of relating other than the struggle for power? Yes, there are other more humane relationship structures where power over the other is not the issue. But for this to happen, we need to get over the gender, status, class, money, race, intelligence, and strength differential issues. In the family structure, the nuclear family with its patriarchal structure is just one option. Men, women, and children are establishing collaborative relationships (Ramos Marcano, 1993a). Women are joining to buy and share homes that would have been prohibitive economically for a female head of household. Women are providing child care for each other in order to gain the much wanted economic independence or the educational requirements for better career opportunities. Women are exchanging services that would otherwise have been way over their income. They are learning about the arts, politics, science, and technology. They are learning handy-person work, making the word *handyman* disappear. In other words, they are providing for their own self-sufficiency. This will translate in alternative family structures and gender role models for future generations.

In the work environment, the first female executives in Puerto Rico followed many of the "rules of conduct" that spelled success for men. The authors of this chapter postulate an integrative theory of genders and agree with Rosener (1990) that a second wave of women is making its way into top management not by adopting the style and habits that have proven successful for men, but by drawing on the skills and attitudes they have developed from their shared experiences. These women are succeeding because of—not in spite of—certain characteristics generally considered to be "feminine." They are drawing on what is unique to their socialization as women and creating a different path to the top.

Men are more likely than women to use the power that comes from their organizational position and formal authority. Women ascribe their power to personal characteristics like charisma, interpersonal skills, hard work, or personal contacts rather than to organizational structure. They tend to encourage participation, share power and information, and enhance other people's feelings of self-worth (Rosener, 1990).

Gender differences are more a result of social construction than biological endowment. Generally, men and women do not receive the same socialization. Women are socially trained to be cooperative, supportive, understanding, gentle, and to provide service to others. They are taught to derive satisfaction from helping others. Men are socialized to appear competitive, strong, tough, decisive, and in control. Because of these differences, some authors conclude women make better managers. Others believe men should "feminize" their leadership styles. What were once labeled women's weaknesses and cited as reasons why they were ill suited for top jobs are suddenly the very traits executives are expected to have (Rosener, 1990).

Yet, while some women may be very domineering and autocratic, some men may be more compromising. The notion of male and female management styles can become stereotypes. There are still some women who feel they have to be more macho than men to be respected in the workplace. Thus, linking leadership styles exclusively to gender is a mistake. But to ignore socially motivated differences is to negate men's and women's identity and, consequently, to negate their contribution to organizations (Ramos Marcano, 1992).

Men and women are capable of making different, but equally valuable, contributions to organizations. Organizations must create enabling conditions for both types of contributions to be made and rewarded within the organization, and look for synergy—ways in which men's and women's contributions can be combined to form new and powerful managerial processes and solutions to the organizations' problems (Ramos Marcano, 1992; Adler and Izraeli, 1988).

The latest participative management theories favoring flatter organizations with authority less concentrated at the top simply represent a more effective way to do business; they are not exclusive to women or men. The integration of the best of both genders in the work environment is what determines success (Ramos Marcano, 1992; 1993b; 1994b).

Conclusions

Puerto Rican women in top management positions integrate and reinforce skills and behavior that are socially constructed as belonging to the masculine gender in the employment environment. The belief that the informal support group of these professional women decreases was not confirmed. In fact, these women reported that they could count on support from relatives, friends, and co-workers throughout their careers. It was also found that their support system includes third persons (women) that take care of their household and child care responsibilities in agreement with a previous study by Colberg and Burgos (1988).

All of the participants move freely with unlimited space for short business trips but they did not show the same willingness to relocate for extended time. It was determined that the majority of the participants (n=7) had limited space if they rejected the business opportunity in critical incident 3 because of partner's career, affective ties to family, or if their decision depended first on others' approval. The answers to critical incidents 2, 3, and 4 about the space of these women do not reflect precisely the subjectivity of each woman. A reading of their complete interviews presents other information that amplifies their answers.

Puerto Rican women in top management positions who had husbands and children assigned equal or greater priority to their employment responsibilities than to their family responsibilities. The results did not establish if women were more willing to relocate for the benefit of their partner's careers than for their own careers because the majority did not have a partner or children.

Implications and Recommendations
for Further Research

The findings have implications for industrial-organizational psychology, social policy, and education. In general, psychologists in the work environment should be more aware of the meaning and consequences of work for women. Because employment and family are both valued highly by women, those whose partners, family, or friends do not support their work outside the home will experience increased conflict and stress in their chosen lifestyle.

The women in this study established how they had to pay for services for child care, household chores, and other tasks in order to be able to keep up with their pace of life. In terms of family arrangements, a support network, both instrumental and emotional, is necessary for employed women, especially those in top management positions. This does not necessarily mean the traditional father-mother family.

Based on this study, it is necessary for schools and educational programs, related to women's health, family, and work, to incorporate in their curriculum content about women's issues. Graduate and undergraduate psychology programs in Puerto Rico are beginning to include courses or units in regular courses on gender.

In the organizational area, employee assistance programs and career development programs need to recognize the importance of work and family issues, and the changes in structure and processes in families and in the work environment. Attention must be given to the contributions of employed women to organizational processes and structures. Support groups for employed women, stress management programs, and innovative interpersonal arrangements are essential in any work environment. In other words, women-friendly environments are required. For these transformations to develop, policy-makers must develop the necessary legislation directed toward creating the conditions for social, health, and work services from the perspective of women.

The limitations of this study lead to suggestions for future research. This study emphasized the description of perceived expected behaviors instead of actual behavior. Therefore the way employed women and women in top management construct their reality deserves further study. As Burgos (1986) states, the construction of reality and expected behavior are in the process of socialization. But the relationship between the social construction of reality and the behavior of employed women is not clear and needs to be documented. There is not necessarily an agreement between expected behavior and actual behavior. More in-depth interviews and ethnographic studies are suggested.

Psychologists, social workers, and educators in Puerto Rico face the challenge of understanding the transition of many Puerto Rican women from traditional family roles to less traditional roles. Special attention must be given to the conflicts and problems women in Puerto Rico face in acquiring these new roles. The implications and suggestions of this study are backed up by previous research (Burgos, 1986). A transcultural analysis of the ways women in other countries manage their families and work, discovering differences in perceptions yet many commonalities, will us help redefine gender, work, and family.

Note

The authors gratefully acknowledge the assistance of the Business Research Center and Academic initiatives of the College of Business Administration, the Department of Psychology, and the Center for Research and Psychological Services (CUSEP) of the College of Social Sciences of the University of Puerto Rico, Rio Piedras, Puerto Rico. Eileen M. Colberg received funding for this study from Institutional Funds for Interdisciplinary Research (FIPI) of the University of Puerto Rico. Both authors of this chapter are principal researchers. Evelyn Ramos, Daisy Diaz, Johanna Kercado, and Magda Rodriguez, graduate students of the Department of Psychology, College of Social Sciences, University of Puerto Rico, Rio Piedras Campus, interviewed the women in top management positions and participated in the design on the study. Eileen M. Colberg designed and coordinated the primary research.

References

Acevedo, L.A. (1987). Politica de industrializacion y cambios en el empleo femenino en Puerto Rico: 1974–1982. *Homines, Tomo Extraordinario (4)*, 40–49.

Adler, N.J., and Izraeli, D.N. (1988). *Women in management worldwide.* New York: M.E. Sharpe Inc.

Azize Vargas, Y. (1987). Mujeres en lucha: Origenes y evolución del movimiento feminista. [Women's struggles: Origins and evolution of the feminist movement]. In Y. Azize Vargas (Ed.), *La mujer en Puerto Rico: Ensayos de investigación.* Río Piedras, Puerto Rico: Ediciones Huracán.

Astin, H.S., and Leland, C. (1991). *Women of influence, women of vision.* San Francisco, Calif.: Jossey-Bass.

Berger, P.L., and Kellner, H. (1970). Marriage and the construction of reality: Patterns of communicative behavior. In H.P. Dreizel (Ed.), *Recent Sociology (No. 2).* New York: Macmillan.

Berger, P., and Luckman, T. (1967) . *La construcción social de la realidad.* [Social construction of reality]. Buenos Aires: Amorrotu Editores.

Burgos Ortiz, N. (1986). Women, work, and family in Puerto Rico. *Journal of Women and Social Work, Affilia, 1*(3), 17–28.

Carreras, A. (1985). *Determinacion de antecedentes del motivo de logro en hombres y mujeres en puestos elecutivos.* Unpublished thesis. Rio Piedras, Puerto Rico: Universidad de Puerto Rico.

Colberg Luciano, E., and Burgos Ortiz, N. (1988). Female headed single parent families in Puerto Rico: An exploratory study of work and family conditions. Work and Family: Theory, Research Applications. *Journal of Social Behavior and Personality 3* (Special Issue) (4), 373–388.

Colón, A. (1985). La participación laboral de las mujeres en Puerto Rico: Empleo o sub-utilización. [The labor participation of women in Puerto Rico: Employment sub-utilization]. *Pensamiento Crítico 7,* 25–30.

Colón, A., García, M., and Alegría, I. (1986). *Análisis de las estadísticas del censo de la población: 1970–1980* [Statistical analysis of the population census]. Río Piedras, Puerto Rico: Centro de Investigaciones, Universidad de Puerto Rico.

Colón, A., Mergal, M. and Torres, N. (1986). *Participación de la mujer en la historia de Puerto Rico (las primeras décadas del siglo viente)* [Participation of women in the history of Puerto Rico (the first decades of the twentieth century]. Río Piedras, Puerto Rico: Centro de Investigaciones Sociales.

Coria, C. (1985). *El sexo oculto del dinero* [The occult sex of money]. Buenos Aires, Argentina: GEL.

Council of Higher Education. (1993). *Compendio estadístico de las instituciones de educación superior en Puerto Rico* [Statistical compendium of the higher education institutions in Puerto Rico]. San Juan, Puerto Rico.

Cristiá, M. (1988) Incorporación de la mujer al trabajo asalariado [Incorporation of women in paid work]. *Comercio y producción* (January/February) 20, 37–38.

De los Reyes, V. (1987) Las mujeres seran el 53% de la fuerza laboral. *El Reportrero,* (September 1) 26.

Departamento del Trabajo y Recursos Humanos. (1983a, rev.). *La participación de la mujer en la fuerza laboral* (Informe Especial E-27) [The participation of women in the work force]. Negociado de Estadísticas del Trabajo. San Juan, Puerto Rico.

Departamento del Trabajo y Recuroso Humanos. (1983b). *Serie estadística sobre empleo y desempleo desde 1970–1982–cifras revisadas* (Informe Especial E-37) [Statistical series of employment and unemployment from 1970–1982–revised

figures]. Negociado de Estadísticas del Trabajo. San Juan, Puerto Rico.
Departamento del Trabajo y Recursos Humanos. (1993). *La participación de la mujer en la fuerza laboral* [The participation of women in the work force]. Negociado de Estadísticas del Trabajo. San Juan, Puerto Rico.
Ferguson, K.E. (1984). *The feminist case against bureaucracy development.* California: Sage.
Frankel, J., and McCarty, S. (1993). Women's employment and childbearing decisions. In J. Frankel (Ed.), *The employed mother and the family context.* New York: Springer.
Gali Bras, S. (1989). Fuerte presencia de la mujer obrera [Strong presence of the working woman]. *El Nuevo Dia* (July), 4.
García Vargas, T., and Muñoz Ramos, M. (1993). *Estudio comparativo de un grupo de mujeres y hombres ejecutivos puertorriqueños: Sus características y estilos en el ejercicio del poder* [Comparative study of a group of Puerto Rican women and men executives: Their characteristics and styles in the use of power]. Unpublished thesis. Río Piedras, Puerto Rico: Universidad de Puerto Rico.
Heilman, M.E., Block, C.J., Simon, M.C., and Martell, R.F. (1989). Has anything changed? Current characterizations of men, women, and managers. *Journal of Applied Psychology 74* (6), 935–942.
Junta de Planificación de Puerto Rico. (1987). *Indicadores socio-económicos de la mujer en Puerto Rico* [Social-economic indicators of women in Puerto Rico]. San Juan, Puerto Rico.
Junta de Planificación de Puerto Rico. (1993). *Boletín social: Informe mensual sobre asuntos sociales de actualidad* [Social Bulletin: Trimonthly report on current social affairs] (September–December). Negociado de Análisis Social.
Long, B.C. (1988). Work-related stress and coping strategies of professional women. *Journal of Employment Counseling 25,* 37–44.
Muñoz, V.M., and Fernández, B.E. (1980). *El divorcio en la sociedad puertorriqueña* [Divorce in the Puerto Rican society]. Río Piedras, Puerto Rico: Ediciones Huracán.
Pacheco, A. (1981). *A study of sex-role attitudes, job involvement and job satisfaction of women faculty at the University of Puerto Rico.* Published dissertation. New York University.
Pereida Díaz, G.M., and Rivera Martínez, J.M. (1989). *Determinantes y antecedentes en el logro de las mujeres ejecutivas en la alta gerencia* [Determinants and antecedents in the achievement of women executives in top management]. Unpublished Thesis. Río Piedras, Puerto Rico: Universidad de Puerto Rico.
Picó, F. (1988). *Historia general de Puerto Rico* [General history of Puerto Rico]. Río Piedras, Puerto Rico: Ediciones Huracán.
Picó, I. (1976). Study on women's employment in Puerto Rico. Paper delivered at the Conferencia sobre la Mujer y el Desarrollo, Mexico City, June 10–16, 14–19.
Ramos Marcano, E. (1992). Feminine traits can gain upper hand in the office. *San Juan Star* (November 23), F4.
Ramos Marcano, E. (1993a). Many divorced businessmen becoming Mr. Moms. *San Juan Star* (June 7), F5.
Ramos Marcano, E. (1993b). The Mission of Management. *San Juan Star* (February 22), F8–F9.
Ramos Marcano, E. (1994a). Balancing your personal and professional life. *San Juan Star* (April 4), F8–F9.
Ramos Marcano, E. (1994b). Nuestras contradicciones [Our contradictions]. *El Nuevo Día* (March 1), S6.
Ramos Marcano, E. (1994c). Non-manager managers. *San Juan Star* (February 28), F8–F9.
Rivera Quintero, M. (1980). Incoporación de las mujeres al mercado de trabajo en el desarrollo del capitalismo [Incorporation of women in the job market in the development of capitalism]. In E. Belen Acosta (Ed.), *La mujer en la sociedad*

puertorriqueña. Río Piedras, Puerto Rico: Ediciones Huracán.

Rivera Quintero, M. (1987). El proceso educativo en Puerto Rico y la reproducción de la subordinación femenina [The educational process in Puerto Rico and the reproduction of the feminine subordination]. In Y. Azize Vargas (Ed.), *La mujer en Puerto Rico: Ensayos de investigación*. Río Piedras, Puerto Rico: Ediciones Huracán.

Rodriguez, I.B. (1984). *Autoconcepto de adultos puertorriqueños y su relación con su aculturación, sexo y clase social* [Self-concept of Puerto Rican adults and their relation with acculturation, sex, and social class]. Unpublished thesis. Río Piedras, Puerto Rico: University of Puerto Rico.

Rosener, J.B. (1990). Ways women lead. *Harvard Business Review* (November–December), 119–125.

Sagardía. (1992). Traban las aspiraciones de las mujeres en las empresas. [Clogging of aspirations of women in organizations]. *El Nuevo Día* (May 1).

Schein, V.E. (1973). Relationships between sex role stereotypes and requisite management characteristics. *Journal of Applied Psychology 57* (2), 95–100.

Schein, V.E. (1975). Relationships between sex role stereotypes and requisite management characteristics among female managers. *Journal of Applied Psychology 60*, 340–344.

Wagenheim, K. (1975). *Puerto Rico: A profile*. New York: Holt, Rinehart and Winston.

Chapter Nine
Families of Employed Mothers in Taiwan

Vincent Shieh, Angela Lo, and Emily Su

In the decades following World War II, Taiwan entered a period of rapid social and economic development. The pace of change accelerated markedly in the sixties and seventies. Industrial and agricultural production rose rapidly, as did per capita real income. There also was an accompanying shift from agricultural to heavily nonagricultural employment, with increased emphasis on urban life. These changes, industrialization and urbanization, have drawn increasing numbers of families into social, economic, and familial relationships that differ from earlier traditional forms. And working women are breaking the restraint of traditional family forms by entering the economic scene.

During the past two decades, there has been a noticeable growth of women's labor-force participation. It is mainly because of the increased educational opportunity, which liberalized women's thoughts and advanced family planning. Birth rate decline resulted in fewer child care duties for women. Also, electric appliances have shortened the time required for housekeeping. With less time spent on child care and housekeeping, women have more time and energy to step out of the private sphere to play a broader social and economic role (Chiang and Ku, 1985). In addition, the transition to high-technology industrialization, with increased automation and computerization, opened jobs to women who had more technical skills. The expansion of the service industries also helped contemporary women to increase their employment opportunities and even start their own businesses. Census data shows that there were roughly three million women in Taiwan at the end of World War II, but only 100,000 women entered the job market (3%). However, by 1992 there were about 8 million women in Taiwan and almost half were employed (Taiwan-Fukien Demographic Fact Book, 1992).

Rapid economic development has expanded women's job opportunities, and, concurrently, has had measurable effects on mothers, children, fathers, family structure, and family policy. This chapter will investigate issues and problems raised by the employment of women in contemporary Taiwanese society.

Taiwan's Background
Historical Background

Taiwan is located between the Philippines and Japan, and lies 100 miles off the coast of southeastern China. Between the fourteenth and seventeenth centuries, pioneering emigrants from Fukien and Kwangtung moved to Taiwan, attracted by the opportunity to own land. By the sixteenth century, Europeans arrived. Portuguese sailors, as they sailed past Taiwan, called it "Ilha Formosa." In 1624 the Dutch established a colony around Tainan (South Taiwan), and Spain established colonies to the north. By late 1948, it became clear that the Kuomintang (KMT) would lose China to the Communists, and hundreds and thousands of refugees fled to Taiwan. The KMT government declared martial law in Taiwan and transplanted the Republic of China onto Taiwan under its control (Shi, 1991).

Historically, Taiwan considers itself a "frontiers culture." Geographically, Taiwanese culture is a kind of a "marine culture" (Cohen, 1992). Under various multicultural upheavals during the past four hundred years, Taiwan has brewed its own unique, multi-influenced culture.

Economic Background

Since the late 1960s, the island has undergone economic growth. Its economic structure has been transformed from a predominantly agricultural to an industrial basis. Over half the work force is presently engaged in nonagricultural occupations. Since 1949, Taiwan's economy has grown radically after adjustment for inflation (Cohen, 1992). Between 1952 and 1987, economic growth averaged 9% per year. Per capita income has increased from U.S. $196 in 1952 to U.S. $10,566 by 1993. Machinery and electronic equipment, textile products, and metals are the major exports. Today, commerce, manufacturing, and service industries employ over 75% of the work force, benefiting many people in the society *(Yearbook of Manpower Statistics, 1994)*. However, there are particular groups within Taiwan's society that have not received their fair share from the "economic miracle." One group includes women.

The pattern of change in the female labor force has been predominantly from agricultural to industrial jobs in the last three decades; cheap labor has played an essential role in Taiwan's rapid industrial development as well as continuing economic growth. Since 1970, as a consequence of rapid industrial development, high demands have been placed on the labor force, and particularly female employees. According to Liu's study (1983), female laborers have been clustered in the lower-level technical work required in manufacturing industries such as the food, textile, and garment industries. Even in the 1990s, fewer female laborers are engaged in more high-end industries such as construction, public enterprises, plastics, and petrochemical industries (Lu, 1994).

Parallel to the increasing labor-force participation of Taiwanese women in general, married women's employment rate is also increasing. Married women's labor-force participation rate was 31.4% in 1981 and reached 42.5% in 1990. In addition, the high labor-force participation rate is not merely that of married women without children. Noticeably, there are more and more mothers with school-aged or preschool children going to work. In 1990, the labor-force participation rate was 52.1% for employed mothers having children between 6 and 17 years of age, and 43.7% for employed mothers with children under 6 years of age (*Social Indicators in Taiwan*, 1990).

The labor-force participation rate does vary with marital status, as the *Yearbook of Manpower Survey Statistics* (1994) reports. Women who have never married have a higher labor-force participation rate than women who are married or cohabit. And women who are divorced, separated, or widowed have the lowest participation rate. Single men and women have near equal labor-force participation rates (56.33% for men and 52.45% for women). But in the married group, there are extremely different labor-force rates between married men (83.97%) and married women (44.29%). *The*

Report on Fertility and Employment of Married Women in Taiwan (1994) reports that 33.5% of women quit their jobs when they marry, while 24% of those women reenter the job market later.

Today in Taiwan, employed women constitute approximately 45% of the labor force. For women, the choice to work is not based entirely on income but also on the social gratifications and the self-esteem they gain from outside employment, or the feeling that they are serving society and putting their education to use. At the same time, women have complaints about the increasing discrimination they meet at work. Women employees suffer disadvantages in the areas of promotion, salary, and fringe benefits when compared with men. Even in government jobs, where legal protections are supposed to be enforced, they are paid on a lower scale and shuttled into dead-end positions.

A particular focus on the transition of women's status in terms of social, educational, and economic situations will be made in the following paragraphs.

Women in Taiwan
Background on Their Status

Historically, the position of women in Taiwan was linked to the structure of family. As a result of patriarchal familial values, inequality between men and women existed, as reflected by the absence of women's right to own property, to hold religious positions, and even to have their full names written in the ancestral records (Chiang and Ku, 1985). Influenced by Confucianism, women's subordination in the family lasted for centuries and their positions were determined by a life cycle throughout which they devoted themselves to the needs of their families (Tsui, 1989).

However, the changing social and economic environment and ideology from the West have offered alternatives to the traditional life for women. In the early twentieth century, the liberation of Taiwanese women was reflected in the acceptance of women in college, work outside the home, and participation in politics, as well as in the changes in law regarding the position of women (Pao, 1991). As a result, these newly acquired educational and nondomestic-employment opportunities enabled women to gain some economic and ideological independence.

The development of Taiwan during the Japanese rule (1895–1945) brought few opportunities for women to improve their position, as the Japanese suppressed women traditionally. Before World War II, the status of Taiwanese women paralleled that of women in agrarian societies (Duley and Edwards, 1986). It was not until 1930 that Taiwanese women had the benefit of constitutional changes in their legal status. While the constitution gave women equal opportunities to participate in politics as well as in education and employment, the traditional ideology toward women has changed very slowly. There are still many regulations existing in civil law that are discriminatory against woman. The Family Law favors granting custody to fathers in the event of divorce disputes and requires women to use their husbands' family names, and husbands preserve their authority over managing family properties, place of residence, and the children's surname. It was not until September 1994 that the Council of Grand Justices ruled unconstitutional Article 1,089 of the civil law, which gave fathers priority in deciding issues related to their children. In the past, judges had given priority to the wishes of men when conflicts arose between fathers and mothers over how to exercise their children's legal rights. Now, the article is revised to reflect the equal status of both parents as well as the best interests of children.

Margery Wolf, who has worked on this subject since 1958, wrote that there are crucial differences in the status of Chinese women according to their position in the family life cycle (1972). Both single and married women were subject to innumerable social constraints, which included women holding multiple roles at home, producing male offspring, carrying out household chores, and obeying their in-laws. Their lives were governed by obedience, forbearance, and tolerance, including tolerance of affairs by their husbands. Disobedience to their husbands and in-laws could result in being expelled from their families, upon whom they were economically dependent. As victims of social mores, their exclusive route to raise their status as women was to produce male offspring (Wolf, 1974).

Both social stability and economic growth in Taiwan contributed to the gradual improvement in women's status during the 1970s.

In 1985, Hu Tai-li, a Taiwanese anthropologist, raised some questions after her anthropological field research in a village near Taichung. She demonstrated that many women increased their autonomy and decision-making rights during the process of industrialization in rural communities. Women earned extra money from jobs other than farming and family, which helped them raise their family status and change the stereotype that "men were in charge of business outside the house and women were the masters of affairs inside the house." In addition, the split of the traditional "stem" family system and the loss of power of the heads of households enabled young daughters-in-law to gain more freedom and autonomy in a more independent family unit. Meanwhile, the power of elderly mothers-in-law was in relative decline (Hu, 1985).

There has been tremendous progress by women in Taiwan in the past two decades. There are many more channels through which women's issues may be voiced, and newly founded women's groups have created support for the development of social and political empowerment. Today, women are pursuing higher education and they are more aware of alternatives outside the family and home provided by the increase in adequate child care and career opportunities. Under pressure from women's groups, legislative reform has taken place in the following areas: revision of the Family Law to improve marital property laws and divorce laws; legalized abortion under the Eugenic Health Law; and the Basic Labor Standards Law, which protects the rights of women workers. Currently, women's groups are lobbying to introduce an equal employment bill into the legislature that would protect women in all fields of employment.

Background of Women's Educational Advancement
Education is one of the more influential factors increasing women's status and has played a critical role in Taiwan's transformation. Taiwanese culture traditionally places an extremely high value on education, and good study habits are cultivated from an early age. The educational system has allowed children from poor rural households to earn university degrees. A nine-year compulsory education for all children ensures equal educational opportunities for boys and girls between six and fifteen years of age. The government claims that 99.9% of all eligible children are enrolled in school. Furthermore,

the quality of primary and secondary education in Taiwan is excellent by world standards (Cohen, 1992). According to the most recently available figures, nearly 80% of Taiwan's students go on to high school, although most go to vocationally oriented schools. Forty-four percent of the high school graduates attend junior colleges or universities, and many of the remaining students receive some form of post-secondary vocational training (Hsieh, 1993).

Although education has always been highly valued in Taiwanese society, Taiwanese parents of the preconstitutional era, however, considered educating daughters beyond the needs of household management (Lang, 1946). Economic and educational investments were made in sons rather than daughters because parents knew a daughter would normally be lost to another family after marriage (Tsui, 1987). There is a famous Chinese saying: "Married daughters are like spilled water which you would not be able to get back." Since sons are expected to take on more responsibilities in the family and take care of their parents, men are expected to go on for more education. The inferior status of women in a family is especially pronounced during financial hardship (Wolf, 1970).

However, the constitution adopted in 1930 gave women equal opportunities to participate in politics as well as in education and employment. Since the beginning of the postwar period, education levels in Taiwan have risen considerably. The literacy rate has increased from 57.9% in 1952 to 91.2% in 1985. While only 2.1% and 0.4%, respectively, of men and women received college and post-graduate education in 1952, this percentage increased to 13.1% and 7.8%, respectively, in 1983 (Tsay, 1987). In addition, statistics indicate that besides an overall improvement in the educational attainment for both men and women, the increase is faster for women than for men at all school levels (Tsay, 1987). In 1992, there were 158,906 men and 121,343 women studying for their bachelor's, master's, or Ph.D. degrees, with roughly 45% of college students being women (*Educational Statistics of Taiwan*, 1993). The advancement in education for women not only reflects better opportunities arising from the prolonged years of compulsory education (since 1957), but also the change of parents' attitudes toward education for girls, who were not as likely to receive an equal opportunity for education in the past. Today, young women are provided with the same educational opportunities as men.

In addition to women's education growing rapidly at all levels of formal education, women have gained more self-esteem and self-confidence through their increasing education. The desire to seek satisfaction beyond the domestic sphere and to obtain a higher living standard has led many of these more highly educated women into the labor force. Better opportunities for education and employment have led to a series of changes in Taiwanese women's life. In the meantime, the high demand for cheap female labor in light industry has provided employment opportunities for many of the women even with little or no education (Yao, 1983). These changes transcend major social, political and economic institutions and relate to psychological and demographic dimensions of behavior (Wilber, 1981). As a consequence, modern working women have achieved a higher position in the family and society than their mothers and grandmothers had, and the relationship between a married daughter and her natal family is also in transition (Tsui, 1987). Such transitions are clearly shown among those married women who have control over their own earnings.

Analyzing the effects of level of education on women's employment, the higher the level of education women achieved the higher their employment rate. The census data also show that the more educated women are, the greater the possibility for them to enter the job market initially and reenter the job market after marriage (*Report on the Manpower Utilization Survey in Taiwan,* 1992). Examining the female labor-force participation rate by educational attainment for the past 15 years, the women who graduated from junior college have always maintained the highest employment rate. For example, in 1993, employment rates were 63.65% for junior college graduates, compared with 55.80% for women who finished college and graduate school, 54.87% for vocational school graduates, 40.51% for senior high school graduates, 44.97% for junior high school graduates, 42.18% for primary school graduates, and 28.70% and 18.27%, respectively, for self-educated and illiterate women.

Public opinion on the compatibility of educational attainment between potential marriage partners and women's age at marriage also prevents many women from attaining as much education as they could. The so-called "Ph.D. phobia" could explain why there were 4,612 men pursuing their doctoral degree yet only 869 women in 1992 (*Educational Statistics of Taiwan,* 1993).

In addition, sex differences influence what field the applicant chooses to study, since social values still support traditional gender role models. A recent survey reveals different educational expectations for men and women in Taiwanese society. For example, teacher education and home economics are considered most suitable for women, while technology, engineering, and medical science are suitable for men. The ratio of men to women in studying engineering is 40 to 1. Conversely, in the field of home economics and nursing, students are almost entirely women (Chiang, 1989). Researchers Lo and Shieh (1992) assert that the trend in study choice results from girls and boys receiving different treatment in their families and schools, as well as from society. For example, boys receive more stimulation and interaction from the school teachers in science and math classes, while girls receive attention and encouragement in the Chinese language and social science lessons. In addition, society expects that girls should receive at least a junior college education and that men should at least finish university studies (Hsieh, 1993).

Government policies in compulsory education have benefited women in Taiwan to a large extent, but what is needed are policies to correct biases in the socialization process, as reflected in differences in the levels of educational attainment between men and women. For instance, although women generally have equal educational opportunities, they have been discouraged from going into the science and technology fields, and most well-educated professional women are still expected to bear the burden of household duties and to care for children.

Familial Background

The traditional Taiwanese family usually includes several generations living under one roof. Following the Confucian social codes, the authority of the eldest generation is supreme in the family hierarchy. Such traditional patrilineal families include all male descendants from common ancestors and their wives and children. The prescribed domestic living style is a "join family" with three or four generations under one roof; however, for various economic and sociodynamic reasons, families almost inevitably divided into smaller units. Traditionally, all sons were entitled to inherit an equal share of family properties; it encouraged the division of the join family into smaller nuclear units upon the death of the eldest male, or sometimes even before the death of the father.

In addition, industrialization affected the family structure in the transition from extended families to nuclear families. The most common types of households in present-day Taiwan are small three-generation "compromise" families, and two-generation nuclear families. The elderly who used to live together under one roof as an extended family now live either with one of their children, usually the eldest son, or on their own. In the trend toward nuclear families, however, proper care for the elderly is becoming a problem.

In Taiwan, 73% to 88% of old people lived with their offspring, compared with 28% in the United States, 20% in Denmark, and 42% in England (Hsiao, Chen, and Chang, 1981). Different family styles have different impacts on family life. Based on the Taiwanese tradition, married women usually live with in-laws. In the extended families, three generations live together and grandparents will normally take care of their grandchildren while both parents are working. But as these extended families are reduced to nuclear families, it becomes one of the factors that affect working mothers' child care arrangements (Tsai, 1993).

Particular to Eastern cultures are relationships to in-laws in an extended family. In Taiwan, those women who are married but without children and who lived in an extended family are usually newlyweds. The sudden change of family style or even simply living with the in-laws puts some stress on the couple and makes them feel that they have to do some extra work to please their in-laws. In Chang's research (1988), 88.9% of married women without children had jobs. The double burden of job and extended family was not easily handled. To highlight the impact of the burden of living with in-laws, Chang's study showed that women without children who lived in an extended family still were 3.27 times more likely to experience "increased workload or work hours" than "married women with preschoolers" who lived in homes separate from in-laws.

When women with children do live with in-laws, grandparents usually share the responsibility of child care. And the presence of grandchildren helped to ease the tense relationships between in-laws. Therefore, married women with preschoolers were less likely to experience increased workload or work hours than married women without children even when they all lived in the same extended family.

The Changing Family Support Systems

According to *Statistical Abstract of Taipei Municipality* (1991), the average number of members in each household in Taipei city was 3.96 persons in 1990. In other words, the type of family structure common in the city is now the nuclear family. Traditional join families or compromise families are declining, and with this decline, the traditional family support system in which dependent grandparents take care of grandchildren. In order to supplement changing family functions, child care institutions are increasing (Wang, 1992). Child care has become an issue, especially in large cities where both parents often have jobs and have less time to spend with their children. Even where grandparents could take care of children, some of the young couples feel uncomfortable with such arrangements. One reason is that young parents do not want their children to absorb their parents' old-fashioned ideas. More and more parents prefer to adopt new methods and child-rearing advice from professional child care services.

Another problem that has arisen with child care is "key-children." The term key-children has been newly adopted within the last few years as a term for those children who return to an empty house with their own keys after school (Tsui, 1987). They are usually between seven and thirteen years old, attending elementary school. How these children spend the hours after school can lead to serious anxieties for parents, such as security concerns, potential behavior problems, and parent-child communication problems.

For preschool-aged children, high quality and affordable child care arrangements are needed. Lack of care sometimes places women in a dilemma, choosing between jobs and being caregivers. If women could find appropriate caregivers for support, most report that they could work or work longer hours (Presser and Baldwin, 1980). Since employed mothers always have a hard time finding proper, high-quality child care assistance, such conflict between work and family accompanies industrialization. Therefore, child care issues have become a new political concern during the 1990s (Wang, 1990).

Child care problems do influence women's employment. The smoothness of child care arrangements is also an important factor affecting employed women's degree of involvement on their jobs. In Taiwan, the choice of care providers (except parents) for nurturing children under three years old, in descending order, are grandparents, babysitters, relatives, preschools, and nursery centers (Feng, 1994; Liu, 1985). The high dependency on family members does not mean that relatives give more nurturing. It merely reflects the difficulty of finding ideal care, and the lack of quality, dependable, safe preschools. How mothers choose their caregivers is also decided by how old their children are. For example, mothers are more concerned about finding appropriate babysitters when children are under three years old. When children are older, mothers put more emphasis on finding someone who could coordinate with their schedule (Kao, Yi, Lai, and Li, 1986).

In addition, Taiwan currently faces a housing crisis. Real estate speculation has raised prices to a level that puts home ownership out of reach for an estimated 21% of the population, and homelessness has become common in the cities (Cohen, 1992). In working-class neighborhoods and rural areas, housing is generally of poor quality. Hence, for the newlywed middle-class couple, it is impossible to buy a house on their own if they merely depend on a single income; this economic pressure has become a major factor in working wives finding jobs and maintaining them. As a result, working wives and mothers find themselves in a new relationship to their traditional society, awaking a new era in women's ideologies.

With all the changes in population, demographics, and economic, educational, social, and familial conditions, we have painted a picture of the increase in the female labor force. Therefore, these researchers are concerned more with the influences of women's employment on such variables as change in family functions, the marriage relationship, child care, nurturing, children's socialization, and parenting education, than whether women should work. How has the culture responded to the changing of the traditional female family role, parenting role, family support system, or the new dilemma of the working role? The following are a series of analyses and discussion of the issues.

Mothers' Employment

Life-Cycle Theory

According to family life-cycle theory, each individual needs to face specific needs and duties to complete different life stages in the family. For an employed woman in a dual-career family, the period of time she wants to develop her career is usually her young adult period. Hence, there is a conflict between her developing career and having a family (Wang, 1992). Lu (1980) found that there is a preference for different hours of work during family cycles. Most women liked to engage in full-time or part-time jobs during the first stage (after she is married and before a first baby is born). Between the period from the birth of the first child until the last child reaches three years of age, most women preferred staying home to take care of the toddlers rather than going out to work. Then they preferred to take part-time jobs until their last child reaches adolescence. Finally, when all the children are independent, mothers chose to return to work as in the first stage, taking full-time or part-time jobs.

Effects on the Child

Female employment has become a common social phenomenon in the decade of the 1990s, and, when mothers work, there are effects on the child. Employed mothers not only have the opportunity to satisfy their own personal needs but also, through work, to improve the economic condition of their families as well (Honig, 1984; Yogev and Brett, 1985). For instance, after gaining employment, women complain less about family, spouse, and children; the interaction between parents and children is more positive. Children in dual-career families are more independent, but it is not conclusive how mothers' employment affects children's academic achievement (Honig, 1984). Some research has reported that the academic achievement of employed mothers' children is lower than that of housewives' children (Hoffman, 1974; Honig, 1984; Yogev and Brett, 1985); however, another study contradicts these results. Researchers Kao, Cheng, and Kao (1981) studied 56 children of employed mothers and housewives. They found no significant difference between these two groups' academic measurements.

In M.H. Sun's study (1982), mothers' employment only slightly influenced children's sex-role stereotype behavior; however, the degree of girls' sex-role behavior is lower than that of boys. The researcher also found that the professional rank of employed mothers is correlated to the achievement motivation of some of the children, and girls' achievement motivation and personality adjustment is higher than boys' in the dual-career families.

Wang's investigation (1992) of employed mothers' attitudes regarding their ability to parent found that these mothers perceived their work resulting in (1) inadequate care for their children; (2) insufficient quality time, and (3) their children's sense of insecurity. These negative feelings are offset if the husbands share household work. It is then easier to establish the parent-child relationship, to discipline, and to reduce their children's sense of insecurity. Concurrently, if husbands spend more time caring for children, they have a more positive attitude toward female employment.

Effects on Mother

There are various reasons why women go to work; sense of accomplishment, self-satisfaction, and self-assurance are three. Also, some women work for family economic needs. However, many kinds of pressures, role conflicts, and family function transitions accompany mothers' employment. It sometimes even produces ambiguity in their maternal role recognition (Yi, 1986; Kao, et al., 1986; Wang, 1992). Struggling in the contradictions between family and career, working women need to keep such circumstances in balance.

Researchers report that a woman's working role is the most influential factor that affects her family role development and her child's development (Hsieh, 1985; Kanter, 1984; Wang, 1992). The nature of her job and the hours of work required are decisive elements affecting family lifestyle and quality (Kanter, 1984). Women's occupational characteristics are related to the degree of their role conflict. Various occupation features (part- versus full-time work, regular and evening hours) cause different degrees of conflict between women's working and mothering roles (Hsieh, 1985).

Influences of Female Employment on Sex-Role Evolution and Family Function Transitions

With the increasing labor-force participation of married women, they spend much less time on their family roles (Wang, 1992). Conflicts within traditional female family role expectations are due to the limitation of time spent on child care (Kao, et al., 1986).

While nearly half of Taiwanese women enter the job market, their opinions about traditional gender role stereotypes are in conflict. In Liao's and Cheng's research (1985), 540 employed women and 392 married women were surveyed. Three of four married women reported that they were in charge of family responsibilities. One-third of them said they handle family work well; however, 38.3% of them felt extremely overburdened by their jobs and under tremendous pressure. Another example of conflicting opinion was that 35% of these working women agreed that their work and bringing their talents into full play were regarded as a modern woman's privilege and duty. But an almost equal number (38.7%) disagreed with that opinion. Also, about half of the women surveyed (47.7%) agreed that as modern women, they could fully concentrate on pursuing a career while not necessarily marrying. Modern Taiwanese women's role recognition is in transition.

Sun (1993) reports that the higher the self-esteem of an employed woman and the higher her position, the more satisfied she feels with her role. The first reason for this result is that the employed mother gets more help from her husband and more opportunities to be involved in family decision-making. Hence she feels higher self-value as a housewife. Second, it is easier to bring her skills and talents into the job domain. In addition, she is more economically independent. Therefore, the working woman feels that she is a useful, capable person and receives more respect from society. This builds her self-confidence. A woman's education and achievement has a great effect upon her gender role attitudes. The higher level of education she has, the more modernized gender role attitude she has (Yi, 1982, 1986; Kao, 1985).

However, the higher education and employment level she has attained, the lower life satisfaction she feels (Sun, 1993). Researchers speculate that with a busy working lifestyle, women feel extremely pressured and strained in their marriages and their daily lives (Wang,

1981; Sun, 1982). The majority of these women take the outside job because they hope to make use of what they have learned and pursue satisfaction from their career. But working women still have their mothering role and housekeeping role, so they feel less satisfied and more pressure and conflict. W.Y. Wang (1981) reported that the less time employed mothers spent on their jobs, the less role conflict and higher life satisfaction they felt.

If the husband helps do family work, the wife feels more satisfied with her marriage and family life (Wang, 1981). This research also found that when employed, married mothers get more social support, help from their relatives, and family support, their role conflict decreases and life satisfaction increases.

Traditionally, Taiwanese wives have always played subordinate roles to their husbands. Their major responsibility was to take care of their husbands' and children's daily lives. They did not work outside the home unless they were in need. But, unlike the traditional view, contemporary values assert that husbands and wives are considered equal and should share their responsibilities in terms of economics, family chores, family affairs, and social responsibilities. Education and occupation are considered important elements for both men's and women's growth. Chen (1983) found that the view of marriage in current Taiwanese society is still quite tradition-oriented; employed women facing the family role conflict usually conform or live with the contradiction. That is, they try their best to uphold the expectations from the society in order to decrease their family role conflicts.

Effects on Father
Traditionally, Taiwanese men did not take on any family chores or child care responsibilities. They had only to play their breadwinner role (Parsons and Bales, 1955). But, as more and more women join the labor market, husbands must adjust to their wives' employment. One piece of research (Lamanna, Riedmann, Lei, and Tsai, 1984) found that husbands in dual-earner families felt their controlling power and self-worth were decreasing. Correspondingly, however, wives increased their self-worth and felt more independent. Many husbands reported that they felt that they had worse communication as a couple since their spouses began to work. However, inter-

estingly, the wives felt their communications with their husbands got better once they were employed.

Will men participate in more family work in view of women's employment? From 1984 to 1988, an investigation of employees who were married and had children found that the frequency of male employees involved in child care had increased from 3 to 9% (Fernandez, 1990). Researchers Yi (1982) and Liao and Cheng (1985) found that men were more able to comprehend the problems of balancing family work and career. In the past, most husbands thought their economic role was the greatest contribution to the family; wives did not ask husbands for help in family work no matter how heavy the load so as not to change father's role and the power distribution in the family. However, as employed women changed their family roles due to their increasing workload, men gradually accepted their role changes as wives in dual-career families were correspondingly asking men to increase their responsibilities for family work. Other researchers (Yi, 1986; Wang, 1990) document role strain problems as men adjust to the new social order.

The above discussion has focused on husbands' passive reactions toward wives' employment. Some social scientists assert that these phenomena are naturally in transition. In response to the lessening of females' family role, men are expanding their roles in the families. Pleck (1984a) asserted a "changing role perspective" to illustrate his optimism that men will change their family role in the future. In order to explain the speed of changes in roles, Pleck quoted from Rapoport and Rapoport (1976) that the changing gender role phenomenon is like a psychosocial lag problem, an adjustment problem during a transitional period, rather than an unchangeable social characteristic. Pleck (1984b) theorized that as society modifies educational and social policy, men will make more efforts to play family roles.

The greater number of career women and the growth of the women's role at work is accompanied by the increase in men's family role. According to Wang's study (1992), the wife is no longer taking full responsibility for rearing the children. Some fathers help in the child-rearing as well as helping with housework. Over one-tenth face the dilemma of work and family, and nearly 30% of men sense that sometimes their jobs conflict with their families. Wang's study also found that over one-third of the informants' husbands (36.7%) share the housework; nearly 43% of the informants sometimes do. Nearly half of the informants (46.3%) report that their husbands take care of the children often; over one-sixth of men have taken paternal leave.

Pleck (1984) is also optimistic about the changing role of men within the family. However, because this change will happen slowly, he is more concerned about social policies and educational matters set by the government for the future. In addition, after marriage men tend to take on the main breadwinning role in the family. They try to enhance their earning ability to meet the growing needs of their family. Wang (1994) has addressed the marriage crises faced by modern Taiwanese men. He says that these crises result from three causes: First, a marriage crisis arises because there is a limitation on the man's social development and financial achievement. A pyramid model explains the capitalist economic structure of Taiwan. Hence, class mobility is more rigid as the opportunities for upward mobility are decreasing. A man's career development frequently becomes static, and he has difficulty in fulfilling his expected role—that is, consistently improving himself and keeping the authoritative role in the traditional family. Hence, both psychological and economic factors can contribute to a marriage crisis.

Second, financial crises and retirement affect the marriage. While women invariably take care of their career and family at the same time, men are more focused on work. They have fewer support networks to aid them when work is terminated due to layoff or retirement. Women have established social networks and relationships to fall back on when work is disrupted; hence, women are able to compensate more easily than their husbands.

Third, the less dependent role of the female in society is new to the culture and the marriage relationship. The role of the man in the traditional family was breadwinner, and it is a role threatened by the increased power of the working wife. She brings expanded knowledge and financial resources to the marriage relationship and demands more for her increasing role. This has raised a role conflict for husbands.

Effects on Societal Structure

Taiwan has changed from a traditional homogeneous society into a modern heterogeneous society. As the traditional lifestyle and moral values have given way to modern ways, conflicts have arisen that in turn lead to personal identity problems. In the patriarchal society (Hu, 1981), women had to take care of all the family tasks, and they sometimes held part-time jobs outside the home to increase the family income. This was especially true of wives of farmers because farmers' work is very laborious.

With the advent of industrialization, even more work opportunities became available for women. This helped working women to gain some financial independence, and has already enhanced their status in the family. However, Yeh and Granrose (1991) found that not all women take their work as seriously as their male counterparts do. Most women still regard work as a way of earning extra money or a way of having fun or killing time. When facing a dilemma of work and family, most women still choose the family as priority. For example, when choosing work, women will consider the work and hours carefully to complement their child care duties. Such women will readily give up individual ambitions. Yeh and Granrose reported that men believe the work goals of contributing to company success, advancement, earnings, and task challenge are more important than women consider them.

In the traditional society, social structure was maintained by relationships between neighbors and relationships between relatives. Relationships inside the nuclear family are not necessarily the only or the strongest ones. However, the situation is changing. The alienated and mobile characteristics in modern society cause a greater dependence between members of the nuclear family. So husbands' and wives' personal problems now have a greater impact on the marriage and nuclear family.

Modern working women have to cope with the extra burden from job as well as the traditional burdens of being a wife and mother. The task of child care has been eased somewhat; the number of public and private kindergartens and day care centers has soared since 1971. For example, public day care centers increased in number from 210 in 1971 to 3,467 in 1992 (Feng, 1994). This increasing number reveals the needs of working women and makes their lives easier.

And yet the demand remains greater than the growth: "Since more than 60% of families in all economic classes, in urban areas are nuclear families, public nurseries remain an urgent need for working women in Taiwan" (Hsieh, 1993).

Implications for Public Policy

As more women enter the labor force and share work opportunities with men, the government must address the changing status of women and families. Seven policy suggestions are suggested:

1. Policy should promote more information and counseling services to facilitate affectionate parent-child relationships. The government and educational institutions need to reinforce parent and child interaction, offer professional counseling in dealing with children, and set evaluation strategies to help children's development.

2. Child care for infants and toddlers and preschoolers, and after-school care, must be a priority to support working women. To ensure the quality of services, policy should focus on training, evaluation, and tuition structure.

3. Policy should encourage and assist employers and entrepreneurs to establish supportive working environments in terms of nursery centers and flexible, family-oriented working times to meet the needs of employees.

4. Parental leave policy and job market reentry programs must meet workers' demands for taking care of infants.

5. Equal employment laws for both sexes to protect women's working rights need to be enacted. It is necessary to encourage more women to participate in political activities, and to enter parliament.

6. Adult education is needed in establishing parenting programs, promoting intergeneration relationships, assisting couples' communication skills and growth, and helping them expand their social lives. Additionally, more research on parenting and fatherhood is needed.

7. The labor, social administration and education departments need to support the concept of gender equity, and stress that husbands and wives are supposed to take the dual responsibilities of family and work.

Summary

There has been tremendous progress in Taiwanese women's status in terms of education, job participation, and independence in the past 30 years. However, occupational segregation, position promotion segregation, and unequal pay policy keep employed women working in a sexually biased environment. Therefore, the government needs to enact equal employment laws for both sexes to protect women's working rights in hiring, wage-earning, and promotion. In addition, well-planned child care service policies are really necessary in order to encourage and support married women with children entering the job market. Taiwan has a long way to go to loosen the fixed male-dominated ideologies and reach an equal and harmonious relationship between the sexes in society.

References

Chang, C.-C. (1988). The stress of married women in Taipei and its relations to family style, life cycle and work-or-not. In Center for Population Studies: *Women's research program, occasional paper no. 2*. Taipei: National Taiwan University.

Chen, M.H. (1983). *Research on married career women's role conflict*. Master's thesis, Taiwan: National Normal University.

Chiang, L.H., and Ku, Y. (1985). *Past and current status of women in Taiwan*. Taipei: Center for Population Studies, Women's Research Program, National Taiwan University.

Chiang, L.H. (1989). The new social and economic roles of Chinese women in Taiwan and their implications for policy and development. *Journal of Development Societies 5*, 96–106.

Cohen, M.J. (1992). *The unknown Taiwan*. Coalition for Democracy, Taipei, Taiwan, and The Northern American Taiwanese Women's Association, U.S.A.

Directorate-General of Budget, Accounting and Statistics (1991). *Statistical abstract of Taipei municipality*. Taipei: Taipei Municipal Government.

Duley, M.I., and Edwards, M.I. (Eds.) (1986). *The cross-cultural study of women*. New York: Feminist Press.

Educational Statistics of Taiwan, 1992. (1993). Taipei: Ministry of Education.

Feng, S.L. (Ed.) (1994). *Child care arrangement for preschool children in Taiwanese employed mothers' families*. Taichung: Social Department, Taiwan Provincial Government.

Fernandez, J.P. (Ed.) (1990). The changing American workforce. In *The politics and the reality of family care in corporate America* (pp. 1–12). Lexington, Mass.: D.C. Heath and Company.

Hoffman, L.W. (1974). Effects on child. In L.W. Hoffman and F.I. Nye (Eds.), *Working mothers*. San Francisco: Jossey-Bass.

Honig, A.S. (1984). Child care options and decisions: Facts and figurings for families. In K. Borman, D. Quaram, and S. Gedeonse (Eds.), *Women in the workplace: Effects on families*. Norwood, N.J.: Ablex.

Hsiao, S., Chen, K., and Chang, L. (1981). The issues of senior citizens in Taiwan: Situations and solutions. *Chinese Journal of Sociology 12*(2), 42–48.

Hsieh, H.C. (1993). Taiwan. In L.L. Adler (Ed.) *International handbook on gender roles* (pp. 374–386). Westport, Conn.: Greenwood Press.

Hsieh, K.C. (1985). Research on the relationships between employed women, house-wives, and family stabilities in Taiwan. *Academic Journal of National Cheng-Chi University 51*, 185–212.

Hu, T.L. (1981). *The Gateway of daughter-in-law*. Taipei: Shi-bau.

Hu, T.L. (1985). The impact of rural industrialization on women's status in Taiwan. In Chiang, N. (Ed.), *The role of women in the national development process in Taiwan* (pp. 339–355). Taipei: Center for Population Studies, Women's Research Program, National Taiwan University.

Kanter, R.M. (1984). Jobs and families: Impact of working roles on family life. In P. Voydanoff (Ed.) *Work and family* (pp. 111–118). Hamilton, Calif.: Mayfield.

Kao, S.K. (1985). A comparison between men and women in Taiwan on the selection of occupations. In N. Chiang (Ed.), *The role of women in national development process in Taiwan* (pp. 357–390). Taipei: Center for Population Studies, Women's Research Program, National Taiwan University.

Kao, S.K., Cheng, M.L., and Kao, T.Y. (1981). The adjustment of mother-child relation-ships in the changing society: A comparison between working mothers and housewives. Research Report of National Taiwan University.

Kao, S.H., Yi, C.C., Lai, E., and Li, A. (1986). *Child care problems of married working women*. Taiwan: Commission of Development and Evaluation, Executive Yuan.

Lamanna, M.A., Riedmann, A., Lee, S.R. and Tsai, W.H. (1984). *Marriages and families* (Mandarin edition). Taipei: Chu-liu.

Lang, O. (1946). *Chinese family and society*. New Haven: Yale University Press.

Liao, L.L., and Cheng, W.Y. (1985). Changing women in Taiwan—an outlook. In N. Chiang (Ed.), *The role of women in the national development process in Taiwan* (pp. 631–656). Taipei: Center for Population Studies, Women's Research Pro-gram, National Taiwan University.

Liu, P.K.C. (1983). Trends in female labor force participation in Taiwan: The transition toward higher technology activities. *Economic Essays 11*(1), 293–323.

Liu, K.P. (1985). The nursery problems in a changing society. *Chinese Journal 229*, 10–13.

Lo, A., and Shieh, V. (1992). *A Study from an Educational Perspective to investigate Sex Equity in the classroom between Teachers and Students at Elementary School Level in Kaohsiung, Taiwan*. Presented at the 7th World Council for Cur-riculum and Instruction Triennial Conference. Cairo, Egypt, July 25–August 2.

Lu, Y.H. (1980). Women's attitudes toward career role and family role [under] Taiwan's social change. *Bulletin of the Institute of Ethnology, Academia Sinica 50*, 25–66.

Lu, Y.H. (1994). Economic development and married women's employment in Tai-wan—A study of female marginalization. *Population Journal 16*, 107–133.

Pao, C.L. (1991). Modern Chinese women's thought (1911–1923). In C.L. Pao (Ed.), *Readings in Chinese woman history volume 2* (pp. 305–336). Taipei: Tao-hsiang.

Parsons, T., and Bales, R.F. (1955). *Family socialization and the interaction process*. New York: Free Press.

Pleck, J.H. (1984a). The work-family role system. In P. Voydanoff (Ed.), *Work and fam-ily* (pp. 8–19). Palo Alto, Calif.: Mayfield.

Pleck, J.H. (1984b). Three perspectives and some new data. In P. Voydanoff (Ed.), *Work and family* (pp. 232–241). Palo Alto, Calif.: Mayfield.

Presser, H.B., and Baldwin, W. (1980). Child care constraints, and bearing on the work and fertility nexus. *American Journal of Psychology 85*(5), 1202–1213.

Rapoport, R., and Rapoport, R.N. (1976). *Dual-career families reexamined*. New York: Harper and Row.

Report on fertility and employment of married women in Taiwan. (1994). Taipei: Direc-torate-General of Budget, Accounting and Statistics, and Council for Economic Planning and Development, Executive Yuan.

Report on the manpower utilization survey in Taiwan, 1991. (1992). Taipei: Directorate-General of Budget, Accounting and Statistics, and Council for Economic Planning and Development, Executive Yuan.

Shi, M. (1991). *Four hundred years history of Taiwanese*. Unpublished manuscript.

Social indicators in Taiwan. (1990). Taipei: Directorate-General of Budget, Accounting and Statistics, Executive Yuan.

Sun, M.H. (1982). *Life satisfaction, children's character adjustment, sex role stereotyping, and achievement motivation between working women and housewives*. Master's thesis, Taiwan: National Normal University.

Sun, M.H. (1993). Psychosocial stress of employed women in Taiwan. *Chinese Journal of Mental Health 6*, 13–35.

Taiwan-Fukien demographic fact book, 1992. (1993). Taiwan: Ministry of Interior.

Tsai, H.C. (1993). Employed mother and child care. *Quarterly Journal of Community Development 62*, 61–83.

Tsay, C.-L. (1987). Status of women in Taiwan: Education attainment and labor force development, 1951–83. *Academia Economic Papers 15*, 153–181.

Tsui, Y.L.E. (1987). *Are married daughters spilled water? A study of working women in urban Taiwan*. Center for Population Studies, Women's Research Program, Monograph No. 4. Taipei: National Taiwan University.

Tsui, Y.L.E. (1989). The changing role of working women in Taiwan. In K.C. Chang (Ed.), *Anthropological studies of the Taiwan area: Accomplishments and prospects* (pp. 285–315). Taipei: National Taiwan University.

Wang, H.W. (1994). *The changes of contemporary gender roles and men's marriage crisis*. Paper presented at the Conference of Marriage System and Gender Role Studies. Taipei, September 3, 1994.

Wang, L.-R. (1990). *Balancing work and family-corporate child care*. Doctoral dissertation, Los Angeles: University of California.

Wang, L.-R. (1992). *The investigation on the needs of employed mothers and children in Taipei*. Taipei City Government: Bureau of Social Affairs.

Wang, W.Y. (1981). *The role conflict and life satisfaction of married career women*. Master's thesis, National Taiwan University.

Wilber, G.L. (1981). *The female labor force in Taiwan*. Paper presented at the annual meeting of the Population Association of America. Washington, D.C., March 26–28, 1981.

Wolf, M. (1970). Child training and the Chinese family. In M. Freedman (Ed.), *Family and kinship in Chinese society* (pp. 37–62). Stanford: Stanford University Press.

Wolf, M. (1972). *Women and the family in rural Taiwan*. Stanford: Stanford University Press.

Wolf, M. (1974). Chinese women: Old skills in a new context. In M.Z. Rosaldo and L. Lamphere (Eds.), *Women, culture, and society*. Stanford: Stanford University Press.

Yao, E.L. (1983). *Chinese women: Past and present*. Mesquite, Tex.: Ide House.

Yearbook of manpower statistics in Taiwan, 1993. (1994). Taipei: Directorate-General of Budget, Accounting and Statistics, Executive Yuan.

Yeh, R.S., and Granrose, C.S. (1991). Work goals of Taiwanese men and women managers in Taiwanese, Japanese and American owned firms. *International Journal of Intercultural Relations 15*(1), 107–123.

Yi, C.C. (1982). The dual roles of married working women: Expectation, conflict, and adjustment. In *Proceedings of the Conference on Social Sciences* (pp. 405–430). Taipei: Institute of the Three Principles of the People, Academia Sinica, Taiwan.

Yi, C.C. (1986). *The gender role attitude of married working women in Taiwan*. Taiwan: Institute of the Three Principles of the People, Academia Sinica, Taiwan.

Yogev, S. and Brett, J. (1985). Perceptions of the division of housework, child care, and marital satisfaction. *Journal of Marriage and the Family* (August), 609–618.

Chapter Ten
Families of Employed Mothers in the United States

Dolores A. Stegelin and Judith Frankel

A major change that has affected families in the United States has occurred in the second half of this century. It is the employment of mothers outside the home in huge numbers that has changed the face of family life, and is beginning to change the values and roles underpinning the place of family in the American society.

Although some mothers have always been employed outside the home, they had been in the minority. Those who had done so had acted upon desperate financial need, rarely from a willing choice. They and their families were looked upon as being in unfortunate circumstances. Mothers who chose to be employed outside the home for reasons other than finances were perceived of by the majority of Americans as unnatural mothers, and their children pitied as being deprived of appropriate maternal care.

Within the last 50 years, since World War II, this situation has changed. Today, more mothers in the United States are employed outside the home than not. From 1950 to 1985, the labor force participation of mothers tripled; for married mothers the rate increased 300% (Hayghe, 1986). Participation rates of women in traditional child-bearing years rose from 34% in 1950 to 73% in 1988 (Rix, 1990). The 1990 Census reports that 72.5% of married women with children between the ages of 6 and 17 years of age were employed outside the home, as were 57.1% of married women with children under 6 years, and 51.9% of those with infants under one year.

Employed mothers in the United States are a very diverse group. The traditional family of past history—the father as breadwinner, mother as stay-at-home caretaker, and several children all living under one roof—is no longer the norm. Only 13% of families fit this description today; the dual earner family structure is institutionalized (Lewis, Israeli, and Hootsman, 1992) for married couples. Other popular forms of family life include single parenting as a function of divorce or as a lifetime choice. In 1991 white single mothers headed 19.3% of white families, black single mothers headed 58% of black households, and 28.7% of Hispanic mothers headed Hispanic households (Women's International Network News, 1993). Bender and Leone (1992) state that 70% of families in the United States today are nontraditional. Stepfamilies with various combinations of children living together, shared custody arrangements, homosexual couple parenting, and the continuation of extended family living arrangements represent other nontraditional family forms. Families living in poverty differ from those living comfortably, and represent another strain of family life.

Thus any examination of the effects of maternal employment families in the United States must take all forms of diversity into account, must be very cautious in making generalizations, working with complex data and even more complex analysis and interpretation of that data. With this caution let us proceed to examine maternal employment effects on family life.

Effects on the Mother

For most mothers in the United States today, being employed outside the home is no longer a choice but an imperative. Financial considerations make a two-income family an economic necessity in many cases and a social prescription in others. Where choice is perceived as possible, it is made on the basis of beliefs about the power of maternal care, career orientation, age and number of children, availability of child care, employment options, domestic obligations and spousal/other support systems (Frankel and McCarty, 1993). According to Nock (1987), the costs of being employed are compared with the costs of not being employed in making maternal employment decisions.

Nature of the Work

How workplace participation affects women depends heavily on the nature of the job. Most women are clustered in female-dominated jobs such as clerical and service positions that are low paying, under-utilizing their skills and offering limited promotion opportunities. Many women are employed in part-time and temporary positions. There has been an increase in the number of professional and managerial women recently, and this affects the satisfaction of the women involved. Mothers who are professional women have the highest labor force participation (Cherlin, 1987 cited in Olson, Fiexe, and Detlefsen, 1990). Clerical/service type jobs and professional jobs have both stressors and rewards, depending upon the nature of the job. According to Baruch, Biener, and Barnett's 1987 study (cited in Sears and Galambos, 1993), the quality of the role will influence whether the consequences are positive or negative for a woman's life.

Negative Job Qualities

When work conditions have been examined by research, many more factors appear to have a negative outcome on worker satisfaction, as cited by Sears and Galambos (1993):

Factors such as shift work, role ambiguity, technical changes, low job control, low or high job complexity, repetition and routinization, supervisory responsibilities, absence of social support, work overload, underutilization of skill, inadequate income, and low occupational status have been negatively associated with employed women's well-being. . . sexual harassment and sexual discrimination are much more likely to be faced by female workers. (p.53)

Jobs that combine high levels of demand with low control over those demands exhibit negative qualities (Caplan, 1985 as cited in Sears and Galambos, 1993).

Many women are employed in the service industry, giving direct care to others. Being employed in direct caring, i.e., as a nurse, teacher or counselor, can be a stressful quality of the job and lead to burnout.

Computerization of office environments, which originally was seen as a positive aspect of employment, now brings with it many problems for female employees. Some of these aspects include eyestrain due to poor lighting and staring at computer screens for hours on end, noise and social isolation (Haynes, 1991 cited in Sears and Galambos, 1993).

Poor physical conditions, chemical and radiologic hazards can lead to infertility, abortions and birth defects (McDonald, 1988 cited in Sears and Galambos, 1993).

Kandel, Davis and Riveis (1985), cited in Sears and Galambos, (1993) summarize Pearlin's life strains model of stress. In addition to Pearlin's four strains they found three others. The four strains are role overload, depersonalization, inadequate rewards, and noxious work environment. The added three strains are "nonreciprocity (feeling exploited in the work situation), constriction of self (nonutilization of skills), and lack of control (undesirable job pressures)" (Sears and Galambos, 1993, p. 55). This analysis seems to encompass most of the negative qualities of jobs that the majority of women in the United States hold at this time.

Positive Job Qualities

So many of the features of typically female positions do seem to be negative, that we must not overlook the positive possibilities of some of the jobs that women hold. Those jobs that are complex (Verbrugge, 1986 cited in Sears and Galambos, 1993), and offer the woman responsibility, a sense of control over her own labor, reasonable pay, promotion possibilities, utilization of skills, security and a sense of equity with male co-workers are jobs with positive qualities.

Many jobs have both negative and positive qualities, and then the situation is idiosyncratic, the results of these qualities being specific to the particular job, time, place and job-holder.

Effect on Health

Sears and Galambos (1993) summarize the research in this area. In spite of the possible negative qualities of jobs that are hazardous to one's health, overall, employed women showed fewer signs of psychological distress than nonemployed women. At midlife, healthy women who continue working increase their well-being.

Married, employed women with 3 or fewer children at home have better mental health than nonemployed mothers. However, these effects are offset in the case of employed mothers with many preschoolers at home.

Work strains were associated with depression in an indirect way through their relation to work stress. They first show specific role stress either at work or at home, then they show more global forms of stress, for example, depression.

Life Satisfaction

General satisfaction does depend upon satisfaction in the various roles one plays in life. Employed mothers play many roles: mother, worker, spouse, daughter, friend, and so on. The way in which these roles are played out and the demands of each role, the support the player receives in meeting the demands and expectations of each role will help determine whether life is satisfying or dissatisfying for the woman involved. Multiple roles can have very positive effects:

1. Self-esteem can be enhanced by doing several things comfortably at the same time.

2. Multiple roles can provide a variety of social contacts.

3. Employment while meeting one's domestic role can enhance the domestic role by increasing one's financial resources (Sears and Galambos, 1993).

4. Job satisfaction can generalize to other areas of life (Crohan, Antonnuci, Perry-Jenkins, Huston and Crawford, 1989 in Sears and Galambos, 1993).

5. Congruence between roles held and roles desired leads to general satisfaction.

On the other hand, multiple roles can lead to role strain. This will occur most generally when the roles held are not a match with the roles desired. A summary of research reports " . . . stress of managing multiple roles is greatest, and the psychological benefits least, when work and family role responsibilities are both heavy" (Emmons, et al., 1990 cited in Williams, K.J., Suls, J., Alliger, G.M., Learner, S.M., and Wan, C.K., 1991). Specifically, role strain has been found to be greatest for mothers with young children and those with spouses who do not share in domestic work and child care. Single mothers face the difficult situation of carrying both work and maternal roles alone.

Married Women and Employment

Married women can experience multiple roles in several ways. They can experience crossover, where the experience in one role, positive or negative, leads to positive or negative interactions with the spouse at home. Or they can experience spillover, where a positive or negative experience in one role carries over to the other role for the person themselves (Bolger, DeLongis, Kessler, and Wethington, 1989 cited in Sears and Galambos, 1993). Marital adjustment is thus affected by the way in which each role is experienced by the women and the effect of this experience on their spouse.

Yogev (1983) found that married professional women had positive attitudes toward their dual rolels. Unlike earlier research, this study showed that professional women do not experience internal ambivalence about combining work and family. The relationship between age and sex-role conflict for professional women in human services was studied by Soled and Blair (1990) but failed to show significant relationships between female age and sex-role conflict. This is an area in need of further exploration.

For wives, work overload and lack of boundedness or the feeling of never being done can lead to high marital strain, psychological distress and low sexual satisfaction (Sears and Galambos, 1993). Husbands exchange inconvenience, more domestic work and less sexual activity due to fatigue—for increased financial resources.

Marital adjustment in general depends on gender role attitudes, the degree to which the couple can manage time and energy constraints, and the ability to set priorities for family and work (Hochschild, 1989).

Single Women and Employment
Life is more difficult for single mothers who are employed because they often lack the support offered by a spouse. They must carry several roles by themselves, resulting in time and energy problems. They lack two incomes and so face financial hardships. Statistically, single mothers with young children are among the poorest population segment in the United States. Yet, in spite of these problems, many of them manage, through hard work and social support from family and friends, to develop increasing self-esteem and social contacts through employment.

African American and Hispanic Mothers
To remind the reader, the United States is a country that contains a large heterogeneous population of over 200 million people, living in

diverse fashion, rural, urban, suburban, wealthy, comfortable, and poor, in a huge landspace with diverse cultural heritages and backgrounds. Any generalizations about the lives of employed mothers must therefore be taken very cautiously. To exemplify this point, we would like to briefly discuss the lives of employed mothers in two important groups of Americans—Hispanics and African Americans—since so very much of the research reported in the literature and summarized here thus far has been about white, middle-class, employed mothers.

African American mothers have been employed outside the home in the United States for many years. Like white women, African American women assume major responsibility for the domestic role in their families. If they feel a lack of resources to meet the demands of their multiple roles, they experience high levels of stress. To cope with this challenge married mothers develop strategies influenced by interrole conflict and marital status, as described by McLoyd (1993). They tend to engage in structural and personal role redefinition, trying to improve the level of their role performance, and rearrange their time to meet children's needs as their first priority. Single mothers, on the other hand, have fewer options, and rely on improving the quality of their role performance to cope with role stress.

While some contemporary scientists continue to emphasize "machismo," the Chicano family as patriarchal and possessing destructive aspects, many other contemporary scholars reject such stereotypes. Valdez and Coltrane (1993) summarize changes that are occurring, noting that Chicano fathers are now engaging more in child care, that gender relations are more equal although not truly egalitarian, with the family maintaining a facade of patriarchy while women assume more daily authority. Extended families continue to be a hallmark of Mexican American families, and in some way affect child care possibilities.

Domestic Responsibilities

A summary of the research shows that daily household chores are still considered the domain of women, to their cost. Stoltz-Loike (1992) says:

The issue of household responsibility is especially important when considering women's status in the workplace. Women with high family in-

comes can hire household help to partially relieve the strain of their multiple roles. For many women . . . relieving the role conflicts . . . means reducing the importance of one of the roles or commandeering more help from other household members or both. (p. 250)

One way that the challenge of housework has been faced by women is to spend less time engaged in domestic tasks (McCullough and Zick, 1992).

Summary on Mothers

The conclusion almost all studies reach about women and their multiple roles is that juggling work and family roles is a major task for women in the United States, one that is highly complex, one that can have negative and/or positive consequences. If there is a match between role expectation and role performance, the outcome for employed mothers tends to be satisfying and self-fulfilling.

Effects on Fathers

There has not been a great deal of research conducted on the effects of maternal employment on fathers, which in itself is very telling. Traditionally, in the recent past, men expected to be the breadwinners for their families, and to have their wives attend to the domestic and childcare chores of the family. According to Parsons the sex role differentiated nuclear family is best suited to the modern urban industrial society (Ritner, 1992), but that has changed. Young men today expect their wives to be employed and to contribute to the family income. They expect them to work outside the home in the same pattern that men follow, a continuous work curve even after the birth of children.

Interest in father's participation in child care and household chores has developed as a function of the vast numbers of women in the work force and research evidence that fathers play a major role in their children's development and socialization (Lamb, Pleck, and Levine, 1987). This image of the "new father" has received news media attention and is a popular one today. However, it is important to note that the older traditional images retain significant power and are still culturally dominant in the United States (Pleck, 1987).

Father's Participation in Family Work

Studies indicate that fathers report low levels of participation in both domestic and child care activities compared with the mother's level of participation (Pittman and Kerpelman, 1993). In dual-earner families, if the wife had a liberal attitude, the husband participated more; if she had a traditional attitude, he participated less in domestic and childcare work (Barnett and Baruch, 1987). Jump and Haas (1987) summarize the research and conclude that fathers in dual career families are more active in child care, ". . . but fall short of egalitarian parenting" (p. 99).

Fathers' involvement with their infants depends on the fathers' personality in single-parent families, but does not in dual earner families (Crouter, Perry-Jenkins, Huston, and Crawford, 1989 cited in Sears and Galambos, 1993). In dual earner families, fathers' participation was predicted by personality (Valling and Belsky, 1991). However, this is an area of research in need of more elaborated investigation.

Fathers' participation in domestic work and child care remains "something of an illusion" (Backett, 1987). And increased paternal participation will not lead to uniform and unambiguous results for the mother (Lamb, Pleck, and Levine, 1987). The cost of mothering under the traditional system was, and remains, high. Giving up some of the power of the traditional domination of the home without gaining equal power from the marketplace leads some women into questioning the sharing of the parental role. However, the majority of mothers are ready for egalitarianism.

Father's Satisfaction in Dual Career Families

Pittman and Kerpelman (1993) report that while wives' satisfaction with their dual earner role is greater when supported by their spouses, the opposite is not always the case. Fathers who are highly engaged in child care sometimes receive ambiguous levels of support from their wives, negatively affecting the fathers' levels of satisfaction. There are many positive effects of paternal participation in child care. Increased participation leads to closer, more satisfying relationships with their children; the opportunity to witness and take part in their development; and a feeling of competency through child care. The negative effects are compelling—diminished earnings; less opportunity for career advancement; marital friction; boredom with the day-to-day household chores; disapproving friends; and social isolation (Lamb, Pleck, and Levine, 1987). Sharing the breadwinner role may have some positive health effects on men. Being the only breadwinner has placed great stress on men, and may be a major cause of their shorter life expectancy in the United States (Ritner, 1992).

Ethnicity, Social Class, and Fatherhood

In the United States, there is great heterogeneity among families along ethnic, religious, racial, and class lines. Does fathering differ along these lines? Until very recently, popular wisdom and the research of social scientists portrayed minority fathers in a very stereotypical way. Today, these narrow portraits are being called into question, and we are finding out that there is no clearcut, monolithic African American, Asian American, Native American, or Hispanic family. There are regional and class differences within each group that are powerful (Mirande, 1991). More recent research reported by Mirande suggests the following:

Black fathers, especially middle-class fathers often are very much involved and play an integral role in the family . . . appear to be authoritative. . . . Latino fathers also play a distinct and unique role in the family, but it is not always the role of strict disciplinarian. . . . Latino and Asian fathers appear to be warm, affectionate and nurturing, especially with very young children (p. 77).

Research from a less ethnocentric perspective is called for to address this issue.

Summary about Fathers

While gender roles are changing in the United States, the change is very slow. With more and more mothers employed outside the home, paternal participation in the family will be forced to change for the family to function effectively. Presently, research shows that fathers do not participate as much as mothers in domestic and child care, but that when they do there are rewards for them. As fathers come to engage in more child care and play a larger domestic role in the family, the entire pattern of familial roles will change as well.

Outcomes of Maternal Employment on Children
Overview

The postwar era in the United States has reflected rapid changes in demographic variables. Since 1975, dramatic changes in maternal employment have been observed. Increasing numbers of mothers have placed their children in nonparental care facilities and such practices have now become normative. Because of social and economic changes, Americans have come to view the development of their children differently. The early psychoanalytic perspective placed the critical aspects of secure emotional development of the child almost entirely upon the mother and the mother-child relationship. Indeed, initial reactions to both maternal employment and nonparental child care were viewed very negatively, both from a moral and psychological perspective. Now, Americans believe that preschoolers can benefit from nonparental care that provides peer interaction, cognitive stimulation, and social/emotional avenues for growth and development. This chapter reviews the literature on outcomes for children of maternal employment and nonparental child care. Most of the research conducted in this area has focused on children placed in child care centers or university lab school settings. Also included in this chapter is a section on family day care, thought to be one of the least understood areas of child care and one in need of further research and investigation.

As recently as 1970, only 3 out of 10 preschool-aged children in the United States had mothers in the work force. By 1990, that proportion had increased to 5 out of 10 preschool children, and it is predicted to increase even further by the year 2000 (Blank, 1992). At the rate of current trends, four out of five women in America between the ages of 25 and 54 will be working by the turn of the century. Thus, a child care crisis confronts this nation and it grows more severe every day. The question no longer is "should a mother work?" but rather "when will mother work or go back to work?" With these startling demographics, it seems appropriate to seek some solutions to the issue of quality of child care and to ask "what effect does maternal employment have on the child?"

Quality of Child Care

The quality of child care that is provided for young children today will help to shape the work force for tomorrow. The millions of children in America that spend a significant part of their childhood in child care are vital to the nation's future economic health and competitiveness. To prepare the next generation to be productive workers, the nation must ensure that every child gets a strong early foundation for learning (Blank, 1992). America's current child care system is somewhat piecemeal and patchwork in its make-up. Families who can afford quality care certainly are at an advantage over those families who must somehow make do. Federal funds for the expansion of Head Start and other government-sponsored early childhood programs are expanding, and this gives us hope for families who cannot afford high-quality child care.

Child Care Needs by Age Group

During the late 1980s, the need for child care for infants and toddlers increased dramatically to 5 million young children. The United States is only beginning to catch up with some European countries that have much more advanced child care policies already in place. The recently passed Parental Leave Act should open doors to those parents who have very young children and who need to have more flexibility in staying home with them. Approximately 50% of mothers of infants up to one year old are working. The cost for this care is high and the choices are usually few. Around the country, waiting lists for infants and toddlers are usually the longest; the average wait is nine months to a year for infant care.

There are also over five million 3- to 5-year olds in the United States in need of care. Although there are more programs in existence for this age group, most of these programs are run on a part-day basis, even though most parents work full time. This results in more fragmented child care services and creates more disruptive lifestyles for both children and parents. Some efforts to increase collaboration among child care providers and other early childhood services may increase the number of full-time programs or at least increase the communications among the various early childhood providers.

One of the age groups of children needing child care and receiving the most attention in the past 10 years has been the 6- to 13-year old group, which numbers over 16 million. An increase in the number of after-school programs is helping to alleviate this child care need. Still, with youth violence on the rise, there remains great concern for the quality of care these children receive or the total absence of such care for many children. Many school-age children loiter in streets or playgrounds after school or go home alone or with other children to an empty house. One report (Wellesley College Center for Research on Women, 1987) found that in Los Angeles nearly one-quarter of 7- to 9-year olds were in self-care after school. Many parents feel uncomfortable with these arrangements but have no alternatives. Elementary school teachers cite isolation of children and a lack of supervision after school as the major reasons children have difficulty in school.

The above demographics simply point out the critical need for child care, the lack of sufficient child care slots for infants and toddlers, the fragmented nature of the preschool programs, and the burgeoning problem of after-school care for children. The need for child care is indisputable. What about the effects of this care on children?

Effects of Child Care on Children: Historical Perspective

Parents, teachers, and child development experts agree that good child care makes a positive and permanent difference to a child's development. Child care that works for children is that which keeps group sizes small and has few children per adult caregiver. Children in these types of settings are more likely to receive more attention and get more chances to improve their cognitive, social, and language skills (Blank, 1992). Numerous research studies validate the need for appropriate child-adult ratios. In addition, good child care is staffed by individuals who have formal training in child development or early childhood education and are familiar with the developmental needs of children. Lack of staff turnover is another positive indicator for a child care setting. Children need stability both at home and in their child care settings. When child care staff average a national turnover rate of approximately 40%, then we have reason to be concerned about this particular aspect of quality child care.

While many states are upgrading their child care standards, there remain many important and serious issues related to the ability of child care centers and family child care homes to deliver and provide really quality care.

With some noteworthy deviations, the history of research on nonparental care in the United States parallels secular changes in the reliance on and attitudes toward nonparental care (Lamb, Sternberg, and Ketterlinus, 1992). In the 1950s, when maternal employment was seen as more harmful to children, there were few relevant studies focusing on maternal employment and its effects. Researchers did not ask about substitute care arrangements or their benefits during this era. By 1970, Caldwell, Wright, Honig, and Tannenbaum (1970) published the first study focusing directly on the effects of day care, in this instance an impressive intervention program at the University of Syracuse. They reported that day care did not harm children or their relationships with their mothers, and because this conclusion ran counter to widespread professional and popular beliefs at the time, it received a great deal of attention and became quite controversial. In late 1973, contrasting results were obtained in research conducted by Mary Blehar (1974). She observed children in a standardized separation-reunion procedure modeled after Ainsworth's and Wittig's Strange Situation and concluded that 2-year olds exhibited detachmentlike behavior and were avoidant of their mothers after being placed in group day care, and that 3-year olds became angry and resistant.

Although the patterns of response differed depending on the children's ages, Blehar's admonition was clear: Day care is harmful for both 2- and 3-year old children and thus, presumably, for infants as well. In spite of Blehar's research, the women's movement and the increased interest in child development research brought about more and more research related to child care. By the mid-1970s, several researchers had attempted to replicate Blehar's original study and findings. Contradictory findings led researchers to believe that Blehar's observations of child behavior may have been more of a reflection of temporary maladjustment rather than true psychopathology. Also, other researchers established that a child in a day care setting can form an attachment to the caretaker, assuming relative consistency and constancy, without supplanting the child's own relationship to parents. These findings came as much relief to parents who were struggling with the uncertainty of the effects of child care on their children. The effects of day care on children's interaction and behavior with their peers were unclear: Some researchers reported that day care, especially early-initiated day care, increased aggressiveness, whereas others reported that day care and the interaction with other children actually could facilitate cooperativeness and sociability. By and large, research out of the 1970s established that day care for children need not have bad effects on them (Belsky and Steinberg, 1978; Clarke-Stewart and Fein, 1983; Scarr and Hall, 1984).

Beginning in the 1980s, and continuing today, researchers in child development are exploring more refined questions about the effects of maternal employment and child care on children. According to Lamb, Sternberg, and Ketterlinus (1992), the research question has now become "What variations in the quality of care affect the outcomes for children?"(p. 217). Because early research regarding the effects of child care on child development did not include definitions and variations of "quality," many children were placed in poor quality day care settings. Child care policy would have been better served if government-sponsored children's programs had been established with high quality indicators in mind, in order to establish a norm for private sector child care facilities.

Another major research thrust that emerged from the earlier research is related to the effects of child care on infants and toddlers. J. Belsky has contributed a great deal to the literature on infant child care. He raised a troubling question: If day care is acceptable for preschool-aged children, does it necessarily generalize to infants? Since 1980 a number of researchers have studied the relationship between day care and infant-mother attachment, utilizing Ainsworth's and Wettig's Strange Situation procedure. Numerous studies and reports seemed to present an unclear picture. In 1986, Belsky, however, surprised the research community when he concluded that he was sufficiently persuaded by new evidence that day care indeed had adverse effects on attachment. Belsky's dramatic conclusion was that placing infants in child care settings for more than 20 hours per week, initiated in the first year of life, increases the risk of insecure infant-mother attachment.

Belsky's conclusions received widespread attention because, by this time, most mothers with infants were now in the labor force. Following Belsky's announcement, other researchers tried to arrive at more representative conclusions, since Belsky's statement was based on relatively few studies that had inconsistent research methodologies and varied samples of mothers and infants. Several researchers reviewed the data and came to more positive conclusions about the outcomes for infants who are placed in child care settings. Among these were Clarke-Stewart (1988, 1989); Lamb and Sternberg (1989); and Thompson, (1988).

Family Day Care

Family day care is receiving more attention in the child care field for several reasons. First, the growing demand for child care, as depicted above, is straining the systems that are in place for the provision of child care. Secondly, the post-Reagan era of privatized funding and reduced governmental regulation explains why family day care is getting more attention. Compared with child care centers, family day care is highly privatized in its funding and more likely to elude (not always intentionally) governmental regulation (Kontos, 1992).

Family day care also provides women with the opportunity to stay at home and care for their own children as well as for others and to earn an income while doing so. Over the years, family day care has existed in the shadow of larger, center-based programs. However, as day care demands increase, parents and policymakers are being forced to pursue all possible options for quality child care. The fact is, while day care centers have received more attention from policymakers and researchers in the past, families continue to rely on family day care more than any other form. Perhaps this fact alone should provide a rationale for better understanding and supporting the family day care system. The most recent family day care licensing study found that there were 223,351 regulated family day care homes (including group homes) in the United States (Kontos, 1992).

Two types of families gravitate toward the use of family day care. These families include those with mothers who are employed part time and families with children under the age of three years. According to Hofferth and Phillips (1987), the increases in use of family day care between 1965 and 1982 can be accounted for by these two groups. Although data indicate that child care use is increasing at a faster rate in child care centers than for family day care, the reasons most cited for the use of family day care include the flexibility of hours, the homelike environment, more affordable rates, and the convenience or closeness to home for the child and parents (Platt, 1991; Stegelin and Frankel, 1994).

In recent years, state and national programs aimed at recruitment and retention of caregivers as well as investigating and promoting the quality of family day care have surfaced. These initiatives are enhancing the perception of family day care and are giving it a new sense of vitality. Indeed, family day care providers need more recognition and support. Family day care has been investigated but in less formal ways. The results of research on family day care centers have been published in journals and magazines that are not traditionally as scholarly as the research done in child care centers. Susan Kontos (1992), in a monograph done for the National Association for the Education of Young Children (NAEYC), does a thorough job of reviewing the current literature base on family day care.

Factors that influence parental choices related to child care vary. Family day care has a solid role in the child care marketplace, and its most loyal and consistent customers are mothers of infants and toddlers and mothers who work part time. Even though the perception is that family day care is almost always less expensive than center-based child care, recent cost estimates suggest that family day care and center-based care are similar in price (Hofferth, 1989). Kahn and Kamerman (1987) point out that the supply of family day care is fairly elastic, able to respond quickly to demand with rapid start-up, little initial investment, and no need for additional buildings or an administrative structure.

Concerns still exist, however, around the issue of licensing, regulation, and monitoring of family day care homes. Serious questions arise as to whether parents are able to recognize poor quality child care indicators, particularly in family day care homes. The issue of quality of care in family day care homes is another reason for expanded research of family day care. If family day care home providers could receive more educational, policy, and financial support, the quality of these centers might become better and there might be more consistency in care from one provider to another. The current milieu of family day care calls upon the parent to be the primary (and sometimes the only) judge of the quality of care. And sometimes these parents are swayed more by geographic location, convenience, lower cost, and homelike qualities of the family day care setting, and they may overlook such dimensions of child care as adult/child interaction, adult/child ratios, and quality of educational and cognitive stimulation.

Summary of Research Findings

In general, the research on the effects of child care on young children is at best inconclusive. The need for more refined research with longitudinal methodologies is indicated. Also, qualitative research approaches that allow the investigator to study the young child in natural settings rather than constructed, artificial research settings such as the Strange Situation (which has been questioned with regard to validity and reliability) allows us to study children in greater detail and within richer contexts. Caution must be followed in the interpretation of the earlier research that showed avoidant behaviors based on the strange situation context. However, there is a need to better understand the course of emotional adaptation of young children in child care settings and to better understand if there is any prognostic value in observing certain types of avoidant behavior when children are first placed in child care. Whether this behavior has long-term effects on the child's development is still not known. There remains an urgent need for further research with more diverse child populations on the antecedents and consequences of individual differences in Strange Situation behavior, as well as for research on alternative measures of studying attachment security.

While the scientific and ideological debate continues as to the effects of maternal employment/nonparental care on children, the fact is that more and more Americans are placing, and will continue to place, their children in child care. Thus, one major goal of both researchers and policy-makers should be to work toward a higher overall standard of care, particularly for infants, since we do know that the earliest life experiences are the most influential. Adverse effects of early child care can be attenuated or reversed if better quality child care were available. In terms of family day care, more research is needed to better understand the rationale for parental selection of family day care, the difference in outcomes for children in family day care versus child care centers, and research related to policy for both family- and center-based child care. Of particular concern is the need to better inform parents of what constitutes quality child care and what specific indicators they should look for in selecting child care for their infant, toddler, preschooler, or school-age children.

Policy Implications

Twenty-one years ago, Congress passed legislation that would have established a national child-care program to provide free day care for poor families and subsidized day care for middle-income parents. In his veto message to Congress, Richard Nixon said that the $2.1 billion-a-year plan demonstrated "fiscal irresponsibility, administrative unworkability and family weakening implications" (Lamb, Sternberg, and Ketterlinus, 1992). Although Congress had passed the bill by a wide margin, the veto could not be overridden. The passage of time has brought about a change in political attitudes toward government support of day care for working parents, and new measures have been introduced that commit federal funds to aid states and cities to expand child care service.

There is a growing concern that providing quality child care must become a high priority for state and federal legislators. In 1988, the U.S. Senate Committee on Labor and Human Resources submitted the following findings to emphasize the serious nature of the problem:

1. The number of children living in homes where both parents work, or living with a single parent who works, has increased dramatically over the last decade.

2. The availability of quality child care is critical to the self-sufficiency and independence of millions of American families, including the growing number of mothers with young children who work out of economic necessity.

3. High-quality child care programs can strengthen our society by providing young children with the foundation on which to learn the basic skills necessary to be productive workers.

4. The years from birth to age six are critical years in the development of a young child.

5. High-quality early childhood development programs are cost effective because such programs can reduce the chances of juvenile delinquency, adolescent pregnancy, and improve the likelihood that children will finish high school and become employed.

6. The number of quality child care arrangements falls far short of the number required for children in need of child care services.

7. The rapid growth of participation in the labor force by mothers of children under the age of one has resulted in a critical shortage of quality child care arrangements for infants and toddlers.

8. The lack of available child care services results in many preschool and school-age children being left without adequate supervision for significant parts of the day.

9. Many working parents are unable to afford adequate child care services and do not receive adequate financial assistance for such services from employers or public sources.

10. A large number of parents are not able to work or to seek the training or education they need to become self-sufficient because of the lack of affordable child care.

These findings clearly indicate that the major issues and problems that need to be resolved include: providing affordable child care, maintaining and regulating the quality of child care, and subsidizing and administrating day care services in an equitable way (Thorman, 1989; Stegelin, 1992).

Eleanor Szanton (1992) states that policy issues related to infants in child care raise three of our nation's most frequently debated domestic policy concerns: work and family issues; efforts to reduce the number of families on welfare; and concerns about an educable labor force for the economy of the twenty-first century. Since 1987, over 50% of mothers of infants are in the labor force (U.S. Bureau of Labor Statistics, 1988). Though a substantial number are not working full time, it is clear that many more than ever are leaving their babies and toddlers in out-of-home care by nonfamily members. Whether this situation is through choice or necessity, it makes parents unusually anxious. Emotionally, it is more difficult for parents to be separated from an infant than from an older child. Also, infants are more vulnerable to errors in care than are older children, thereby heightening the parents' level of concern. Szanton (1992) writes, "Infant child care suffers not only from society's blurred vision of what it is, but also from the fact that all problems of child care are heightened for infant care." (p. 91). One of the major policy issues confronting the United States today is parental leave at child-birth or adoption. Broad availability of paid parental leave would greatly reduce the pressure of numbers in infant day care. It would also provide parents and their babies the time they need to become firmly attached to each other—for parents to know the child's individual sensitivities and possible special needs in order to make a more intelligent placement into child care. Paradoxically, policy-makers, many of whom express concern about the possible ill effects of early child care, have not adopted the measure that would most powerfully alleviate that concern, and which is law in 80 countries and all developed countries, except South Africa and the United States (Kamerman, Kahn, and Kingston, 1983).

According to Blank (1992), there are glaring gaps in America's child care system. Meeting the nation's child care crisis calls for a working partnership among the federal government, the states, the private sector, and America's families to ensure an adequate supply of quality child care and to provide help to lower-income families so they can keep working. According to Blank:

1. The federal government has been the missing partner in child care policy. Despite the demographic and economic variables that make child care a pressing national concern, the nation still has no broad federal policy or program that addresses the availability, affordability, and quality of child care. Federal tax breaks do not build a good child care system. The credit allows families to offset some of their federal tax bill by claiming a portion of their child care expenses; but the credit does little for the lower-income families that most desperately need child care assistance, because these families have little or no federal income tax liability to offset, and because the credit covers only a fraction of the cost of care. Nor does the tax credit have any impact on the two other key child care problems: availability and quality of care.

2. States cannot handle the child care crisis alone. Some states are struggling to address the child care crisis by boosting state con-tributions to Title XX–funded child care or by launching new child

care programs. But more states are sliding backwards; in 1988, 26 states spent less in real dollars for child care funded through the Title XX Social Services Block Grant than they did in FY 1981. Only 20 states are serving more children than they did in 1981, while 23 states are serving fewer (Blank, 1992). Even California, which yearly invests more than $300 million in child care, serves only 7% of the children eligible for child care assistance.

3. Private sector efforts are growing, but still are very scarce. While employers are increasing their involvement in child care, only approximately 4,500 employers out of 6 million across the United States provide any child care help to their employees.

An Action Plan for Federal and State Policy Development

Both the federal and state governments need to be involved in the policy solution to child care in the United States. At the national level, more funds could be appropriated to fund the Child Care and Development Block Grant in order to help states improve the quality of child care in the Licensing and Monitoring Grant Program. Also, the federal government has made very recent gains in Head Start funding; these funds need to be continued and increased so that Head Start can be available for all eligible children.

At the state level, administrators can carefully implement the two new federal child care programs—the Child Care and Development Block Grant and the "At-Risk" Child Care Program. Also, states can make sure that new federal child care funds are not used to supplant (replace) existing state child care investments and consider supplementing these federal funds with additional state monies. States can also provide supplemental money to the federal expansion funds for Head Start or support state-initiated programs that provide comprehensive services to preschool children and operate full days throughout the year. States can also provide more leadership in putting into place strong health and safety standards that are presently not monitored carefully regardless of the sponsor of the child care program or the numbers of children served.

Requiring child care centers and family child care homes to comply to licensing regulations is essential; therefore, states must be more willing to invest in the hiring of adequate numbers of individuals to provide monitoring and enforcement of regulations. States can also expand the supply of trained child care workers by establishing scholarships and loan forgiveness programs for individuals seeking early childhood development credentials, thus improving the supply of training opportunities as well as individuals who are professionally trained to work with young children. The Family Support Act can be implemented effectively, thus allowing for better payment mechanisms, meaningful standards, and child care counseling (resource/referral) sources.

Stegelin (1992), discussing the evolution of early childhood policy in the United States, describes the evolving policy process as a mirror of the changing definition of the child in our culture. As the 1990s emerge, the way in which Americans view the young child reflects deeply rooted changes in the fabric of our society. The growing need for policy awareness for young children and their families is reflected through new family forms and parenting styles, business and corporate involvement in child care and family and parent support roles, new federal and state legislation that addresses the needs of young children, the awareness of politicians that early childhood issues impact all of America's families, a growing awareness of multicultural influences and sensitivity to a diverse world, expansion of early childhood programs and enrollments across the United States, and the increased professionalism associated with child care and other occupations related to young children. Perhaps the clearest message of all being sent today by employed mothers is the need for viable alternatives for safe, secure, consistent, and affordable child care (Stegelin, 1992; Broberg and Hwang, 1992).

References

Backett, K. (1987). The negotiation of fatherhood. In C. Lewis and M. O'Brien (Eds.), *Reassessing fatherhood* (pp. 74–90). London: Sage.

Barnett, R.C., and Baruch, G.K. (1987). Determinants of fathers' participation in family work. *Journal of Marriage and the Family, 49*, 29–40.

Belsky, J. (1986). Infant day care: A cause for concern? *Zero to Three, 7* (1), 1–7.

Belsky, J., and Steinberg, L.D. (1978). The effects of daycare: A critical review. *Child Development, 49*, 929–949.

Bender, D., and Leone, B. (Eds.). (1992). *The family in America*. San Diego, Calif.: Greenhaven Press.

Blank, H. (1992). Emerging child care policy issues. In D. Stegelin (Ed.), *Early childhood education: Policy issues for the 1990s*. Norwood, N.J.: Ablex.

Blehar, M.C. (1974). Anxious attachment and defensive reactions associated with day care. *Child development, 46*, 801–817.

Broberg, A.G., and Hwang, C.P. (1992). The shaping of child-care policies. In Michael Lamb, et al. (Eds.), *Child care in context*. Hillsdale, N.J.: Erlbaum.

Caldwell, B., Wright, C., Honig, A., and Tannenbaum, J. (1992). Infant day care and attachment, *American Journal of Orthopsychiatry, 69*, 690–697.

Clarke-Stewart, K.A. (1989). The effects of infant day care reconsidered: Risks for parents, children and researchers. *Early Childhood Research Quarterly, 3*, 293–318.

Clarke-Stewart, K.A., and Fein, G.C. (1983). Early childhood programs. In M.M. Haith and J.J. Campos (Eds.), *Handbook of child psychology: 2. Infancy and developmental psychology* (4th ed., pp. 917–999). New York: John Wiley and Sons.

Clarke-Stewart, K.A. (1989). Infant day care: Maligned or malignant? *American Psychologist, 44*, 266–273.

Crouter, A.C., MacDonald, S.M., McHale, S.M., and Perry-Jenkins, M. (1990). Parental monitoring and perceptions of children's school performance and conduct of dual- and single-earner families. *Developmental Psychology, 26*, 649–657.

Frankel, J., and McCarty, S. (1993). Women's employment and childbearing decisions. In J. Frankel (Ed.), *The employed mother and the family context* (pp. 31–46). New York: Springer.

Hayghe, H. (1986). Rise in mother's labor force activity includes those with infants. *Monthly Labor Review, 109*(2), 43–45.

Hochschild, A. (1989). *The second shift*. New York: Viking Press.

Hofferth, S.L. (1989). What is the demand for and supply of child care in the United States? *Young Children, 44*(5), 28–33.

Hofferth, S.L., and Phillips, D.A. (1987). Child care in the United States, 1970 to 1995. *Journal of Marriage and the Family, 49*, 559–571.

Hwang, C.P., and Broberg, A.G. (Eds.) *Child care in context*. Hillsdale, N.J.: Erlbaum.

Jump, T.L., and Haas, L. (1987). Fathers in transition: Dual-career fathers participating in child care. In M.S. Kimmel (Ed.), *Changing men* (pp. 98–114). Newbury Park, Calif.: Sage.

Kahn, M., and Kamerman, S. (1987). *Child care, family benefits, and working parents*. New York: Columbia University Press.

Kamerman, S., Kahn, A., and Kingston, P. (1983). *Maternity policies and working women*. New York: Columbia University Press.

Kontos, S. (1992). *Family day care*. Washington, D.C.: National Association for the Education of Young Children.

Lamb, M.E., Pleck, J.H., and Levine, J.A. (1987). Effects of increased paternal involvement on fathers and mothers. In C. Lewis and M. O'Brien (Eds.), *Reassessing fatherhood* (pp. 109–125). London: Sage.

Lamb, M., Sternberg, K.J., and Ketterlinus, R.D. (1992). Child care in the United States: The modern era. In M. Lamb, K.J. Sternberg, S. Lewis, D. Israeli and H. Hootsman (1992). *Dual-earner families*. London: Sage.

McCullough, J., and Zick, C.D. (1992). The roles of role strain, economic resources, and time demands in explaining mothers' life satisfaction. *Journal of Family and Economic Issues, 13*(1), 23–44.

McLoyd, V.C. (1993). Employment among African-American mothers in dual-earner families: Antecedents and consequences for family life and child development. In J. Frankel (Ed.), *The employed mother and the family context* (pp. 180–226). New York: Springer.

Mirande, A. (1991). Ethnicity and fatherhood. In F.W. Bozett and S.M.H. Hanson (Eds.), *Fatherhood and families in cultural context* (pp. 53–82). New York: Springer.

Nock, L. (1987). The symbolic meaning of childbearing. *Journal of Family Issues 8*(4), 373–393.

Olson, J.E., Frieze, I.H., and Deltefsen, E.G. (1990). Having it all? Combining work and family in a male and a female profession. *Sex Roles, 23* (9/10), 515–533.

Pittman, J.F., and Kerpelman, J.L. (1993). Family work of husbands and fathers in dual-earner marriages. In J. Frankel (Ed.), *The employed mother and the family context* (pp. 89–112). New York: Springer.

Platt, E.B. (1991). *Scenes from day care: How teachers teach and what children learn.* New York: Teachers College Press.

Pleck, J.H. (1987). American fathering in historical perspective. In M.S. Kimmel (Ed.), *Changing men* (pp. 83–97). Newbury Park, Calif.: Sage.

Reeves, D.L. (1959). *Child care crisis.* Santa Barbara, Calif.: ABC-CLIO.

Ritner, G. (1992). *Fathers' liberation ethics.* Lanham, Md.: University Press of America.

Rix, S.E. (1990). *The American women: 1990–1991.* New York: W.W. Norton.

Scarr, S., and Hall, E. (1984). What's a parent to do? *Psychology Today 18* (May), 58–63.

Sears, H.A., and Galambos, N.L. (1993). The employed mother's well-being. In J. Frankel (Ed.), *The employed mother and the family context* (pp. 49–67). New York: Springer.

Soled, S.W., and Blaird, E.D. (1990). Relationship of age and sex-role conflict for professional women in human services. *Psychological Reports, 67,* 523–527.

Stegelin, D.A. (1992). Early childhood policy: An introduction. In D. Stegelin (Ed.), *Early childhood education: Policy issues for the 1990s.* Norwood, N.J.: Ablex.

Stegelin, D.A., and Frankel, J. (1994). *Scenes from day care: A photographic study of home-based child care centers in Greater Cincinnati.* A presentation to the Southern Early Childhood Association, April 15, 1994, New Orleans, Louisiana.

Stoltz-Loike, M. (1992). The working family: Helping women balance the roles of wife, mother, and career woman. *Career Development Quarterly 40* (March), 244–256.

Szanton, E. (1992). Issues related to infant child care policy. In D. Stegelin (Ed.), *Early childhood education: Policy issues for the 1990s.* Norwood, N.J.: Ablex.

Thompson, R.A. (1988). The effects of infant day care through the prism of attachment theory: A critical appraisal. *Early Childhood Research Quarterly 3,* 273–282.

Thorman, G. (1989). *Day care . . . An emerging crisis.* Springfield, Ill.: Charles Thomas.

U.S. Bureau of the Census. (1990). Statistical abstract of the United States. Washington, D.C., U.S. Government Printing Office.

U.S. Bureau of Labor Statistics. (1988). Facts about working women. Washington, D.C.: U.S. Government Printing Office.

Valdez, E.O., and Coltrane, S. (1993). Work, family, and the Chicana: Power, perception, and equity. In J. Frankel (Ed.), *The employed mother and the family context* (pp. 153–179). New York: Springer.

Valling, B.L., and Belsky, J. (1991). Multiple determinants of father involvement during infancy in dual-earner and single-earner families. *Journal of Marriage and the Family, 53* (May), 461–474.

Wellesley College Center for Research on Women. (1987). Columbus explores child care territory. *School-age Child Care Project Newsletter, 4* (3).

Williams, K.J., Suls, J., Alliger, G.M., Learner, S.M., and Wan, C.K. (1991). Multiple role juggling and daily mood status in working mothers: An experience sampling study. *Journal of Applied Psychology, 5,* 664–674.

Women's International News Network. (1993). *19*(4), 73–75.

Yogev., S. (1983). Judging the professional woman: Changing research, changing values. *Psychology of Women Quarterly, 7,* 219–234.

Index

Reference Books
on Family Issues

Postpartum Depression
A Research Guide and International Bibliography
by Laurence Kruckman and Chris Asmann-Finch

Adoption
An Annotated Bibliography and Guide
by Lois Ruskai Melina

Resources for Middle Childhood
A Source Book
by Deborah Lovitky Sheiman and Maureen Slonim

Children and Adjustment to Divorce
An Annotated Bibliography
by Mary M. Nofsinger

One-Parent Children, The Growing Minority
A Research Guide
by Mary Noel Gouke and Arline McClarty Rollins

Child Abuse and Neglect
An Information and Reference Guide
by Timothy J. Iverson and Marilyn Segal

Adolescent Pregnancy and Parenthood
An Annotated Guide
by Ann Creighton-Zollar

Employed Mothers and Their Children
by Jacqueline V. Lerner and Nancy L. Galambos

Children, Culture, and Ethnicity
Evaluating and Understanding the Impact
by Maureen B. Slonim

Prosocial Development in Children
Caring, Helping, and Cooperating
A Bibliographic Resource Guide
by Alice Sterling Honig and Donna Sasse Wittmer

Hispanic Children and Youth in the United States
A Resource Guide
by Angela L. Carrasquillo

Family Addiction
An Analytical Guide
by Douglas H. Ruben

The Social Correlates of Infant and
Reproductive Mortality in the United States
A Reference Guide
by Ann Creighton-Zollar

Children of Poverty
Research, Health, and Policy Issues
by Hiram E. Fitzgerald, Barry M. Lester, and Barry Zuckerman

Families of Employed Mothers
An International Perspective
by Judith Frankel